Introducing the Quran to Non-Muslims

By

Prof. M. Shamim

Islamic Book Service (P) Ltd.

Introducing the Quran to non-Muslims

By Prof. M. Shamim

ISBN 81-7231-907-X

1st Edition : 2015

Published by *Abdus Sami* for :

Islamic Book Service (P) Ltd.

1511-12, Pataudi House, Darya Ganj, **New Delhi**-110 002 **(INDIA)**
Tel.: +91-11-23244556, 23253514, 23269050, 23286551
e-mail: info@ibsbookstore.com
Website: www.ibsbookstore.com
(ebooks) www.bit.do/ebs
amazon.com www.bit.do/ibs

Our Associates

Angel Book House FZE, **Sharjah (U.A.E.)**
Azhar Academy Ltd., **London (United Kingdom)**
Lautan Lestari (Lestari Books), **Jakarta (Indonesia)**
Husami Book Depot, **Hyderabad (India)**

Printed in India

OF WHAT USE IS THIS BOOK?

A non-Muslim, when he is presented a copy of the Quran, accepts it gladly, looks over it with reverence, casts a glance at this and that page and keeps it at a safe and respectful place in the shelf. At some other time of leisure, if he finds himself inclined to this Book he picks it up goes through some passages from here and there, finds nothing worth interest. He feels disenchanted, keeps the Book again in the shelf and considers that it is just an 'another book on religion' which subscribes some moral lessons and nothing more. However, he places this Book prominently in the shelf to show to his friends his generosity and open-heartedness to all religions. Sadly the most beneficial book which could have alleviated many of his problems remains unfolded to him!

For non-Muslims (and for ignorant Muslims too), it is difficult to read the Quran cover to cover, and in actuality, to expect this from them, is beyond practical considerations. On this ground it is humble advice of the author to all those who are eager to present the Quran to their friends and to all those who are ever ready to distribute the Quran generously on mass scale; *to present along with it an introductory book of the Quran*. This book in your hand now, is such an endeavor in the direction of presenting a proper introduction of the Quran. In this introductory book, it has been tried to present all salient aspects of the Quran which could give a panoramic view of it. The other motive to author this book is to arouse in the reader two feelings viz. of "amazement" and "curiosity". Going through different chapters particularly on those discussing scientific aspects the reader will be "amazed" that fourteen hundred years back such descriptions were given which are discovered only today. There are many verses, as we have indicated at various places, which make the reader "curious" to know more about these. It is expected that these two feelings aroused by such an introduction will drive the reader to come closer to the Quran.

Today we are living in a world, where it is quite easy in the comfort of middle-class life to live on the surface of existence, focusing on getting the right clothes, mixing with friends, hunting after degrees, house, job and so on. Opportunity for contemplation is seldom offered. Work in offices or in businesses consume the energies of the day, and at night one either flops down in front of the television (with its sleep inducing effect), or goes to the nightclub, where drink and loud music prevent one from thinking. "The loud music" that haunts public space and home theatre and an un-ending number of TV channels all these create an environment that precludes deep thought. The Quran refers to this phenomenon in the verses that describe "the life of this world is but play and amusement … the goods and chattels of deception." (57:20). "Quench your thirst" (in whatever manner, right or wrong) is the slogan of the day. In such an environment who cares to read a serious book drawing attention to a religion. Who needs a God after all? Who wants to shackle himself to the strictures laid down by a Book? Today it is really a difficult task to draw the attention of a man to read the Quran. Here we need to evolve some techniques *to draw him near the Quran* cautiously and gradually and this much is sure that to hand over 'The Quran' as such should be avoided.

There are other persons who are in search of 'some solace', 'some comforting hands' to come out of the present day 'worrisome' world. But they are in search of some easy-to-understand materials as they don't have much time to spare.

To all such persons this introductory book will prove to be a helping guide.

This book is written in a manner as if the reader is sitting with the author engaged in a dialogue. The presentation of the book is not in academic form but it is more akin to a student's handbook; understandable to laypersons, to persons with initial knowledge of Islam.

Classification of Chapters

In writing this introductory book, the author has kept in mind that he is presenting it to a person whose knowledge of Islam is at minimal level but who is eager to know the main points of the Quran in clear plain and unambiguous language. In the present day busy world, there is evidently an urgent need for a panoramic view of the numerous aspects and side issues related to the Quran and one obtainable in a concise volume which can be read by common men, a book which may answer the principal questions lingering at the backyard of the reader's mind about this Book.

For the purpose of introduction to the Quran, out of numerous topics the author has picked up only a few with following ideas in mind:

(i) Those topics of the Quran which may arouse in the reader a feeling of 'curiosity'; when the reader will find that such and such topics of modern-day concern are present in this scripture, he will like to see these in the main Scripture. Chapter no. 1 to 6 are its examples.

(ii) Those topics of which a general reader has either heard about or read superficially regarding the Quran or of which some misunderstandings are likely to be harbored. Chapters no.7 to 11 are its examples.

(iii) The third set of chapters are concerned with the actual introduction of the Quran, the Prophet and the relationship between the two. Chapters 12 to 23 deal with it.

Some Words of Caution

It may be pointed out that the Quran at the time of the Prophet was lively, vibrant and guiding. The companions of the prophet were ever ready to "listen" to the revelations coming from God directly to them via the medium of the Prophet; at occasions he called and they acted. It was a lively process. It were these people who, well trained by him to sustain adversities for the cause of whole mankind (3:110- *you are indeed the best community that has ever been brought forth for [the good of] mankind: you enjoin the doing of what is right and forbid the doing of what is wrong, and you believe in God.*) and to adhere to the injunctions of the Quran marched outside the Arabian peninsula; wherever they went the people found in them the perfect embodiment of the Quran. This was the secret of the spread of Islam then ; but now what has happened? The so called torchbearers of the Quran "*chained*" it with beautiful glossy silken coverings and strings, placed it at the very top of the shelf beyond easy reach, "*lest it not interact with them*!" Alas! now the followers of the Quran and Muhammad(pbh) have no relevance with the two. They do speak in favour of them but in action neither are they ready to obey the commands of the Prophet nor are they ready to heed to the injunctions of the Quran. The present scenario of the Muslim world is the fitting example of the verse 30 of Surah 25 which depicts the complaint the Prophet will present to Allah on the Day of Judgment : 25:30- *Then the Messenger will say: "O my Lord! Truly my people took this Quran as something [that ought to be] discarded!"*

To the readers of this Introductory book it is a word of caution that the fruitfulness of the Quran be not judged by seeing the present day Muslims who have drifted far from the principles laid down by the Quran in almost all walks of life. Indeed in this sense it is more difficult to come closer to the Quran than it was in early days of Islam when the Quran was lively and vibrant.

An another reason why the Quran became 'un-lively' and 'dormant' for last few centuries is the sectarian attitude of the 'Ulema' (scholars taking their degrees from traditional madrasahs). They gave more weightage to the studies of the principles of 'their sects' than the studies in the Quran. It must be known that these sects are not based on basics of Islam but some petty ramifications; in that way they ignored the call of the Quran, they forsook it.

> ***All these pitfalls must be known to the person who wants to embark on the journey to the Quran.***

A major misunderstanding is prevalent not only among non-Muslims but among Muslims too that this Book, the Quran is *of* Muslims or *for* Muslims. This is far removed from reality. This Book addresses to all mankind, keeps a treasure open to anyone who approaches to it with open heart and unprejudiced mind.

May Allah Reward Them All

While writing this book, for the last four years, I have gone through huge amount of great work done by lot of respectable scholars, (available in physical form or available on credible websites) and have tried to bring their works to the readers at finger tips, wherever required. My sincere and immense gratitude goes to the learned scholars like A. A. Maududi, Abdullah Yousuf Ali, Muhammad Asad, Maurice Bouccaille, HarunYahya,.......and prominent Islamic websites like, Islamicity.com, taz-keer.org, openburhan.net, studyquran.co.uk, corpus.Quran.com, qurango.com/seerat.html, islamicstudies.info/tafheem.php. The treasure of knowledge in their books have been of tremendous help in order to convert the idea and inspiration behind this book to reality. In writing this book we are highly indebted to various websites, a few mentioned above, we have tried to quote them at most of the places. While going through an article the reader will find it very convenient to go to the website quickly and gather more knowledge.

I feel obliged, with pleasure, to mention the name of Prof. Shahid N Hyder without his tremendous help, cooperation, and encouragement, it would have been almost impossible to complete this book. I am extremely grateful to Allah who has blessed me with a very supportive wife who has been a great support for me in writing this book with her continuous encouragement and letting me provide full focus to this endeavor by taking care of everything else. Another person who deserves special recognition is my son Tasin who despite being extremely busy as an IT Manager in a Bank abroad, snatched time to edit the whole book and pass on valuable suggestion off and on. Finally, my deepest gratitude to Almighty Allah for providing me with the opportunity and privilege of embarking on this topic; whatever faults are present in this book are entirely my own; and whatever pleases Him is for His Glory alone. I pray that He will accept this work as a sincere effort on His behalf and on the Day of Judgment raise me and all those who helped me in any way in this endeavor and all those of whose works I have benefited, among the assembly of those about whom the Prophet said ***"Khairukum man ta'allamal Qur'ana wa allamahu"*** (best among you are those who learn the Quran and teach it to others).

M. Shamim
(Rtd. Professor of Mech. Engg., BITSindri)

FOREWORD

This book 'Introducing the Quran to non-Muslims' is not an interpretative work on the Quran, rather it is a well-researched introductory endeavor covering many aspects of the Book. Apart from dealing with the usual social, moral, spiritual, legal, military and political frontiers, it also touches authentically upon scientific spheres. An amalgamation of around thirty chapters and sub-chapters all well researched and critically examined articles, this book may be esteemed as one of the finest handbooks of reference not only for non-Muslims but for even the Muslim readers curious to study the Quran other than holy purposes. Professor Shamim, the retired professor of Mechanical Engineering in B I T Sindri, a premier technical institute in Eastern India, since his early days has been passionately engaged in researches on the diverse Quranic aspects. His book is the output of his patient study and fruitful consultation of materials available on the internet which is laboriously sorted out and assembled in a book form.

The one traditional approach to the study of the Quran is limited to its metaphysical constituent. But Prof Shamim true to his professional scientific background in engineering endeavored to break himself free from discussing solely the metaphysical components of the Quran and he addressed to the dynamics of the Quran in scientific references.

Scientific descriptions in the Quran are just 'amazing' to common readers. It seems unbelievable to them that there are statements and words mentioned in the Quran which indicate scientific truths discovered only in recent times. The author of this introductory book being a teacher of Mechanical engineering has been in touch with various fields of Science including Life sciences and is well aware with recent trends in different fields of sciences. At the same time he has been a student of the Quran for a long time with a searching eye on such words and statements indicating some aspects of science. Chapters 1 through 6 are those which will surely attract those readers who have even a slight interest in science. Thus modern cosmologists for instance, are amazed to hear from the Quran the divinely revealed verdicts on what the physicists term as Big Bang, the ever expanding edges of the Universe; the entropic decay of it; and an incredible existence of extraterrestrial life in outer space. One is amazed to know that the Quran tells that in between the celestial bodies it exists no total vacuum as laypersons generally believe; now science agrees that there exists inter stellar dust in the space between celestial bodies.

The chapters, "Wars and Fighting as described in the Quran" and "The Quran on Man Woman relationship" are deep study of the concept and relevance of jihad and what in the Islamic parlance a woman is assumed to be. His article dismisses the Woman's existing confusion of her liberty vis-à-vis the feminist movement. In Islam a woman is complete in all respect and that her emancipation does not demand any reshuffling of femaleness or maleness. Prof Shamim does not agree with marauding aspect of Jihad that has rocked the world today but at the same time points out those factors under which the Quran enjoins fighting.

In the article, "The Practicality of the Quran", the author emphatically talks of the up righteousness and eradication of evil in the individual so that holistic life turns beneficial to all alike. The author discusses pointedly on issues of common nature including what the Quran says on Islamic law, fornication, bribery, marriage and divorce, alcoholism and other legal and corrupt practices.

The chapter, "Why the Muslims are lagging behind?" naturally pinches a curious reader. The author raises question why the Quran that is believed to be a book of enlightenment that shook Arabia and made it conquer half of the World of its time, is not reflecting its shine and glory through the behavior and life style of present day Muslims. This chapter convincingly answers all doubts, as the author pin points that a huge difference lies between the religion explained and the religion practiced.

The chapter, "How to Study the Quran: guide to a person quite new to it" is an endeavor on its part to guide the reader in matters of Quranic study. The author's exclusive approach to Quran is that, one cannot gain the best of it if one divorces oneself from understanding the Prophet. The chapter on "Structure and Style of the Quran" is complex but it is explained lucidly. Another chapter which deems special mention here is "Preservation and Authenticity of the Quran". To explain this topic the author raises an interesting hypothetical question: "if a companion of the Prophet happens to come today, will he be able to read the present day-Quran and answers that he won't- -why? It is an eye-opening historiography of the Quran and it presents a convincing proof that the text of the Quran in our hands today is the same as the one handed over by the Prophet to us although there has been a change in the script, this chapter is indeed worth serious perusal.

The presentation of the whole book is, as if the author is engaged in direct talk with the reader, he raises a question from the side of the reader and replies it, conforming all rules of logic. Coming to the science of Logic a full chapter "the Quran appeals to man's logic and intellect" is devoted on this topic. This is a very interesting chapter and people of all segments will find it a bit "awaking" as to why one believes in something? Reading this chapter a common man who is so overwhelmed by Science finds that there is a limit beyond which Science is helpless—it cannot solve the riddle of "why"; a very interesting discussion indeed.

Even a cursory glance over the index of this introductory book will give an idea of the varied topics discussed and which will surely arouse in the readers an 'inquisitiveness' to dig into the book.

Shahid N Hyder

(Assistant Professor of English in Birsa College a constituent unit of Ranchi University, Ranchi & author of internationally sold fiction "Love, Jihad and Terrorism", "Muslim Women: Tradition and Modernity" and "I lost my Faith")

The Quran is the book without inconsistencies; one part of its text (or doctrine) does not clash with the other. In fact, it sets the absence of contradiction, irrationality, and incoherence, as one of the criteria for checking the authenticity of any divine revelation. It states

أَفَلَا يَتَدَبَّرُونَ الْقُرْآنَ ۚ وَلَوْ كَانَ مِنْ عِندِ غَيْرِ اللَّهِ لَوَجَدُوا فِيهِ اخْتِلَافًا كَثِيرًا ﴿٨٢﴾

"Do they not ponder the Quran (with care)? Had this book been from anybody but Allah, you would have found many inconsistencies."

[Surah Nisa : 82]

If the allegation against Muhammad (pbh) that he imitated from several books like the Bible, the Torah etc, or that some anonymous persons helped him in supplying the source materials then he must have been adopting a "pick and choose" technique in writing the Quran. If that had been the case such a technique must have led to a large number of discrepancies. But to the surprise of all there is none.

{A passage from the book}

NOTE:

It is a long established and cherished tradition among Muslims to follow the mention of a prophet's name by the benediction,

"May peace be upon him"
(Arabic: alaihissalaam).

This high respect is shown not only to the last Messenger, Muhammad, but all prophets mentioned in the Quran this is why Jesus is alwasys called Eisa alaihissalm and Moses as Musa alaihissalm –no such regard is shown even by their own followers. A word for those prophets whose names don't appear in the Quran and who came in different lands: they all are also given full regard and shown utmost respect however they are not followed with "alaihissalam".

We have used the abbreviation (pbh) for "peace be upon him" along with the name of the Prophet, Muhammad all through the book but not where only 'the Prophet' is written.

INDEX

- Of What Use Is This Book .... (*iii*)
- FOREWARD..(*ix*)

1. Scientific Descriptions in the Quran 1
2. What We Observe in the Universe.............................. 27
3. What the Quran says about the Theory of Evolution 49
   - I. Brief Introduction of Theory of Evolution 49
   - II. Arguments Against the Theory of Evolution .. 53
   - III. Theory of Evolution in the Quranic perspective 64
4. The Quran on Cosmology 68
   - I. A Very Brief Introduction to Modern Cosmology 68
   - II. The Quran on Cosmology 103
5. The Quran Appeals to Man's Logic and Intellect... 120
   - I. Logical Reasonings (An elementary Introduction) 120
   - II. The Quran Appeals to Man's Logic and Intellect 131
6. The Quran – An Amazing Book 148
7. Islamic Laws – Outdated, Barbaric or Useful 157
   - I. An Important Prerequisite to Islamic Laws 157
   - II. Islamic Laws – Outdated? Barbaric? or Useful? 172
8. Man-Woman Relationship 185

9. Wars and Fightings as Described in the Quran 208
   I. Quran on War, Fighting, Persecution & Jihad 208
   II. Wars and Fightings as Described in the Quran 212
10. The Quranic Directives in Politics 227
11. The Quran on Economics 241
12. The Quran & Muhammad – the two are entwined 259
   I. Brief Life Sketch of the Prophet 259
   II. The Quran and Muhammad – the Inter-relationship 266
   III. How the Quran presents Muhammad 274
13. Main theme, Structure and Style of the Quran 280
   I. Main Theme, Structure and Style of the Quran 280
   II. What kind of a book is the Quran 288
14. Preservation & Authenticity of the Quran 298
15. Translation of the Quran is not the Quran, why? .. 321
16. Distinguishing Features of the Quran among the World Scriptures 332
17. The Quran and Muhammad (pbh) under the scanner of the Orientalists 343
18. Why the Quran is believed to be a divine book? ... 355
19. Present day World: Why it needs the Quran? 380
20. The Practicality of the Quran 395
21. How to Study the Quran: a guide to a person quite new to it 406
22. The Quran at the time of despair 417
23. Why the Muslims are Lagging Behind? 430
- APPENDIX 1. Islam Basics 436
- APPENDIX 2. Where to go from here? 460

1

Scientific Descriptions in The Quran

While in recent times some scientific discoveries have dealt a deathblow to many religious beliefs, it is amazingly the same discoveries of science have highlighted various aspects of the Quran and they are found compatible with them.

The Quran contains widely dispersed references on a variety of subjects which are not only scientifically accurate, but in some cases, quite advanced relative to the time of the Prophet Muhammad (pbh) and to the surprise to many, there are some references such as 'extra-terrestrial-life', which are yet to be discovered. For the Muslim who reads and understands these references, they serve to strengthen his or her faith of course. For the non-Muslim who questions the authenticity or authorship of the Quran, these references provide some interesting answers.

Three Categories of Verses in The Quran Related to Science

There are various verses in the Quran which indicate scientific phenomena. For ease of understanding we may categorize them in three heads:

✧ The First Category

In the first category are those verses which indicate a **general description** of the comprehensible natural phenomenon going on in the Universe and various objects scattered all over the world. These are presented by the Quran as "SIGNS" ("***ayaats***" in Arabic): something which *indicate* 'Control', 'Power', 'Organization' in the system mentioned in the verse; moreover it indicates coordination, interlinking and interdependence among different systems operating in the nature; all these to the highest perfection, without any flaw. For example read the following verse carefully:

[Quran 2:164] Behold! in the creation of the heavens & the earth, in the alteration of the Night & the Day, in the sailing of the ships through the Ocean for the profit of mankind, in the rain which Allah sends down from the skies and the life which He gives there with to an earth that was dead; in the beasts of all kinds that He scatters through the earth; in the change of the winds and the clouds which they trail as subservient between the sky and the earth; *(Here) indeed are SIGNS for a people that are Wise.*

[Quran 10:6] For, verily, in the alternating of night and day, and in all that God has created in the heavens and on earth there are messages indeed for people who are conscious of Him!

In chapter 30 named Surah Rum (spelled as 'room' indicating the Roman Empire) there is a long list of very interesting nine verses indicating many signs worth reading minutely. (For dearth of space we are not quoting these here) as an example see this verse:

[Quran 30:22] And among His Signs is the creation of the heavens and the earth, and the variations in your languages and your colours: verily in that are Signs for those who are possessed of [innate] knowledge!

Mark that each verse starts with *'And among His Signs is'* and ends with such clauses as 'verily, in that are indeed Signs for people who contemplate', 'who listen', 'who use their intellect'

✧ The Second Category

In this category there are verses which contain certain **words** indicating some scientific facts. See a few examples:

[10:5] He it is who has made the sun a [source of] radiant light *(ziya)* and the moon a light *(noor)* [reflected], and has determined for it measured *(qaddarahu)* phases so that you might know how to compute the years and to measure [time]. None of this has God created without [an inner] truth. Clearly does He spell out these messages unto people of [innate] knowledge.

Here the word *'Ziya'* in Arabic for 'shining' attributed to the sun as its qualifier, it indicates a light which comes out of something blazing but the word *'Noor'* attached to the Moon ascribed to soothing cool light. Again the word

"*Qaddarahu*" (measured it) comes from the root word '*qadara*' in Arabic which means "a very calculated and measured quantity in due proportion". As we know the planet earth and its satellite moon are so well calculated and are at measured distances and angles of axis of rotation with reference to the sun that even a slight change in any parameter will change the whole eco system of the earth.

[Quran 78:6 &7] Have we not made the earth a resting-place [for you], and the mountains [it] pegs?

In these verses, the words *'Mehad'* (resting place) and *'Autada'* (pegs) are very significant from a scientific point of view, the first indicates that the earth with all its high speed of rotation (1670 Km/hr at the equator about its axis of rotation and the speed of 107,000 Km/hr along its orbit around the Sun) amazingly seems to be a very comfortable place for the mankind. The term *Autada* word indicates that the mountains are not just heavy rocky masses kept over the surface of earth but they are 'pegged into the earth'. The researchers found roots under each mountain which penetrate the depths of the Earth. Researchers were amazed when they found that this fact has been revealed in the Quran which says "And the mountains as pegs?"

(Mountains have roots deep under the surface of the ground. (*Earth,* Press and Siever, p. 413)

Schematic section. Mountains, like pegs, have deep roots embedded in the ground. (*Anatomy of the Earth,* Cailleux, p.220)

Another illustration shows how mountains are peg-like in shape, due to their deep roots. (*Earth Science,* Tarbuck and Lutgens, p.158)

[Quran 79:32] The Quran says "And the mountain has He firmly fixed" "Yet in another verse: "He set on the earth mountains standing firm lest it should shake with you" [Quran 31:15]

[Quran 16:68] And [consider how] Your Sustainer has inspired the bee: "Prepare for yourself dwellings in mountains and in trees, and in what [men] may build [for you by way of hives];

[Quran 16:69] And then eat of all manner of fruit, and follow humbly the paths ordained for you by thy Sustainer." [And lo!] There issues from within these [bees] a fluid of many hues, wherein there is health for man. In all this, behold, there is a message indeed for people who think!

The remarkable points here are the words used for the verbs (in Arabic verse) for the Bee are such that indicate *feminine gender of the bee:* the researchers have found it very recently that indeed it is the feminine bees which do their jobs mentioned above.

✧ The third category

There are many verses which reveal the direct descriptions of the scientific facts showing compatibility with the modern science.

[Quran 36:38] And the sun runs his course for a period determined for him: That is the measuring of the Mighty, the Wise.

[Quran 13:2] It is God who has raised the heavens without any support that you could see, and is established on the throne of His Almightiness;

and He [it is who] has made the sun and the moon subservient [to His laws], each running its course for a term set [by Him]. He governs all that exists. Clearly does He spell out these messages, so that you might be certain in your innermost that you are destined to meet your Sustainer [on The Judgment Day].

In these two verses and on many other occasions in the Quran are mentioned that the sun and moon are running unto their destinations (i.e. for a predetermined time) and that this movement is an *orbit* (Arabic word used for it is 'falak; it is clearly mentioned at two places 21:33 and 36:40)

[Quran 21:33] It is He who created the Night and the Day, and the sun and the moon: all (the celestial bodies) *swim along, each in its orbit.*

[Quran 36:40] It is not permitted to the Sun to catch up the Moon, nor can the Night outstrip the Day: **Each (just) swims along in (its own) orbit.** The cosmologists tell us that in the sun the actual fuel burning is hydrogen with a fast rate and it will all exhaust in about 200 million years.

[Quran 41:12] And We adorned the skies nearest to the earth with lamps, and made them secure: That is the *measuring* of the Mighty, the Knower.

Three remarkable points are to be noted:

(*a*) Stars are described as lamps which imply that stars are burning bodies.

(*b*) The earth is made secured (from harmful elements though not mentioned here by name) but emphasis falls upon the word "secured"; justified by scientific discoveries how harmful cosmic rays are barred to enter our atmosphere, the Ozone Layer acting as a shield.

(*c*) With the word measuring Arabic : *"taqdeer" (this word coming from the root 'qadara', mentioned above meaning 'ordering something with the sophisticated measuring and proportionality).* It is emphasised here that some stars are set near the Earth as an adornment and that this planet is made protected in the best possible measured way. All these are scientific facts well known to us today.

(*d*) All heavenly bodies are running for a predetermined period.

Here worth mentioning are four consecutive passages from chapter 21 (Surah Anbiya):

[Quran 21:30] Do the Unbelievers not see that *the heavens and the earth were joined together, before we clove them asunder?* We made from water every living thing. Will they not believe then?

[Quran 21:31] And We have set on the earth mountains standing firm, lest it should shake with them, and We have made therein broad highways (between mountains) for them to pass through: that they may receive Guidance.

[Quran 21:32] And We have made the heavens as *a canopy well-guarded:* yet do they turn away from the Signs which these things (point to)!

[Quran 21:33] It is He Who created the Night and the Day, and the sun and the moon: *all (the celestial bodies) swim along,* each in its *rounded course.*

This whole passage of four verses is packed with facts closely compatible with the latest scientific data. In short, the following facts are indicated above as described here:

(*a*) That the whole universe was assembled at one junction and God caused it to explode and disperse: an indication of the **Big Bang Theory,** the latest theory among the modern cosmologists for the Creation of the Universe. Currently, the Big Bang model of the origin of the universe is the cosmological paradigm most widely accepted by astronomers. It holds that about 15 billion years ago the universe began with the explosive expansion of a single, extremely dense matter, the primordial mass. It was only after the development of radio telescopes in 1937 that, the necessary observational precision was achieved so that the astronomers could arrive at the above conclusion.

(*b*) That every living organism was created from water: it is a conclusion to our latest knowledge in biological science.

(*c*) That mountains were formed by Him to keep the earth in a dynamic balance (this term 'dynamic balance' we use in Engineering parlance, as the earth is rotating from its own axis and at the same time it is revolving around the sun with a speed far greater than that of a bullet from an AK-47 rifle; and yet amazingly it is perfectly balanced.

(*d*) That the 'sky of the earth' was made protected from such harmful elements. The word sky here refers to the Arabic word used 'samaa' conveys a meaning of 'canopy' apart from the usual meaning 'heavens'.

(*e*) That each heavenly body, planets, stars and galaxies revolve in its own **"falak"** (orbit). This was not known at the time of the Prophet *that all celestial bodies are moving and that too 'moving in orbits'; this is a finding of the recent times.*

(*f*) Day and night; the sun and the moon were created and that each of them (and by corollary each star) is swimming in its orbit. Descriptions of 'orbit' is remarkable but the word **"yasbahoon" (swimming)** really is amazing. "Swimming" implies that there must be some fluid (liquid or gas) in which the celestial objects are moving. It is the very latest information in the field of cosmology that between the stars and galaxies exists no 'vacuum' but is filled with 'inter- stellar dust 'Interstellar Gas.

[Approximately 99% of the interstellar medium is composed of the interstellar gas, and of its mass, about 75% is in some form of hydrogen (either molecular or atomic), with the remaining 25% as helium. The interstellar gas consists partly of neutral ***atoms*** *and* ***molecules,*** *as well as charged particles, such as* ***ions*** *and* ***electrons.*** *This gas is extremely dilute, with an average density of about 1 atom per cubic centimetre. (For comparison, the air we breathe has a density of approximately* 30×10^{18} *molecules per cubic centimetre.) Even though the interstellar gas is very dilute, the amount of matter adds up over the vast distances between the stars. See the detail on* http://www-ssg.sr.unh.edu/ism/what1.html]

This fact is also indicated in the following verses where a clause *"the heavens and the earth* ***and all in between them (Arabic:wa ma bainahuma)"*** is used at 19 places: 15:85, 19:65, 20:6, 21:16, 25:59, 26:24, 30:8 and many other verses; see one example:

[Quran 30:8] Do they not reflect in their own minds? Not but for just ends and for a term appointed, did Allah create the heavens and the earth, and all between them.

Everything in The World is in Due Proportion and Balance

[Quran 13:8] Allah does know what every female (womb) does bear, by how much the wombs fall short (of their time or number) or do exceed. *Every single thing is before His sight, in (due) proportion.*

[Quran 54:49] **Behold, everything have We created in due measure and proportion;**

These are very remarkable statements everything in the whole universe, from the configurational details of an atom to the movements of stars and galaxies; from the design of DNA to the sophisticated balance of hormones in a man; all indicate a very sophisticated proportion, well balanced design in each of the things we see in the world. A slight alteration in any dimension will thoroughly upset the proportion and order causing havoc not only in the thing concerned but entire inter-linked systems as well. (This topic has been dealt with in the Quran at several places, we have discussed it in another chapter "What We Observe in the Universe")

Everything is Running for an Appointed Term:

A corollary of the Second Law of Thermodynamics

This is our common observation: everything in the world is perishable. Going one step further, the Quran declares that everything in the universe, the sun, the stars rather the whole universe is running only for an appointed term; there are many verses (13:2; 31:29; 35:13; 39:5) related to this topic. Please see an example shown below.

[Quran 39:5] He created the heavens and the earth in true (proportions): He makes the Night overlap the Day, and the Day overlap the Night: He has subjected the sun and the moon (to His law): ***Each one follows a course for a time appointed.*** Is He not the Exalted in Power - He Who forgives again and again?

Materialists, in general, have been in history of opinion that this universe is eternal and everlasting. But the recent concept advanced by the Second Law of Thermodynamics shows that all the Irreversible processes going on in the universe are causing to increase the Entropy of the universe which in turn causes to decrease the Available Energy. Thus causing the End of the Universe. For those unacquainted with the Laws of Thermodynamics, which are well established laws of science, this description may seem a bit cumbersome but is now well accepted by the scientists. (For those interested in this topic read: http://www.answers.com/topic/entropy)

Gender Determination in an embryo-Man is Responsible Not a Woman

The concept of "Gender Determination" as being described by geneticists is one of the outstanding information revealed in the Quran. This information is universally acknowledged that sperms are the deciding factors in determining the gender (male or female) in the embryo.

This determination through the male sperm is due to the fact that sperms have X and Y chromosomes, while the female ovum has only X Chromosomes (X, X). Through the Quran, The Almighty informs us that it is the male sperms that determine the type of gender for the new offspring:

[Quran 75:37] Was he not a drop of sperm emitted (in lowly form)?

[Quran 75:38] Then did he become a leech-like clot; then did (Allah) make and fashion (him) in due proportion.

[Quran 75:39] And *fashioned out of it* (Arabic in the Quran: ja'ala minhu—meaning 'making, fashioning out of the sperm to which *'minhu'* indicates) the two sexes, the male and the female.

These verses indicate that the sex of the child in the womb of a mother is determined by the ***'nutfa'*** (a very small quantity of semen) of man and it is not dependent on the ovum of the woman. This is a statement from the Quran which surprises us as it is the latest finding of recent times. This statement of the Quran amazes the modern man as to how the Quran could mention such a sophisticated fact which could be known now only after the invention of the Electron Microscope.

On Human Embryological and Foetal Development

The science of Embryology as we know it today did not discover many of the detailed aspects of the human embryonic development until the 1970s, using powerful microscopes, ultra sound and fibre optics technology. See how the Quran described **the stages of the embryonic development.**

The Quran has an extensive amount of information on the growth of the human embryo and foetus, especially the former. Before presenting this information, it may be helpful to provide a brief outline of the human development in the womb as modern science understands it today:

An unfertilized egg is produced by the female, and is subsequently placed in her Fallopian tubes.

- ❖ The male cohabits with the female, and a single sperm cell fertilizes the egg.
- ❖ The fertilized egg retreats into the uterus, and attaches itself to the uterine wall.
- ❖ Embryological growth (roughly 3 months).
- ❖ Foetal growth (6 months).
- ❖ Birth

We will examine some of these stages in greater detail as per the verses in the Quran, see how this Book deals with this subject

A General Overview of the Human Development:

[Quran 71:14] Seeing that it is He, (Allah) who has *created you in stages.*

[Quran35:11] And Allah created you from dust, then from a drop.

The first verse is a very general, yet accurate description of our creation as happening in stage-wise (see the six-step outline above). The second verse puts some perspective on the whole affair: how man originally came from dust (First human being, Adam created from dust), and then from a drop of semen.

Specific Details Regarding the Human Development

There are at least four specific details regarding human development in the Quran which modern science has revealed only within the last few centuries and in some cases only in this present century. The first concerns the emission of semen:

[Quran 75:37] Was he (man) not a drop of semen emitted?

In spite of the large amount of fluid emitted during sexual intercourse, this verse emphasizes that only a small drop of it is significant.

The second important detail in the Quran on foetal development is the description of the fertilizing fluid (i.e. semen):

[Quran 86:6] He (man) is created from *a gushing liquid.*

[Quran 76:2] We created the human from a drop which is a *mixture.*

[Quran 32:8] Then He (Allah) made his (Adam's) progeny from *a quintessence of a despised liquid.*

<u>Two Arabic words ***"nutfa"*** and ***"sulalah"*** clarified</u>

The word in the Quran is *"nutfa"* which means a very small quantity of a large amount, its root is *"natafa"* which according to the dictionary meaning is to 'dribble, trickle, drip'. Obviously, this is a very pertinent word and *nutfatin amshajin,* used in the second and third verses are related to the contents of the semen. Modern science has established that semen is infact a composition of different secretions which come from four different glands during ejaculation: the testicles, the seminal vesicles, the prostate gland, and the urinary tract glands; out of these secretions the actual sperm cells come from the testicles.

The Quran goes farther than just informing us that semen is a mixture of liquids. It tells us in [Quran 32:8] that only the *"sulalah"* meaning "quintessence" (The Dictionary meaning: purest and most concentrated essence of something) of the fluid emitted is used (the "despised" comes from the fact that semen is emitted from the same place as urine, and thus may be despicable in some people's sight). The Arabic word for "quintessence" in this verse signifies extracting the absolute best out of something. The numbers tell the story: a normal ejaculation involves about 3 ml of fluid containing between 120,000,000 and 150,000,000 sperm cells. Of these cells, only one fertilizes the egg in the female, and this is the point which [Quran 32:8] elucidates.

"Alaqah": A Clinging Substance

A third detail of foetal development mentioned in the Quran concerns the newly fertilized egg, the fertilised ovum or zygote, in the parlance of Genetics. The Quran uses a word "alaqah" which literally means *'something which clings'*. This is mentioned in the Quran at least seven times: 96:2, 22:5, 23:14 (two times in this verse), 40:67, 75:38, 4:129

[Quran 75:37-38] Was he (man) not a drop of semen emitted? Then he did become something leech-like which clings.

Recent study reveals that the fertilised ovum literally implants itself into the uterine wall. It "clings" in the strongest sense, and it remains stuck there in the early stages of development. On top of that, the developing foetus behaves as a leech on the female host in the sense that it draws its sustenance directly from its mother's body.

Embryological Development

Finally, the Quran gives a fascinating account of embryological development (the first three months) in the following two verses (certain words have been transliterated directly from the Arabic):

[Quran 23:14] We made the drop into an *"Alaqah"* (a clinging substance, leech-like structure), and then we changed the *"Alaqah"* into a *"Mudghah"* (chewed-like substance), then We changed the *"Mudghah"* into "Idhaam" (bones, skeleton), then We clothed the *"Idhaam"* with "Lahm" (flesh, muscles), then We caused him to grow and come into being as another creation.

[Quran 22:5] O mankind! if ye have a doubt about the Resurrection, (consider) that We created you out of dust, then out of sperm, then out of "alaqah" a clinging substance(leech-like clot), then out of a morsel of flesh, *partly formed and partly unformed,* in order that We may manifest (our power) to you; and We cause whom We will to rest in the wombs for an appointed term, then do We bring you out as babies (the verse continues further).

The above verses divide embryological development into four stages.

The *first stage* picks up right after fertilization ("drop"), and is characterized by an Alaqah or "leech-like structure" which describes how the egg implants itself into the uterus (see above). The <u>*second stage*</u> describes the embryo as evolving into a *Mudghah* which means something which has been chewed (especially a piece of meat), or which has the appearance of having been chewed. This seemingly crude description is in fact quite accurate: after the fertilized egg lodges itself in the uterus, it begins to receive its first nutrients and energy from its mother. Consequently, it begins to grow especially rapidly, and after a week or two it looks like a ragged piece of meat to the naked eye. This effect is enhanced by the development of the small buds and protrusions which will eventually grow into complete organs and limbs.

The <u>*next two stages*</u> described in verse [23:14] tell, of bones being made from the *"Mudghah"*, followed by the "clothing" of the bones with flesh or muscles. If we follow the progress of the embryo with our own eyes, we find that after approximately four weeks, a process called 'differentiation' begins, where groups of cells within the embryo transform themselves to form certain large organs. One of the earliest structures to develop in this stage is the cartilaginous basis of the human skeleton (in subsequent months, the cartilage hardens or ossifies). It is followed soon after by the appearance of a host of other organs including muscles, ears, eyes, kidneys, heart, and more. This maintains the order described in the Quran. Verse [23:14] concludes with the growth of the organism in the womb (and simple growth is the primary characteristic of the foetal stage) followed by its birth.

These verses indicate the various stages of the embryological evolution, compatible with the recent findings.

Embryo Behind Three Veils

[Quran 39:6] "He creates you in your mothers' wombs, one act of creation after another, ***in three veils of darkness.*** Thus is God, your Sustainer: unto Him belongs all dominion: there is no deity save Him: how, then, can you lose sight of the truth?"

In three veils of darkness? What does this mean? It means three anatomical layers: abdominal layer, the uterus itself and the surrounding of the foetus (placenta, embryonic membranes, amniotic fluid).

Comments on the above Quranic statements by some experts

Dr. E. Marshall Johnson : Professor of Anatomy, concluded after studying the verses from the Quran: "The Quran describes not only the development of an external form but emphasizes also the internal stages - the stages inside the embryo of its creation and development, emphasizing major events recognized by contemporary science. So, I see nothing in conflict with the concept that divine intervention was involved...

Keith L. Moore : A noted embryologist and expert in his field, upon being presented with all the statements made in the Quran regarding the stages of the formation of the embryo from the mixing of the male and female gametes up to the embryo's full development was impressed so much that he presented his findings to scientists at several conferences. Several Canadian periodicals published many of Moore's statements and in addition he presented three television programmes in which he highlighted the compatibility of the modern science with what has been revealed in the Quran 1400 years ago. Consequently, he was asked: "Does this mean that you believe that the Quran is the word of God?" to which he replied "I find no difficulty in accepting this."

In fact, Professor Moore was so amazed at the accuracy of the descriptions and the terminology used for the various stages of the development of the embryo ***that he modified his own textbook on the subject. He incorporated all the relevant Quranic passages and authentic statements of the Prophet Muhammad into his book,*** **"The Developing Human: Clinically oriented embryology"** which was published by WB Saunders in 1987 and was a standard university textbook in the United States. The book now contains passages of the Quran and the Hadeeth (verified statements of the Prophet Muhammad) for every stage of development and Professor Moore has also adopted the classification used in the above two sources. (http://www.-quranandscience.com/human/135-dr-keith-moore-confirms-embryology-in-Quran.html)

Dr. T.V.N. Persaud : Professor and Head of the Department of Anatomy, University of Manitoba, Canada, who received in 1991, the most distinguished award presented in the field of Anatomy in Canada, the J.C.B. Grand Award says: "You have an illiterate person (Prophet Muhammad) making profound statements that are amazingly accurate, of a scientific nature. I personally can't see how this could be a mere chance, there are too many accuracies and like Dr. Moore, I have no difficulty in my mind reconciling that this is a divine inspiration or revelation which led him to these statements".

Expanding Universe

In 1925, Edwin Hubble (after whom the Hubble Space telescope is named) provided the observational evidence for the expansion of the universe. Stephen Hawking (author of 'A Brief History of Time') states: "The universe is not static, as had previously been thought, it is expanding". So what did God reveal in the Quran, 1400 years ago?

[Quran 51:47] "And the firmament, We constructed with power and skill and verily We are expanding it.

We discuss this topic again in another chapter "The Quran on Cosmology"

Extra Terrestrial Life (ET)

At the end of this article, I quote verses which indicate a very surprising description that there are living beings in other places besides this earth. Extra Terrestrial life (ET) is the current topic of discussion in scientific circles. The scientists are in a vigorous search of some kind of Intelligent Beings; the name of such a project is SETI (The **search for extraterrestrial intelligence (SETI)** is the collective name for a number of activities people undertake to search for intelligent extraterrestrial life. SETI projects use scientific methods in this search. For example, electromagnetic radiation is monitored for signs of transmissions from civilizations on other worlds) (http://en.wikipedia.org/wiki/Search_for_extraterrestrial_intelligence) Refer these verses in the Quran, for brevity, we show the translations of the first two only: 42:29, 65:12, 16:49, 17:44, 24:41, 22:18.

- [Quran 42:29] *(Asad)* And among His signs is the [very] creation of the heavens and the earth, **and of all the living creatures which He has caused to multiply throughout them:** and [since He has created them,] He has [also] the power to gather them [unto Himself] whenever He wills.

- [Quran 42:29] *(Y. Ali)* And among His Signs is the creation of the heavens and the earth, and **the living creatures that He has scattered through them:** and He has the power to gather them together when He wills.

"in both" (Arabic word used is 'feehima' meaning 'in both' denoting the heavens and the earth. In the Quran, the expression "the heavens and the earth" invariably denotes the universe in its entirety. (see explanatory note of Asad in http://www.islamicity.com/QuranSearch/)

[Quran 16:49] "<u>All the living creatures</u> in the heavens and the earth and all the angels prostrate themselves in adoration before Allah; they do not show any arrogance at all; (http://www.islamic studies.-info/tafheem.php?sura=16&verse=41&to=50)

[Quran 65:12] Allah is He Who created seven Firmaments and <u>*of the earth a similar number.*</u> Through the midst of them (all) descends His Command: that ye may know that Allah has power over all things, and that Allah comprehends, all things in (His) Knowledge.

(Most commentators of the Quran are of view that 'seven' mentioned here and at many places in the Quran mean as 'many in number' (We have discussed this word 'seven' in length in the chapter "The Quran on Cosmology"). The translation *"of the earth a similar number"* is for the Arabic words used in the text which are "wa minal ardi mithlahunna"

وَّمِنَ الۡاَرۡضِ مِثۡلَهُنَّ ؕ

See the translation and commentary of this verse by the renowned exegetist A.A.Maududi below: (refer to http://www.quranenglish.com/tafheem_Quran/065.htm). The explanatory note on this verse is worthy of due attention of the modern cosmologists and very interesting to laymen.

[Quran 65:12] Allah it is He Who created seven heavens, and, like them, the earth. His commandment descends among them. (All this is being stated so that you know) that Allah has power over everything, and that Allah encompasses all things in His knowledge.

- See explanatory note on this verse at the above site—we note here some of the points.

"Also their like-- does not mean that He created as many earths as the heavens, but it means that He has also created several earths as He has created several heavens. "Of the earth- mean that just as this earth which is inhabited by man is serving as a bed and cradle for the creatures living on it, so has Allah made and set other earths also in the universe, which serve as beds and cradles for the creatures living on them. Moreover, there are clear pointers in the Quran to the effect that living creatures are not found only on the earth but also in the heavens. (For instance, sec. Ash-Shura: 29 and E.N. SO on it). In other words, the countless stars and planets seen in the sky are not all lying desolate, but like the earth there are many among them which are inhabited."

The Protected Roof

In the Quran, God calls our attention to a very interesting attribute of the sky: [Quran 21:32] We made the sky a preserved and protected roof yet still they turn away from Our signs.

This attribute of the sky has been proved by a scientific research carried out only in the 20th century. The atmosphere surrounding the earth serves crucial functions for the continuity of life.

(*i*) While destroying many meteors, big and small as they approach the earth, it prevents them from falling to the earth and harming the living things.

(*ii*) In addition, the atmosphere filters the light rays coming from space that are harmful to the living things. Interestingly, the atmosphere lets only harmless and useful rays– visible light, near ultraviolet light, and radio waves pass through. All of this radiation is vital for life. Near ultraviolet rays, which are only partially let in by the atmosphere, are very important for the photosynthesis of plants and for the survival of all living beings. The majority of the intense ultraviolet rays emitted from the sun are filtered out by the **ozone layer of the atmosphere** and only a limited–and essential–part of the ultraviolet spectrum reaches the Earth.

(*iii*) The atmosphere also protects the earth from the freezing cold of the space, which is about minus 270 degree Celsius.

(*iv*) In addition to the atmosphere, the **Van Allen Belt**, a layer caused by the magnetic field of the Earth, also serves as a shield against the harmful radiation that threatens our planet. This radiation, which is constantly emitted by the Sun and other stars, is deadly to living things. If the Van Allen belt did not exist, the massive outbursts of energy called solar flares that frequently occur in the Sun would destroy all life on Earth. Dr. Hugh Ross has this to say on the importance of Van Allen Belts to our lives: In fact, the Earth has the highest density of any of the planets in our Solar System. This large nickel-iron core is responsible for our large magnetic field. This magnetic field produces the Van-Allen radiation shield, which protects the Earth from the radiation bombardment. If this shield were not present, life would not be possible on the Earth. The only other rocky planet to have any magnetic field is Mercury - but its field strength is 100 times less than the Earth's. Even Venus, our sister planet, has no magnetic field. The scientists only learned about the Van-Allen radiation recently, yet centuries ago, God informed us in the Quran of the world's atmosphere functioning as a protective shield.

We have indicated above some scientific descriptions in the Quran, there are many more verses which contains either words or statements that convey directly or indicate indirectly some scientific facts.

Anyone interested may go through them by consulting **Google: "Scientific descriptions in the Quran"**;

Youtube: Quran: Top scientists comment on scientific miracles in the Quran,
scienceislam.com, quranandscience.com,
http://www.missionislam.com/science/book.htm
http://www.sultan.org/
http://www.miraclesofthequran.com/scientific_94.html

Extra Note:

Dr. Maurice Bucaille, a French Surgeon, scientist and university scholar, and the author of one of the most popular books about scripture and science, "The Bible, The Quran and Science" and "What is the Origin of Man" writes:

In '***La Bible,, le Coran et la Science***' [***The Bible, the Quran and Science***], which first appeared in the original French in 1976 and which subsequently appeared in English in 1978, I set forth the main points of these findings. On November 9, 1976, I gave a lecture to the ***Academic de Medecine*** [***French Academy of Medicine***] in which I explored the statements on the origins of the man contained in the Quran; the title of the lecture was '***Donnees physiologiques et embryologiques du Coran***' [***Physiological and Embryological Data in the Quran***]. I emphasized the fact that these data, which I shall summarize below, formed part of a much wider study. The following are some of the points, which arise from a reading of the Quran:

- ❖ A concept of the creation of the world which while different from the ideas contained in the Bible, is fully in keeping with today's general theories on the formation of the universe;
- ❖ Statements that are in perfect agreement with today's ideas concerning the movements and evolution of the heavenly bodies;

- A prediction of the conquest of space; notions concerning the water cycle in nature and the earth's relief, which were not proven correct until many centuries later.

All of these data are bound to amaze anyone who approaches them in an objective spirit. They add a much wider dimension to the problem studied in the present work. The basic point remains the same, however: we must surely be in the presence of facts which place a heavy strain on our natural propensity for explaining everything in materialistic terms, for **the existence in the Quran of these scientific statements appears as a challenge to the human explanation."**

"It makes us deem it quite unthinkable for a man of Muhammad (pbh)'s time to have been the author of such statements, on account of the state of knowledge in his day. Such considerations are part of what gives the Quranic revelation its unique place among religious and non-religious texts, and forces the impartial scientist to admit his inability to provide an explanation based solely upon materialistic reasoning."

(See the detailed interesting discussion in "What is the origin of Man?" And "the Bible, the Quran and Science" now available on the Internet: search these titles in Google and see: http://www.sultan.org/articles/QScience.html)

2

What We Observe in The Universe

{In this chapter, scientific description are mentioned and the verses are quoted in Arabic text for anyone to check the veracity}

The Quran asks its readers, be Muslim or non–Muslim to observe the different phenomena going on in the Universe and further asks to apply their intelligence, infer logical conclusions and asks them not to be blind followers. It even says that to observe and ponder over the creation of the Universe is a praise worthy quality of a wise person; and on the other hand it rebukes those who don't apply their intellect:

إِنَّ فِي خَلْقِ السَّمٰوٰتِ وَالْأَرْضِ وَاخْتِلَافِ الَّيْلِ وَالنَّهَارِ لَآيٰتٍ لِّأُولِي الْأَلْبَابِ ﴿١٩٠﴾
الَّذِينَ يَذْكُرُونَ اللّٰهَ قِيٰمًا وَّقُعُودًا وَّعَلٰى جُنُوبِهِمْ وَيَتَفَكَّرُونَ فِي خَلْقِ السَّمٰوٰتِ
وَالْأَرْضِ ۚ رَبَّنَا مَا خَلَقْتَ هٰذَا بَاطِلًا ۚ سُبْحٰنَكَ فَقِنَا عَذَابَ النَّارِ ﴿١٩١﴾

[Quran 190-191] Verily, in the creation of the heavens and the earth, and in the succession of night and day, there are indeed messages for all who are endowed with insight, [and] who remember God when they stand, and when they sit, and when they lie down to sleep, and [thus] *reflect on the creation of the heavens and the earth:* "O our Sustainer! Thou hast not created [aught of] this without meaning and purpose. Limitless art Thou in Thy glory! Keep us safe, then, from suffering through fire!

وَيَجْعَلُ الرِّجْسَ عَلَى الَّذِيْنَ لَا يَعْقِلُوْنَ ﴿١٠٠﴾

[S.Yunus 10:100] and [that] it is He who lays the loathsome evil (or uncleanness) upon those who will not use -their reason.

وَكَاَيِّنْ مِّنْ اٰيَةٍ فِي السَّمٰوٰتِ وَالْاَرْضِ يَمُرُّوْنَ عَلَيْهَا وَهُمْ عَنْهَا مُعْرِضُوْنَ ﴿١٠٥﴾

[Quran 12:105] (But [then] - how many a sign is there in the heavens and on earth which they pass by [unthinkingly], and on which they turn their backs!

On such an appeal, as we observe the Universe, we find some very interesting and peculiar facts and further we are surprisesd that many of which are reffered to in the Quran. Perhaps in the future, some more observations and their references will be found ;as the Quran predicts :

سَنُرِيْهِمْ اٰيٰتِنَا فِي الْاٰفَاقِ وَفِيْٓ اَنْفُسِهِمْ حَتّٰى يَتَبَيَّنَ لَهُمْ اَنَّهُ الْحَقُّ ۭ

[Quran 41:53] (Soon will we show them our signs in the farthest regions of the earth and in their own souls, until it becomes clear to them that this is the Truth.)

The Following are The Most Observable Facts of The Universe:

1. Creating Everything in Pairs

سُبْحَٰنَ ٱلَّذِى خَلَقَ ٱلْأَزْوَٰجَ كُلَّهَا مِمَّا تُنۢبِتُ ٱلْأَرْضُ وَمِنْ أَنفُسِهِمْ وَمِمَّا لَا يَعْلَمُونَ ٣٦

[Quran 36:36] Glory to ALLAH who created **pairs in all things** that the Earth produces and in their own (humankind) and ***things of which they have no knowledge.***

وَمِن كُلِّ شَيْءٍ خَلَقْنَا زَوْجَيْنِ لَعَلَّكُمْ تَذَكَّرُونَ ٤٩

[Quran 51:49] (*And of everything we have created in pairs so that you may reflect (contemplate, think, ponder)*.

ٱلَّذِى جَعَلَ لَكُمُ ٱلْأَرْضَ مَهْدًا وَسَلَكَ لَكُمْ فِيهَا سُبُلًا وَأَنزَلَ مِنَ ٱلسَّمَآءِ
مَآءً فَأَخْرَجْنَا بِهِۦٓ أَزْوَٰجًا مِّن نَّبَاتٍ شَتَّىٰ ٥٣

[Quran 20:53] "He Who has, made for you the earth like a carpet spread out; has enabled you to go about therein by roads (and channels); and has sent down water from the sky." With it have **We produced diverse pairs of plants each separate from the others.**

وَهُوَ ٱلَّذِى مَدَّ ٱلْأَرْضَ وَجَعَلَ فِيهَا رَوَٰسِىَ وَأَنْهَٰرًا ۖ وَمِن كُلِّ ٱلثَّمَرَٰتِ جَعَلَ
فِيهَا زَوْجَيْنِ ٱثْنَيْنِ ۖ يُغْشِى ٱلَّيْلَ ٱلنَّهَارَ ۚ إِنَّ فِى ذَٰلِكَ لَءَايَٰتٍ لِّقَوْمٍ يَتَفَكَّرُونَ ٣

[Quran 13:3] And it is He who has spread the earth wide and placed on it firm mountains and running waters, **and created thereon two sexes of every [kind of] plant**; [and it is He who] causes the night to cover the day. Verily, in all this there are messages indeed for people who think!

The pairs are not there only in living beings but in all objects, animate or inanimate. In engineering, there are male & female joints without which no structure can stand and work. There are positive and negative charges, electron and proton and such several examples.

2. Everything in The Universe is in Motion

Everything in the universe, from a subatomic particle to stars to galaxies, all are moving:-

اَللّٰهُ الَّذِیْ رَفَعَ السَّمٰوٰتِ بِغَیْرِ عَمَدٍ تَرَوْنَهَا ثُمَّ اسْتَوٰی عَلَی الْعَرْشِ وَسَخَّرَ
الشَّمْسَ وَالْقَمَرَ ؕ كُلٌّ یَّجْرِیْ لِاَجَلٍ مُّسَمًّی ؕ یُدَبِّرُ الْاَمْرَ ؕ

[Quran 13:2] and He [it is who] has made **the sun and the moon subservient [to His laws], each running its course for a term set** [by Him]. He governs all that exists.

'He controlled the SUN and the MOON, each runs unto an appointed term.'

وَالشَّمْسُ تَجْرِیْ لِمُسْتَقَرٍّ لَّهَا ؕ ذٰلِكَ تَقْدِیْرُ الْعَزِیْزِ الْعَلِیْمِ ﴿۳۸﴾

[Quran 36:38] "And the sun runs on unto a resting place for him. That is the *measuring* of the Mighty, the Wise". There is NOTHING which is at Absolute Rest.

As we know today, ALL stars including the Sun are moving, a general value is as below:

- The speeds of stars: 50,000 km/hr to 600,000 km/hr.
- The speed of Sun 72,000 km/hr completing its orbit in 220 million years.

- The speed of electron, depending upon in which orbit around the Nucleus is : Electron in H – atom : 20,000 km/hr ~ 72 lakh km/hr.
- The speed of the Earth around its spining axis 1675 km/hr and around the sun at 1,07,000 km/hr.

3. Change/ Growth/ Decay

كُلُّ مَنْ عَلَيْهَا فَانٍ ﴿٢٦﴾

[Quran 55:26] All that lives on earth or in the heavens is bound to pass away: *every thing runs for an appointed term.*

[Quran 13:2] Allah is He Who raised the heavens without any pillars that ye can see; He is firmly established on the throne (of authority); He has subjected the sun and the moon (to his Law). Each one runs (its course) *for a term appointed*. He does regulate all affairs, explaining the signs in detail that ye may believe with certainty in the meeting with your Lord.

يُولِجُ الَّيْلَ فِي النَّهَارِ وَيُولِجُ النَّهَارَ فِي الَّيْلِ ۙ وَسَخَّرَ الشَّمْسَ وَالْقَمَرَ ۖ كُلٌّ يَّجْرِي لِأَجَلٍ مُّسَمًّى ۚ ذٰلِكُمُ اللّٰهُ رَبُّكُمْ لَهُ الْمُلْكُ ۚ وَالَّذِيْنَ تَدْعُوْنَ مِنْ دُوْنِهٖ مَا يَمْلِكُوْنَ مِنْ قِطْمِيْرٍ ﴿١٣﴾

[Quran 35:13] He merges Night into Day, and he merges Day into Night, and he has subjected the sun and the moon (to his Law): each one runs its course for a term appointed. Such is Allah your Lord: to Him belongs all Dominion. And those whom ye invoke besides Him have not the least power.

خَلَقَ السَّمٰوٰتِ وَالْاَرْضَ بِالْحَقِّ ۚ يُكَوِّرُ الَّيْلَ عَلَى النَّهَارِ وَيُكَوِّرُ النَّهَارَ عَلَى الَّيْلِ
وَسَخَّرَ الشَّمْسَ وَالْقَمَرَ ۭ كُلٌّ يَّجْرِيْ لِاَجَلٍ مُّسَمًّى ۭ اَلَا هُوَ الْعَزِيْزُ الْغَفَّارُ ⑤

[Quran 39:5] He created the heavens and the earth in true (proportions): He makes the Night overlap the Day, and the Day overlap the Night: He has subjected the sun and the moon (to His law): <u>Each one follows a course for a time appointed</u>. Is not He the Exalted in Power - He who forgives again and again?

Every living & non- living thing manifests this quality. It is clearly evident in living things e.g. mankind, trees, animal, etc., but one should know that it is also happening to everything from atomic particles to stars & galaxies. Every time new stars are being born, they grow, shine and fade away and so called die. Our SUN is also said to be losing its energy and will die in about 200 million years. Even machines show this pattern of their working - they start, grow and decline with time. Now, this pattern, start / birth, grow, decline, decay has a direction, so it is unidirectional, with the passage of time, hence called the **Arrow of Time**.

Time flows in one direction and it is irreversible. It gives rise to some very interesting conclusions:

(*a*) All processes going on in the universe are undergoing *irreversible process*es.

(*b*) With irreversibility is linked a property called ***Entropy*** which is a measure of the disorder, whenever an irreversible process occurs, its entropy increases the useful energy of the system decreases.

(*c*) The famous **'Second law of Thermodynamics'** which deals with Entropy gives rise to a very important corollary called the "law of degradation of energy of the universe". Thus, it is proved scientifically that the end of this world, as claimed by the Quran, is going to happen with all certainty

4. Emphasis and Importance of *'Very Small'*

It is to be noted that in the universe, everything, I repeat everything, either animate or inanimate, living or nonliving, from a small blade of grass to a rocket, a small microprocessor to super galaxies, all these rest for their genesis and maintenance or sustenance on a very small amount / particle / or object. See the following examples:

- **Embryology** : A man is created by a sperm and an ovum hardly seen even by a good microscope (Detail is coming in passages below).
- **Physics** : Galaxies are composed of stars. Stars are basically places of burning Hydrogen atoms almost like H- bombs: the process of fusion taking place between Hydrogen atoms.
- **Chemistry** : See the configuration of an atom, of basic elements : displacing a single electron from its orbit around the nucleus, changes the character of the element.
- **Medical** : A slight change of any hormone in micro or milli-micro – gram amount may change the health of a man drastically.
- **DNA** : It is just a marvel, how a very large number of information is packed at a microscopic level.

In everything, ALL THE TIME, A CHANGE IS GOING ON, TOWARDS ITS DECAY, ON MICRO – LEVEL. It affects the working of that substance in a long way and for all the time, such microscopic particles are demonstrations of how ALLAH has packed in such a small space, some mind–blowing marvels.

As an example, ALLAH has described the creation of man at many places in the Quran as to how it goes on at a microscopic level.

[Quran 32:7-9] Who makes most excellent everything that He creates. Thus, He begins the creation of man out of clay; [Quran 32:8] then He causes him to be begotten out of the essence of a humble fluid (Arabic word used here is "**sulalah** min maa maheen": quintessence amount). And then He forms him in accordance with what he is meant to be, and breathes into him of His spirit: and [thus, O men,] He endows you with hearing, and sight, and feelings as well as minds: [yet] how seldom are you grateful!

This word (***sulalah***) used here means a ***very small drop***. It means an essence of something; the best part or an extraction of something.

The semen ejaculated is the extraction of the body and as we know, out of more than a million 'spermatozoon', a single one fertilizes the ovum.

In male humans, **sperm** cells consists of a flat, disc shaped **head** 5 μm by 3 μm and a tail 50 μm long. An **ovum** is about 100 microns (or micrometers) in diameter.

A sperm of that small size contains 24 chromosomes which in turn contains 20,000 Gene. Egg 1/200 inch diameter, it also contains 20,000 genes.

In one cubic cm. of semen there are (100 million sperms). Thus, in one ejaculation of man, of about 5 ml. There are 500 million sperms & out of this only one goes to fertilize].

{Allah is the best knower of what is going on in the micro level of everything}

5. Symmetry and Asymmetry

Allah has kept beauty in a symmetry. In nature, in all living creatures, in fruits and flowers, butterfly to whales, we find a symmetry in the construction and the structure.

However, there is also an element of *ASYMMETRY* : the heart in man, in slightly leftward, the left kidney is slightly higher than the right and so on, such an asymmetry is there in the leaves of trees and the wings of the butterfly, the two parts are not *EXACTLY* similar; the two hands of a man are not having equal strength of grip (dexterity): adeptness, facility in using hands and writing skills with both hands are not balanced; similar is the case with feet, one foot (right) is stronger than the other. It's this cause that people who are blind folded or if lost in wilderness, they walk in circles.

6. Everything in this Universe is in Due Proportion

One of the most remarkable things of the universe is its "***fine tuning***", that all things here are well designed and well balanced and with due proportion. This fact is considered by the present day scientists in the following words:

In fact, this "**fine-tuning**" is so pronounced, and the "coincidences" are so numerous, many scientists have come to espouse The Anthropic Principle, which contends that the universe was brought into existence intentionally for the sake of producing mankind. Even those who do not accept The Anthropic Principle admit to the "fine-tuning" and conclude that the universe is "too contrived" to be a chance event.

Dr. Dennis Scania, the distinguished head of Cambridge University Observatories stated:

If you change a little bit of the laws of nature, or you change a little bit of the constants of nature -- like the charge on the electron -- then the way the universe develops is so changed, it is very likely that intelligent life would not have been able to develop.

Dr. David D. Deutsch, Institute of Mathematics, Oxford University stated:

If we nudge one of these constants just a few percent in one direction, stars burn out within a million years of their formation, and there is no time for evolution. If we nudge it a few percent in the other direction, then no elements are heavier than the helium form. No carbon, no life. Not even any chemistry. No complexity at all.

Dr. Paul Davies, noted author and professor of theoretical physics at Adelaide University stated:

"The really amazing thing is not that life on Earth is balanced on a knife-edge, but that the entire universe is balanced on a knife-edge, and would be total chaos if any of the natural 'constants' were off even slightly. *You see," Davies adds, "even if you dismiss man as a chance happening, the fact remains that the universe seems unreasonably suited to the existence of life -- almost contrived -- you might say a 'put-up job'."* (http://www.geraldschroeder.com/FineTuning.aspx)

Now see what the Quran says on this topic:

اِنَّا كُلَّ شَىْءٍ خَلَقْنٰهُ بِقَدَرٍ ۞

[Quran 54:49] **Behold, everything have** *We created in due measure and proportion*: -

"*Verily, all things have we created in PROPORTION & MEASURE" And our COMMAND is but a single word like the twinkling of an eye*".

> Allah's creation is not haphazard. Everything follows (or in other words, is bound by) a LAW, is constituted in due proportion and measure. Everything has its appointed time and occasion. Nothing happens but according to a plan and design.

The word 'qadara' used in the verse above, appears in the Quran in various grammatical forms at 132 places.

This is a very comprehensive word, it includes in it at least these fine shades of meaning :

it follows some *LAW, it is in accordance with PROPORTION & MEASURE, it* runs for an appointed term, occurs at an appointed occasion or time.

وَخَلَقَ كُلَّ شَىْءٍ فَقَدَّرَهٗ تَقْدِيْرًا ۞

[Quran 25:2] It is He who <u>created all things, and ordered them in due proportions</u>. (It is he who created all things and ordered (arranged) them in due proportion.)

هُوَالَّذِىْ جَعَلَ الشَّمْسَ ضِيَآءً وَّالْقَمَرَ نُوْرًا وَّقَدَّرَهٗ مَنَازِلَ لِتَعْلَمُوْا عَدَدَ السِّنِيْنَ وَالْحِسَابَ ۚ مَا خَلَقَ اللّٰهُ ذٰلِكَ اِلَّا بِالْحَقِّ ۚ يُفَصِّلُ الْاٰيٰتِ لِقَوْمٍ يَّعْلَمُوْنَ ۞

[Quran 10:5] "He it is who has made the sun a [source of] radiant light and the moon a light [reflected], *and has determined for it phases so that you might know how to compute the years and to measure [time].* None of this has God created without [an inner] truth. Clearly does He spell out these messages unto people of [innate] knowledge"

وَالشَّمْسُ تَجْرِي لِمُسْتَقَرٍّ لَّهَا ۚ ذَٰلِكَ تَقْدِيرُ الْعَزِيزِ الْعَلِيمِ ﴿٣٨﴾

[Quran 36:38] "And [they have a sign in] the sun: it runs in an orbit of its own **[and] That is the measuring of** the Mighty, the Wise".

The distance of the Earth, the Moon and the Sun from each other, the orbit, the angle of the axis of the spining Earth, the rotation and the revolution of it around the Sun, all such details are **set** and **measured** and are bound by a strict **law**.

The same marvel is observed in the rotation of electrons around the Nucleous and the similar phenomenon in the galaxies as well.

This marvel of having all things in **due proportion (Qaddar)** is better observed in the creation of man himself.

اللَّهُ يَعْلَمُ مَا تَحْمِلُ كُلُّ أُنثَىٰ وَمَا تَغِيضُ الْأَرْحَامُ وَمَا تَزْدَادُ ۖ وَكُلُّ شَيْءٍ عِندَهُ بِمِقْدَارٍ ﴿٨﴾

[Quran 13:8] "Allah knows what every female bears in her womb. He is fully aware of what decrease or increase takes place in the womb. *Every single thing is before His sight, in (due) proportion*".

The detail of the human anatomy and stages in the embryological development are to be noted here.

7. Balance, Interdependence, Interlinking & Co-ordination of Different Systems in the Universe

There are various systems working in the universe, at times they seem to be working separetly and independently but when digging deep into their workings, they all are found to be interdependent and interlinked. A slight increase or decrease in any one parameter pertaining to a system will affect the other system. We know, how the bread we are eating is linked to the inclination of the axis of the rotation of the earth of 23 and ½ degrees because a slight variation in this value will drastically change the seasonal variables.

وَالْأَرْضَ مَدَدْنٰهَا وَأَلْقَيْنَا فِيهَا رَوَاسِيَ وَأَنْۢبَتْنَا فِيهَا مِنْ كُلِّ شَيْءٍ مَّوْزُوْنٍ ﴿١٩﴾

[Quran 15:19] And the earth -We have spread it out wide, and placed on it mountains firm, *and caused [life] of every kind to grow on it in a balanced manner,* -

Every type of a thing on the earth is in due balance & measure. The mineral kingdom supports the vegetable and they in turn support the animal and there is a link of mutual dependence between them.

Excess of one is eliminated by the other and vice versa.

وَإِنْ مِّنْ شَيْءٍ إِلَّا عِنْدَنَا خَزَآئِنُهٗ ۚ وَمَا نُنَزِّلُهٗٓ إِلَّا بِقَدَرٍ مَّعْلُوْمٍ ﴿٢١﴾

[Quran 15:21] And there is not a thing but its (sources and) treasures (inexhaustible) are with Us; but **We only send down thereof in due and ascertainable measures**.

وَكَأَيِّنْ مِّنْ دَآبَّةٍ لَّا تَحْمِلُ رِزْقَهَا ۖ اللّٰهُ يَرْزُقُهَا وَإِيَّاكُمْ ۚ وَهُوَ السَّمِيْعُ الْعَلِيْمُ ﴿٦٠﴾

[Quran 29:60] And how many living creature are there that takes no thought of its own sustenance; [the while] God provides for it as [He provides] for you - since He alone is all-hearing, all-knowing. –

وَعِندَهُ مَفَاتِحُ الْغَيْبِ لَا يَعْلَمُهَا إِلَّا هُوَ ۚ وَيَعْلَمُ مَا فِي الْبَرِّ وَالْبَحْرِ ۚ وَمَا تَسْقُطُ مِن وَرَقَةٍ إِلَّا يَعْلَمُهَا وَلَا حَبَّةٍ فِي ظُلُمَاتِ الْأَرْضِ وَلَا رَطْبٍ وَلَا يَابِسٍ إِلَّا فِي كِتَابٍ مُّبِينٍ ﴿٥٩﴾

[Quran 6:59] "With him are the keys of the unseen treasures that no one knows but He. He knows whatever is there on the earth and in the sea. Not a leaf does fall but with His knowledge. There is not a grain in the darkness (or depths) of the earth, nor any thing fresh or dry (green or withered) but is inscribed in a Record clear".

As we observe, all types of man's physical, mental, sexual, spiritual needs are provided to him at appropriate times of his needs, thus sexual urge is aroused in him/her only when his / her physical body is fully grown. Such is the case in all living beings.

وَآتَاكُم مِّن كُلِّ مَا سَأَلْتُمُوهُ ۚ وَإِن تَعُدُّوا نِعْمَتَ اللَّهِ لَا تُحْصُوهَا ۗ إِنَّ الْإِنسَانَ لَظَلُومٌ كَفَّارٌ ﴿٣٤﴾

[Quran 14:34] And [always] does He give you something out of what you may be asking of Him; and should you try to count God's blessings, you could never compute them. [And yet] Behold, man is indeed most persistent in wrongdoing, stubbornly ingrate!

Not only mankind but all creatures are taken care of. Describing the creation of the earth, it is said in S.41 Haam Mim Sajdah 41:9

(And bestowed blessing on the earth and measured there in its sustenance).

وَإِن مِّن شَيْءٍ إِلَّا عِندَنَا خَزَائِنُهُ وَمَا نُنَزِّلُهُ إِلَّا بِقَدَرٍ مَّعْلُومٍ ﴿٢١﴾

[Quran 15:21] "And there is not a thing but its (sources and) treasures (inexhaustible) are with Us. But We only send down there of in due and ascertainable measures "

All the gifts, forces and energies which we see in the world, around us, have their fountainhead with Allah, these treasures are unravelled by Him according to *His greater Plan*. As an example, we see, how Petrol was unravelled by Allah as a gift of Nature. Only three centuries back, we were not at all knowing about it. Imagine if petrol was discovered three centuries back, of what use could it be, there was no petrol engine as there was no Thermodynamic Laws, no Gas Laws, no material to sustain the high temperature inside the combustion chamber and so on. The petrol at that time could be of no use. **Allah plans everything as to which treasure has to be opened to mankind, at what place, at what age of time and how much in quantity.**

[Quran 32:5] "He regulates (every) affair from the heaven to the earth".

And we at present don't know the doors of which and what type of treasure will be opened by Him in the coming days. Although, out of our folly and ignorance and by deviating from Allah's path, we have misused them. Allah warns:

ظَهَرَ الْفَسَادُ فِي الْبَرِّ وَالْبَحْرِ بِمَا كَسَبَتْ أَيْدِي النَّاسِ لِيُذِيقَهُم بَعْضَ الَّذِي عَمِلُوا لَعَلَّهُمْ يَرْجِعُونَ ﴿٤١﴾

[Quran 30:41] [Since they have become oblivious of God,] corruption has appeared on land and in the sea as an outcome of what men's hands have wrought: and so He will let them taste [the evil of] some of their doings, so that they might return [to the right path].

8. Variety

A very noticeable thing we find in the Universe is that in every creature there is a wide ***variety*** in everything, ants to whales, grass to fruits, trees to mountains and in the humankind itself. Further, that kind of variety is not repeated in the chain of new reproduction. Variety is a classification of organisms into groups based on similarities of structure or origin etcetera and it exists in everything—the Quran states:

اَلَمۡ تَرَ اَنَّ اللّٰهَ اَنۡزَلَ مِنَ السَّمَآءِ مَآءً ۚ فَاَخۡرَجۡنَا بِهٖ ثَمَرٰتٍ مُّخۡتَلِفًا اَلۡوَانُهَا ؕ وَمِنَ
الۡجِبَالِ جُدَدٌۢ بِيۡضٌ وَّحُمۡرٌ مُّخۡتَلِفٌ اَلۡوَانُهَا وَغَرَابِيۡبُ سُوۡدٌ ﴿۲۷﴾ وَمِنَ النَّاسِ
وَالدَّوَآبِّ وَالۡاَنۡعَامِ مُخۡتَلِفٌ اَلۡوَانُهٗ كَذٰلِكَ ؕ اِنَّمَا يَخۡشَى اللّٰهَ مِنۡ عِبَادِهِ الۡعُلَمٰٓؤُا ؕ
اِنَّ اللّٰهَ عَزِيۡزٌ غَفُوۡرٌ ﴿۲۸﴾

[Quran 35:27-28] (Do you not see that Allah sends down rain from the sky? With it we bring out the productions of *various colours*, and in the mountains are tracts white and red, of various shades of colors and black intense in hue. And so (is the case) among men and beasts and cattles of various colors. Those among His servants are they who truly fear of Allah, Who have knowledge, for Allah is exalted and forgiving.

Among various creatures, there are a large number of species, whereas each species has large number of types and each individual of a type has different characteristics. Moreover, each species has its own type of systems such as digestive, nervous, blood circulatory and reproduction systems etc which is quite different from those of other species. **This variety in different systems in species is a strong issue against the theory of evolution which we are**

not turning up at this place. (We have discussed this in another chapter: "What the Quran says about Theory of Evolution")

As we know each man is different from the other by difference of characteristics, in hair, finger prints, DNA, speech, gait in walking and so on, as Allah mentions in the chapter Room (30:22).

وَمِنْ اٰيٰتِهٖ خَلْقُ السَّمٰوٰتِ وَالْاَرْضِ وَاخْتِلَافُ اَلْسِنَتِكُمْ وَاَلْوَانِكُمْ ۭ اِنَّ فِيْ
ذٰلِكَ لَاٰيٰتٍ لِّلْعٰلِمِيْنَ ۝۲۲

[Quran 30:22] And among His signs are the creation of the heavens and the earth, and the diversity of your tongues and colours: for in these, behold, there are messages indeed for all who are possessed of [innate] knowledge!

9. Each and Everything is Functioning Under a Law

This is the most remarkable thing observed in the universe that each and every single thing here is functioning and working under a LAW, namely physical law, chemical law or biological law etc. But what is a Law? What are the characteristics of 'LAW'?

1) Laws are what we observe '**how**' a phenomenon occurs in the Nature.

2) By minutely observing a phenomenon, we characterize the 'factors/parameters' on which that law is dependent and then 'formulate' a formula or 'enunciate' it in form of a statement (Example : law of gravitation $F = \frac{G.m_1m_2}{r^2}$ in form of a formula or 'statement of Second Law of Thermodynamics' in statement form)

3) Laws' cannot be 'deduced', we cannot apply principles of logic to deduce it or we cannot 'invent' a law, because LAWS as such are there in the Nature operating. What we do is only to observe it in a phenomenon and put it in proper 'words' and / or put it into mathematical formulation.

4) We cannot answer 'WHY' a particular law is operating only in the way we observe. (Example : 2nd law of thermodynamics heat energy flows from a higher to a lower temperature, 'why' so, why not from lower temperature to a higher one?), Science cannot answer this.

5) All 'laws' of nature are pervasive in Nature, uniformly applicable in any corner of the Universe.

6) Also, the 'Laws' do not change with time, however they are not 'eternal' as the laws were 'created' simultaneously with the creation of the universe and these laws, as we see operating now, will be ceased to work with the destruction of the universe *(and during and after the Qiyamah (Resurrection) these laws will not be in operation as is indicated in the various verses and chapters of the Quran.*

➢ What we say 'law' in Science, in the words of the Quran, this is ***"AMR of Allah"***. Everything in the Universe, every plant and animal, every rock and mountain, every particle of matter and galaxy, sound wave or electro-magnetic wave is bound by the *COMMAND (AMR)* of Allah. **Thus, Allah by His command has made each and every object to function and work under a particular Law**. This is mentioned in various verses:

➢ Indicating towards the **law of gravitation**, that how the heavenly bodies are working.

وَسَخَّرَ لَكُمُ الَّيْلَ وَالنَّهَارَ ۙ وَالشَّمْسَ وَالْقَمَرَ ؕ وَالنُّجُومُ مُسَخَّرٰتٌۢ بِاَمْرِهٖ ؕ اِنَّ فِيْ ذٰلِكَ لَاٰيٰتٍ لِّقَوْمٍ يَّعْقِلُوْنَ ۝١٢

[Quran 16:12] He has made subject to you the Night and the Day; *the sun and the moon; and the stars are in **subjection by His Command**:* verily in this are Signs for men who are wise.

[30:25] **And of His Signs is that the sky and the earth stand firm by His command.**

Referring to the **laws of governing floatation** of ships, the Quran says :

اَللّٰهُ الَّذِىْ خَلَقَ السَّمٰوٰتِ وَالْاَرْضَ وَاَنْزَلَ مِنَ السَّمَآءِ مَآءً فَاَخْرَجَ بِهٖ مِنَ الثَّمَرٰتِ رِزْقًا لَّكُمْ ۚ وَسَخَّرَ لَكُمُ الْفُلْكَ لِتَجْرِىَ فِى الْبَحْرِ بِاَمْرِهٖ ۚ وَسَخَّرَ لَكُمُ الْاَنْهٰرَ ۝٣٢ وَسَخَّرَ لَكُمُ الشَّمْسَ وَالْقَمَرَ دَآئِبَيْنِ ۚ وَسَخَّرَ لَكُمُ الَّيْلَ وَالنَّهَارَ ۝٣٣

[Quran 14:32] It is Allah Who has created the heavens and the earth and sends down rain from the skies, and with it brings out fruits wherewith to feed you; *it is He Who has made the ships subject to you, that they may sail through the sea by His command;* and the rivers (also) has He made subject to you.

(There are several ayats related to floatation of ships: S. Ibrahim 14:32, S. Baqrah 2:164, S. Hajj 22:65 S. Rum 30:46 and so on).

7) To show another aspect of the 'law' of Nature that it is pervasive, uniformly applicable to all corners of the Universe, the Quran states:

الَّذِىۡ خَلَقَ سَبۡعَ سَمٰوٰتٍ طِبَاقًا ؕ مَا تَرٰى فِىۡ خَلۡقِ الرَّحۡمٰنِ مِنۡ تَفٰوُتٍ ؕ فَارۡجِعِ
الۡبَصَرَ ۙ هَلۡ تَرٰى مِنۡ فُطُوۡرٍ ۞

[Quran 67:3] Who created the seven heavens one above another; you see no incongruity in the creation of the Beneficent Allah; then look again, can you see any break (anywhere)?

This is well demonstrated by the functioning of the spaceships namely Voyager I and Voyager II, sent far beyond into the space; the instruments in these, designed *according to the 'Laws' operating in the Earth* are well working in space, confirm the existence of those very Laws operating in the outer space.

- All the seven points indicated above, regarding the "Laws", make it somewhat 'mysterious' and 'beyond comprehension', yes we do comprehend but we can't go beyond a limit into the range of 'why'. Beyond a limit it becomes elusive i.e. difficult to detect or grasp. This is why the Quran calls these 'Laws' (amr) of Allah - and this comes under the preview of *mutashabihaat* category in the parlance of the Quran (the truths which lie beyond the range of human perception). This topic is interesting and inquisitive but at this point we can't dig into it because, here, we are only indicating 'what we observe' in the Universe and not discussing the details of each.

10. Mathematical Formulation of Nature

As scientists record what they observe, most often they are not just using words and paragraphs. The laws of nature can be documented with numbers. They can be measured and computed in the language of mathematics. Physicist

Eugene Wigner confesses that "**the mathematical underpinning of Nature is something bordering on the mysterious and there is no rational explanation for it.**" (Eugene Wigner, "The Unreasonable Effectiveness of Mathematics in the Natural Sciences," in Douglas Campbell and John Higgins, eds., *Mathematics* (Belmont, CA: Wadsworth, 1984), Vol. 3, 117)

➢ Physicist Paul C. Davies comments, "...to be a scientist, you had to have faith that the Universe is governed by dependable, immutable, absolute, universal, mathematical laws of an unspecified origin. You've got to believe that these laws won't fail, that we won't wake up tomorrow to find heat flowing from cold to hot, or the speed of light changing by the hour. Over the years I have often asked my physicist colleagues why the laws of physics are what they are? The favourite reply is, 'There is no reason they are what they are–they just are.'" (Paul C. Davies, physicist, cosmologist, astrobiologist, at Arizona State University; quoted in edge.org/3rd_culture/davies07/davies07_ index.html)

Conclusion

The above discussed are some of the very remarkable and noticeable facts of the Universe, when we contemplate over all of these separately or interlinking each or only some of them, we are but compelled to accept the following:-

(*a*) That this Universe is a highly *ORGANISED* entity.

(*b*) That there is a meticulous *COORDINATION* among several or all wings of the creation.

(*c*) That all these are created as per a very ***PERFECT DESIGN***.

(*d*) That a well-organized, well-coordinated, perfect designed body cannot come into being mere by ***Chance***.

(*e*) How was it that with the strike of the Big Bang, all the Laws of the Nature, Physical, Chemical, Gravitational and so on, started functioning in the most perfect order; and after all who knew that such and such laws will be required at such and such juncture?

(*f*) How is it that, for example, in human beings, variety and pairing has been maintained for years and years, in the most flawless manner, that you can recognize an Indian among all the people of the world and you can say of which part of India he may belong to, and even you can say which tribe he belongs to, over and above all these, two own brothers are different from each other; and it never happens that a Mexican is born in a Bengali family, yes you may say it is all the play of DNA!

Coming to DNA, the revelations of the modern genetics, has astounded the modern scientist and seeing its complexity and intricacy and the marvellous packaging of a large number of Information in a tiny space, hardly seen by an advanced electron microscope, the existence of Allah cannot be hushed up by saying that it all happened by *Chance*.

3

What the Quran says about the Theory of Evolution

(I) Brief Introduction of the Theory of Evolution

In 1859, Charles Robert Darwin published his book "The origin of species by means of Natural selection" and claimed that all living beings had a common ancestor and that they evolved from one another by means of natural selection. Those that best adapted to the habitat transferred their traits to subsequent generations and by accumulating over great length of time, these advantageous qualities transformed individuals into totally different species from their ancestors. The human body was thus the most developed product of the mechanism of natural selection. (see here an introduction of Theory of Evolution: http://www.talkorigins.org/faqs/evolution-research.html)

The fanciful ideas of Darwin were at first seized upon by those, at that period of time, who were seeking something to oppose the religionists (who were culprits of persecuting the scientists declaring them as apostate, going against the Bible), thus the theory gained popularity. Another reason was that at that stage of time, science itself had not advanced to an extent where 'Genetics', 'microbiology' and 'Biochemistry' had not emerged yet which later proved to be deadly to Darwin's theory.

"Neo- Darwinism", this model of the Theory says that species evolved as a result of MUTATIONS, minor changes in their genes and the fittest one survived through the mechanism of natural selection. Later on, they came up with another idea of "Punctuated Equilibrium" – stating that living beings suddenly evolved into other species without any transitional forms. Thus, they came near to the idea of 'CREATION"

Note:

1) You notice above that they use the word "Natural selection" - how is it carried out? Now, when we come to know the rules of 'genetics', 'biophysics', 'biochemistry' and the intricate process of 'mutations' in the light of 'DNA' and such related topics, we can easily hush up the fantasies carried by the evolutionists.
2) 'Theory of Evolution' - by logic, requires that there must had been a large no. of fossils of the "transitional formers", but to the dismays of the evolutionists, inspite of their fervent search they could not find a SINGLE fossil of the transitional form.

Cambrian Period

The oldest stature of earth in which fossils of living creatures have been found is that of the "Cambrian", (roughly 530 – 520 million yrs) - they appear to be those of a vast mosaic of living organisms, made up of such great numbers of complex creatures without any pre– existing ancestors.

Deception & Forgeries

(see the detail here:

http://www.nwcreation.net/evolutionfraud.html,

http://theevolutionimpasseii.wordpress.com/tag/the-see-the-chemical-evolution-deception-and-the-primordial-soup-fantasy-theory-of-favored-races/,

http://darwinismwatch.com/index.php?git=makale&makale_id=147941,)

Unable to find valid evidences in the fossil record, some evolutionists ventured to fabricate of their own– there are several instances of such forgeries recorded in the internet and encyclopedias. In school books and charts, they produced such pictures of a family of half –man, half–ape, trying to cook on wood–fire, giving a very deceptive impression on the minds of children.

"PILTDOWN MAN" In 1912, a doctor Charles Damson, claimed that he found a "jawbone and a cranial fragment in a place pill down, England, said to be 500 thousand years old. For 40 years scientists carried it as a great evidence - but later on using "fluorine Dating Method" it was found that the skull belonged to a 500 yrs old man ; the teeth in the jawbone belonged to an orangutan and the teeth had been artificially worn-down and were stained with potassium dichromate to give them an old dated appearance.

Nebraska Man

Based on a single tooth discovered by H.F Osborn, Director of American Museum of Natural History, in 1922, it was claimed to bear the common characteristics of both man and ape. It was named that of the Nebraska man (after the name of the place in U.S. where it was forced). To impress the public, they showed a whole family of the Nebraska man - all this based on a SINGLE TOOTH - and that tooth was later proved to be, hold your breath, that of an extinct wild American pig called prosthennops.

OTA BENGA—The African Native Put in to a Cage

The most tragic story is that of a short height man, captured in Congo in 1904'he had a family and children, but so called scientist, caged him, brought gatherings of scientists and claimed to be a transitional form, not in fossil but found living - a marvelous achievement. One can imagine the agony of a man, put in to a cage and declared an animal. Dr. William T. Hornady, the director of the Zoo in New York was proud to have such an exceptional piece of scientific evidence. Ota Benga eventually committed suicide!

See the details of Deceptions in Google:- *Theory of evolution: Evolution Forgeries*.

Ota Benga will remain a blot on the face of modern scientists; It shows how low they can fall in pursuit of proving their speculations and conjectures.

_Australopithecus

Evolutionists call the so called common ancestors of men & apes: Australopithecus (meaning South African ape): They are considered to be more developed than anstralopitheseous giving way to the modern man, "Homosapiens" the latest stage of evolution.

Now examine this scientifically:

The movements of men and apes are completely different. **Human Beings are the only Living creatures that move freely on two feet.** Some other animals do have a limited ability as they have bent skeletons. So only humans and no other animal are Bi-pedals.

The evolutionists earlier claimed that the Australopithecus, being ancestor of men was bipedal– then so feting the claim, said that these walked in bent rather in an upright posture (like men). But this claim of "bipedal" was refuted in mid-70's by some evolutions themselves (see a "Brief History of time" by Stephen Hawkings) and in 1996 by Robin Crompton who, by computer simulation demonstrated that Living creatures can walk either upright or on all fours. A type of in between stride cannot be sustained for long periods because of the extreme energy consumption:

- ❖ This means Australopithean could not have been both BIPEDAL and HAVE BENT SKELETON, thus have a bent walking posture.

(II) Arguments Against The Theory Of Evolution

Basic Arguments Against the Theory of Evolution

It explains, rather tries to explain - how a simpler form of life (amoeba) goes on acquiring the characters of a complex organism and changing from one species to another.

But it does not explain how the 'Life' itself started- the theory does not even try to explain 'what is life' and the genesis of it. The cell of a living being is more complex than all of the technological products produced by man. Today, even in the most developed laboratories of the world, a living cell cannot be produced by bringing organic chemicals together. The conditions required for the formation of a cell are too great in quantity to be explained away by coincidences. **Till now with all advancements of the modern science, no laboratory in the world has been successful in creating even a SIMPLE LIFE (a simple form of life).**

"Evolution cannot satisfactorily account for the genesis of life, the genetic code, or the ingenious synchronization process needed to produce life from a single fertilized human egg. Nor can evolution satisfactorily explain how physical processes can produce metaphysical realities such as consciousness and spirituality."

1) This theory does not explain, how the "psychological characters" were acquired by the human beings e. g. weeping, laughing, etc. which characters are not there, even partially, in its so called ancestors.

2) This theory does not explain the *instincts and intuitions*, inherently present in the animals and human beings. Based on these qualities, spiders and bees make their homes in the most sophisticated ways, suitable only to them; there are many such examples unexplained.

3) This theory does not explain the presence of the ***diverse*** *digestive systems, circulatory systems, reproductive systems and other such systems in different*

species - neither it throws any light on the gradual change of these systems from one type to another as this theory claims.

4) It also does not explain how and at what stage the capability of "speech" was acquired by man. "Speech" is the quality only human beings possess.

5) There are certain organs in human beings (and in some animals also) which function only when all of its components work together i.e. if any component does not work the whole organ will stop working. E.g. Eye or Wings.

Human Eye

The human eye is enormously complicated - a perfect and interrelated system of about 40 individual subsystems, including the retina, pupil, iris, cornea, lens and optic nerve. For instance, the retina has approximately 137 million special cells that respond to light and send messages to the brain. About 130 million of these cells look like rods and handle the black and white vision. The other seven million are cone shaped and allow us to see in color. The retina cells receive light impressions, which are translated to electric pulses and sent to the brain via the optic nerve. A special section of the brain called the visual cortex interprets the pulses to color, contrast, depth, etc., which allows us to see "pictures" of our world in 3-Dimension. Incredibly, the eye, optic nerve and visual cortex are totally separate and distinct subsystems. Yet, together, they capture, deliver and interpret up to 1.5 million pulse messages a milli-second! It would take dozens of Cray supercomputers programmed perfectly and operating together flawlessly to even get close to performing this task. (Lawrence O. Richards, *It Couldn't Just Happen*, Thomas Nelson, Inc., 1989, p.139-140.)

For instance, if an eye happened to have lost its eyelid, but still had all other parts e.g. cornea, conjunctivae, pupil, eye lenses, retina, choroids, eye muscles, tear glands, it would be greatly damaged and lose its seeing function. In the same manner, even all its organelles were present, but the tear production were stopped, the eye would soon dry out and become blind. Thus, the Eye has a multi sectioned complex system; all of these individual sections had to come in to existence <u>*All at the same time*</u>. Further, keep in view that different species have different types of eyes.

How did the lens, retina, optic nerve, and all the other parts in vertebrates that play a role in seeing suddenly come about? Because natural selection cannot choose separately between the visual nerve and the retina. The emergence of the lens has no meaning in the absence of a retina. The simultaneous development of all the structures for sight is unavoidable. Since parts that develop separately cannot be used, they will both be meaningless, and also perhaps disappear with time. At the same time, their development all together requires the coming together of unimaginably small probabilities. (Dr. Ali Demirsoy, *Inheritance and Evolution*, Meteksan Publications, Ankara, 475)

Similar is the case with WINGS of birds. "The common trait of the Eyes and the Wings is that they can only function if they are fully developed - a half way developed eye cannot see, a bird with half formed wings cannot fly. This aspect of the developments of the organs is completely ignored by this Theory.

The Missing Link between "Required and Acquired"

In schools, the students are taught how giraffes acquired a long neck; they used to eat leaves of trees by striking out their necks so they "required" long necks so gradually they "acquired" it in due course - this story is so imprinted in the minds of children in the name of science that they never ask the links between " required " and "acquired"

- Now consider the peculiarities of the neck of a giraffe - the heart of a giraffe is well formed and equipped to supply blood to the head, so high, requiring a high pressure but when the animal bows his head to say, drink water, that much high B. P. will harm its brain, so there are valves in the neck vessels which are shut down in this posture, and prevent excess blood flowing to the brains.
- Again, turn your attention to that stage, the first stage, when the giraffe's neck was short as of other similar animals - it desired to have a long neck - desired out of its requirement.

Now answer the Questions:

(*i*) How did the unconscious cells of its brain gained consciousness to think to change the functions of its organs?

(*ii*) One animal thought such a thing or the whole lot of all the giraffes of the world thought at the same level of time?

(*iii*) How did they get the thought that they should have such and such length of necks which will be suitable for them?

(*iv*) How did they get the thought of that such high lengths of necks will require a sophisticated system of pumping blood?

(*v*) To acquire these, how did they direct their own DNA/genes to '***make***' such valves?

The DNA and related rules of genetics will further raise many after questions very difficult for evolutionists to answer.

Mutation and DNA- A New Challenge to the Evolutionists

Mutations

Mutations are defined as breaks or replacements taking place in the DNA molecule, which is found in the nucleus of the cell of a living organism and which holds all the genetic information. These breaks or replacements are the result of external effects such as radiation or chemical action. Every mutation is an "accident" and either damages the nucleotides making up the DNA or changes their locations. Most of the time, they cause so much damage and modification that the cell cannot repair them.

Mutation, which evolutionists frequently hide behind, is not a magic wand that transforms living organisms into a more advanced and perfect form. The direct effect of mutations is harmful. The reason for this is very simple: DNA has a very complex and a sophisticated structure and random effects can only cause harm to this structure. Mutations are small, random, and harmful at best possibility they may be ineffectual. Mutations cannot lead to an evolutionary development. **A random change in a**

highly specialized organism is either ineffectual or harmful.

Developments in the science of genetics and the discovery of the nucleic acids (DNA and RNA) a new look on Mutation and have produced brand-new problems for the theory of evolution. *The DNA molecule located in the nucleus of cells of living beings is an example of this. The DNA is a sort of databank formed of the arrangement of four different molecules in different sequences. This databank contains the codes of all the physical traits of that living being. When the human DNA is put into writing, it is calculated that this would result in an encyclopedia made up of 900 volumes.*

Some Very Basic Information on the Structure and Function of DNA:

The molecule called DNA, which is found in the nucleus of each of the 100 trillion cells in our body, contains the complete construction plan of the human body. Information regarding all the characteristics of a person, from the physical appearance to the structure of the inner organs, is recorded in DNA by means of a special coding system. The information in DNA is coded within the sequence of four special bases that make up this molecule. These bases are specified as A, T, G, and C according to the initial letters of their names. All the structural differences among people depend on the variations in the sequence of these bases. There are approximately 3.5 billion nucleotides, that is, 3.5 billion letters in a DNA molecule. The DNA data pertaining to a particular organ or protein is included in special components called "genes". For instance, information about the eye exists in a series of special genes, whereas information about the heart exists in quite another series of genes. The cell produces proteins by using the information in all of these genes. Amino acids that constitute the structure of the protein are defined by the sequential arrangement of the nucleotides in the DNA.

➤ At this point, there is an important detail that deserves attention. An error in the sequence of nucleotides making up a gene would render the gene completely useless. When we consider that there are twenty thousand genes in one human cell, it becomes more evident how improbable it is for the millions of nucleotides making up these genes to be formed by accident in the right sequence. This improbability can be easily seen mathematically.

➤ A medium protein might include about 300 amino acids. The DNA gene controlling this would have about 1,000 nucleotides in its chain. Since there are four kinds of nucleotides in a DNA chain, one consisting of 1,000 links could exist in 4^{1000} (4 to the power 1000) forms. In fact, the probability of the random formation of a protein and a nucleic acid (DNA, RNA) is 1 divided by 4^{1000} which is inconceivably small. The chances against the emergence of even a particular protein chain are just insignificant.

➤ In addition to all these improbabilities, DNA can barely be involved in a reaction because of its double-chained spiral shape. This also makes it impossible to think that it can be the basis of life.

➤ Moreover, while DNA can replicate only with the help of some enzymes that are actually proteins, the synthesis of these enzymes can be realized only by the information coded in DNA. **As they both depend on each other, either they have to exist at the same time for replication, or one of them has to be "created" before the other.**

In short, the theory of evolution is unable to prove any of the evolutionary stages that allegedly occur at the molecular level.

Intelligent Design – DNA: (an extra note from http://www.allaboutscience.org/intelligent-design.htm)

An excellent example of intelligent design is the DNA molecule. Since its discovery by James Watson and Francis Crick in 1953, evolutionists have faced an insurmountable hurdle.

Anyone who truly investigates the mystery of the *DNA molecule – this incredible micro, digital, error-correcting, redundant, self duplicating, information storage and retrieval system, with its own inherent language convention, that has the potential to develop any organism from raw biological material – understands that life is the result of Intelligent Design*. In light of recent discoveries such as the DNA molecule, the absurdity of the evolution argument is readily apparent

To summarize what we have said so far, neither amino acids nor their products, the proteins making up the cells of living beings, could ever be produced in any so-called "primitive atmosphere" environment. Moreover, factors such as the incredibly complex structure of proteins, their right-hand, left-hand features, and the difficulties in the formation of peptide bonds are just parts of the reason why they will never be produced in any future experiment either.

Second Law of Thermodynamics Falsifies 'Theory of Evolution'

The First Law of Thermodynamics, commonly known as the Law of Conservation of Matter, states that matter/energy cannot be created nor can it be destroyed. The quantity of matter/energy remains the same. It can change from solid to liquid to gas to plasma and back again, but the total amount of matter/energy in the universe remains constant.

Second Law of Thermodynamics– Law of Increased Entropy

The Second Law of Thermodynamics is commonly known as the Law of Increased Entropy. While quantity remains the same (First Law), the quality of matter/energy deteriorates gradually over time. How so? Usable energy is inevitably used for productivity, growth and repair. In the process, a part of the usable energy is converted into unusable energy. Thus, usable energy is irretrievably lost in the form of unusable energy.

This famous law of physics is also known as the "law of entropy." In physics, entropy is the measure of the disorder of a system. A system's entropy increases as it moves from an ordered, organized, and planned state towards a more disordered, dispersed, and unplanned one. The more disorder there is in a system, the higher its entropy is. **The law of entropy holds that the entire universe is unavoidably proceeding towards a more disordered, unplanned, and disorganized state.**

It is now accepted in the world of Science that the (three) Laws of Thermodynamics have influence over every scientific discipline, every biological or geological process, and every interstellar system. We can immediately test certain ideas against the Laws of Thermodynamics to see if they follow some of the universe's most basic rules. Ideas that don't follow those rules are either wrong or must be caused by some supernatural influence. (see the detailed discussion: http://www.allaboutscience.org/three-laws-of-thermodynamics-faq.htm)

- Coming to the Theory of Evolution, we find that this theory ignores this fundamental law of physics. The mechanism offered by evolution totally contradicts the second law. The theory of evolution says that disordered, dispersed, and lifeless atoms and molecules spontaneously came together over time, in a particular order, to form extremely complex molecules such as proteins, DNA, and RNA, whereupon millions of different living species with even more complex structures gradually emerged. *According to the theory of evolution, this supposed process which yields a more planned, more ordered more complex and more organized structure at each stage—was formed all by itself under natural conditions.*

So Theory of evolution proceeds from disordered, dispersed, and lifeless atoms and molecules to a highly organized structure whereas the law of entropy makes it clear that all natural processes tend towards disorganization and decay. Thus this theory utterly contradicts an established law of physics.

(III) Theory of Evolution in the Quranic perspective

This theory tells that the first living creature in the simplest form came into being in WATER by just a combination of certain elements in a suitable environment. It ignores the question as to wherefrom those elements came, how the suitable environment could be available, and most important question: what is "life" itself? And if "chance" plays a vital role what is the factor of probability of this chance from a mathematical perspective.

➢ This theory by its essence negates the existence of an external supernatural agency in the process of creation while the essence of the Quran is just the opposite. The Quran presents:

(*i*) Allah as the sole creator of the universe out of nothing.

(*ii*) Allah as the creator of Adam as a new entity in unequivocal terms and not as a link of previous creatures.

(*iii*) There are clear wordings that Allah not only created once and went out of scene but controls each and every affairs of each of His creatures.

(*iv*) As per Quranic description, living creatures did come from water but not by its own; but Allah caused them so.

(*v*) **Variety** is one of the many important 'signs' of Allah in the Nature, in animate and in inanimate beings. The Quran says that the 'variety' in species and 'variety' of systems operating in each species quite different from others is not due to 'chance' but caused by and controlled by Allah.

- Theory of Evolution rests its edifice on "chance"; it tries to explain 'the *change* from one species to another in the attractive name of "MUTATION", thus an abrupt change to take place in DNA. For those unknown to the recent advances in the field of Biochemistry and Genetics, these words mutation and DNA may seem catching but the truth is just the opposite. Now the experts in these disciplines raise such questions to the evolutionists which make them dumbfounded. Thus, it does not and cannot answer as to **how** this "mutation" proceeds in a 'desired' and always in a 'better' direction; and as to **how** all the systems operating in a living being proceed in that direction in a well co-ordinated manner?

- The Quran says that it is Allah Who 'plans' and 'controls' each and every affair of each creature and also co-ordinates, and makes them inter-linked and inter-dependent not only in each of the creatures but also in the whole eco-systems of the world. [Quran 32:5] He governs all that exists, from the celestial space to the earth;)

Now contemplate over an entirely novel aspect:

It is a scientific fact that what we "see", "hear" and "touch" are just sensory perceptions, a variety of signals perceived by "Brain"; stimulations coming from an object are converted into electrical signals and cause an effect in the brain. When we "see", we in fact view the effects of these electrical signals in our mind. If the thing we acknowledge as the material world is merely comprised of perceptions shown to us, then what is this brain, by which we hear, see and think? Isn't the brain, like everything else, a collection of atoms and molecules?

But what is this "brain": only a heap of tissue slightly more than one kilogram. Who is there in it which really "sees", "hears" & "touches"? Certainly it is not the material "cells". Here comes the Quran to lead us to the reality : the man is not simply a heap of a variety cells but a summation of matter and SPIRIT ("rooh"). As Allah says in S. Sajdah v.7-9 (shown below)

He Who has created all things in the best possible way. He commenced the creation of man from clay; then produced his seed from an extract of base fluid; then formed him and breathed His Spirit into him and gave you hearing, sight and hearts. What little thanks you show! (S. Sajdah:32: 7-9)

The theory of evolution does not bring this "spirit" into consideration under its gambit; it tries to explain the "life" only on materialistic basis. Here is not the right place to discuss what this spirit is; here we only want to present why this theory is not compatible with the Quranic concept of creation.

See a glimpse of what the scientists say about "life" originating out of chance:

Could life evolve randomly from inorganic matter? Not according to mathematicians.

In the last 30 years a number of prominent scientists have attempted to calculate the odds that a free-living, single-celled organism, such as a bacterium, might result by the chance combining of pre-existent building blocks. Harold Morowitz calculated the odds as one chance in $10^{100,000,000,000}$. *Sir Fred Hoyle* *calculated the odds of only the proteins of an amoebae arising by chance as one chance in $10^{40,000}$.*

The odds calculated by Morowitz and Hoyle are staggering. The odds led Fred Hoyle to state that the probability of spontaneous generation 'is about the same as the probability that a tornado sweeping through a junk yard could assemble a Boeing 747 from the contents therein.' Mathematicians tell us that any event with an improbability greater than one chance in 10^{50} is in the realm of metaphysics - i.e. a miracle (Mark Eastman, MD, Creation by Design, T.W.F.T. Publishers, 1996, 21-22.)

Regarding the origin of life, Francis Crick, winner of the Nobel Prize in biology for his work with the DNA molecule, stated in 1982: *An honest man, armed with all the knowledge available to us now, could only state that in some sense, the origin of life appears at the moment to be almost a miracle, so many are the conditions which would have had to have been satisfied to get it going.* (Francis Crick, *Life Itself -- Its Origin and Nature*, Futura, 19)

4

The Quran on Cosmology

(I) A Very Brief Introduction to Modern Cosmology

(For commoners it is pointed out that Cosmology is different from Astronomy; the first is related to the branch of astrophysics that studies the origin and evolution and structure of the universe whereas the latter is a branch of study of celestial bodies of the universe as a whole. In preparing this article we have quoted heavily from Google, Wikipedia and other sites, although checked from some standard books, only for the reason that readers may quickly refer to and accumulate more information on any topic just by accessing their computers. Another point to indicate: Cosmology is a very wide field and a day to day changing field of knowledge; practically it is not possible to introduce it in a short article, we have concentrated here on such topics which have some indications however remotely to the Quranic descriptions; while going through the article "The Quran on Cosmology" one has to keep the following descriptions in view.)

- At the outset, we should state that the Cosmology is a difficult subject for a layman to comprehend. To make this clear just take 'distance', here it is not that simple distance you are accustomed to: there are many 'types of distance' as all the objects are moving in different directions, light which is the main 'tool' of measuring here, has its own speed over and above the universe itself is expanding. Here plane or spherical geometry is not applicable because of expansion of the universe. The subject is although interesting as the terms used are complex. Here we have tried to present some main points briefly but in simplified manner. (**for Basics of Astronomy and cosmology please see an easy to understand site:** http://www.universeadventure.org/)

Big Bang Theory

(http://www.newscientist.com/article/)

Cosmologists study the universe as a whole: its birth, growth, shape, size and eventual fate. The vast scale of the universe became clear in the 1920s when Edwin Hubble proved that "spiral nebulae" are millions to billions of light years distant and are moving away.

Hubble found that most galaxies are red shifted: the spectrum of their light is moved to longer, redder wavelengths. This can be explained as a doppler shift if the galaxies are moving away from us. Fainter, more distant galaxies have higher red shift, implying that they are receding faster, in a relationship set by the hubble constant.

The discovery that the whole universe is expanding led to the big bang theory. This states that if everything is flying apart now, it was once presumably packed much closer together, in a hot dense state. A rival idea, the steady-state theory, holds that new matter is constantly being created to fill the gaps generated by expansion. But the big bang largely triumphed in 1965 when Arno Penzias and Robert Wilson discovered cosmic microwave background radiation (CMB). This is relic heat radiation emitted by hot matter in the very early universe, 380,000 years after the first instant of the big bang.

Objects Created After Big Bang

(http://en.wikipedia.org/wiki/Physical_cosmology)

The **Big Bang** theory is the prevailing cosmological model that explains the early development of the Universe. But nobody knows what was **before** the Big Bang and **why** it happened, but it is assumed that just after this enigmatic cataclysm, the universe was so dense and hot that all four forces of nature (strong, electromagnetic, weak, and gravitational forces) were indistinguishable and therefore gravity was governed by quantum laws, like the other three types of interactions. A complete theory of quantum gravity has not been constructed yet, and this very first *epoch* of our history remains as enigmatic as the Big Bang itself. According to the most recent measurements and observations, the Big Bang occurred approximately 13.75 billion years ago, which is thus considered the age of the Universe. After its initial expansion from a singularity (a state in which density of matter is infinite and volume zero—an state beyond human conception), the Universe cooled sufficiently to allow energy to be converted into various subatomic particles, including protons, neutrons, and electrons. While protons and neutrons combined to form the first atomic nuclei only a few minutes after the Big Bang, it would take thousands of years for electrons to combine with them and create electrically neutral atoms. The first element produced was hydrogen, along with traces of helium and lithium. Giant clouds of these primordial elements would coalesce through gravity to form stars and galaxies, and the heavier elements would be synthesized either within stars or during supernovae. Now the Big Bang is widely accepted within the scientific community. It offers a comprehensive explanation for a broad range of observed phenomena. Since its conception, abundant evidence has been uncovered in support of the model.

Observable Universe

(http://en.wikipedia.org/wiki/Physical_cosmology)

In the Big Bang cosmology, the **observable universe** consists of the galaxies and other matter that humans can in principle observe from Earth in the present day, because light (or other signals) from those objects has had time to reach the Earth since the beginning of the cosmological expansion. Assuming the universe is isotropic, the distance to the edge of the observable universe is roughly the same in every direction—that is, the observable universe is a spherical volume (a ball) centred on the observer, regardless of the actual shape of the universe as a whole. Every location in the universe has its own observable universe which may or may not overlap with the one centred on the Earth.

The age of the universe is about 13.75 billion years, but due to the expansion of space humans are observing objects that were originally much closer but are now considerably farther away (as defined in terms of cosmological proper distance, which is equal to the comoving distance at the present time) than a static 13.75 billion light-years distance. The diameter of the observable universe is estimated to be about 28 billion parsecs (93 billion light-years).

Fine –Tuned Universe

(http://en.wikipedia.org/wiki/Fine-tuned_Universe)

In fact, this "fine-tuning" is so pronounced, and the "coincidences" are so numerous, many scientists have come to espouse **The Anthropic Principle**, which contends that the universe was brought into existence intentionally for the sake of producing mankind. Even those who do not accept The Anthropic Principle admit to the "fine-tuning" and conclude that the universe is "too contrived" to be a chance event. In his best-selling book, "A Brief History of Time", Stephen Hawking (perhaps the world's most famous cosmologist) refers to the phenomenon as "remarkable."

As long as the Universe has a beginning, we can assume that it had a creator, said Hawking.

- **A created Universe needs much information, many initial conditions, many Physical and Chemical laws. It seems that charges and the masses of elementary particles, which were about to form after the explosion, were "thought of" from the initial conditions, before the birth of the Universe. The expansion was achieved with such a rate so that the**

chemical elements, indispensable for any living creature such as H, C, N and O, can have time to produce.

At an atomic level, energy is quantified. The smallest quantum of action, named the Planck constant, has the value h = 6.67 * 10^{-34} J. s. If energy hadn't been quantified, infinity of chemical compounds would have formed, but they would have been unstable. The formation of proteins or of nucleic acids, without which life would not exist wouldn't have been possible.

Are the few data presented here the result of chance or are they well-thought of from the initial conditions so as the Universe should look the way we see it today? (J.M. Maldamé, *Christos pentru întreg Universul [Christos for the Whole Universe]*, Cartimpex Publishing House, Cluj, 1999, p. 102)

The remarkable fact is that the values of these numbers (i.e. the CONSTANTS OF PHYSICS) seem to have been very finely adjusted to make possible the development of life". "For example," Hawking writes, "if the electric charge of the electron had been only slightly different, stars would have been unable to burn hydrogen and helium, or else they would not have exploded. It seems clear that there are relatively few ranges of values for the numbers (for the constants) that would allow for development of any form of intelligent life. Most sets of values would give rise to universes that, although they might be very beautiful, would contain no one able to wonder at that beauty." Hawking then goes on to say that he can appreciate taking this as possible evidence of "a divine purpose in Creation and the choice of the laws of science (by God)" (ibid. p. 125). (http://en.wikipedia.org/wiki/A_Brief_History_of_Time)

Example of Proton & Electron:

Consider protons, for a simple example. Protons are the positively charged subatomic particles which (along with neutrons) form the nucleus of an atom (around which negatively charged electrons orbit). Whether by providence or fortuitous luck (depending on your perspective), protons just happen to be 1,836 times larger in mass than electrons but has equal charge of $1.602176565 \times 10^{-19}$ coulombs that of electron but of opposite nature. If they were a little bigger or a little smaller, we would not exist (because atoms could not form the molecules such as C(Carbon), N(Nitrogen), we require). So how did protons end up being 1,836 times larger than electrons? Why not 100 times larger or 1000 times? Why not smaller? Of all the possible variables, how did protons end up being just the right size? And why exactly equal charges? Why opposite charge, why not same type? Was it chance or contrivance? If protons did not balance electrons and vice versa, we would not exist. They are not comparable in size, yet they are perfectly balanced in case of charge. Did nature just stumble upon such a favourable relationship, or did some external Agent ordained it for our sakes?

Anthropic Principle

(http://en.wikipedia.org/wiki/Anthropic_principle)

Anthropic means "relating to human beings or their existence." *Principle* means "law." The Anthropic Principle is the Law of Human Existence as explained in the following words: It is well known that our existence in this universe depends on numerous Laws and Cosmological constants and parameters and mathematical formulations whose numerical values must fall within a very narrow range of values. If even a single variable were off, even slightly, we would not exist. The extreme improbability that so many variables would align so auspiciously in our favour merely by chance has led some scientists and philosophers to propose instead that it was God who providentially engineered the universe to suit our specific needs. It is just a small sample of the many factors which must be just right in order for life to exist on Earth. We are very fortunate to live on a privileged planet in a privileged solar system in a privileged galaxy in a privileged universe.

Intelligent Design theorists hail the Anthropic Principle as further evidence in support of their thesis that life was engineered by a transcendent Mastermind. Not only do biological systems bear the hallmarks of design (the information content of DNA, specified complexity, irreducible complexity, etc.), but the universe which supports and provides a context for life appears to have been designed as a means to that end. (See the detail here: http://www.gotquestions.org/anthropic-principle.html)

Looking Out in Space is Looking Back in Time

We see our universe not as it is, but as it used to be

The telescope is a kind of time machine; it lets us see our distant past. **As a matter of fact whatever you see NOW in the sky is not a picture of Present as such but it is a picture of Past**. Looking a star you think it is at its place but actually it is not; *it was at this place some time back*, during the time light from the star travelled to your eye, that star shifted to some other place. To understand this take the example of the nearest star from the Earth, Proxima Centauri 4.22 light year distance away. It took light rays to travel 4.22 years to reach to us; in that duration that star travelled (moved) to some other place of course with very high velocity.

Speculations and Conjectures in Modern Cosmology

1) Many observations are not answered definitively by **known physics**. According to the prevailing theory, a slight imbalance of matter over antimatter was present in the universe's creation, or developed very shortly thereafter, possibly due to the CP violation that has been observed by particle physicists. Although the matter and antimatter mostly annihilated one another, producing photons, a small residue of matter survived, giving the present matter-dominated universe. Several lines of evidence also suggest that a rapid cosmic inflation of the universe occurred very early in its history (roughly 10^{-35} seconds after its creation).

2) Recent observations also suggest that the cosmological constant (Λ) is not zero and that the net mass-energy content of the universe is dominated by a dark energy and dark matter that have not been characterized scientifically. They differ in their gravitational effects. Dark matter gravitates as ordinary matter does, and thus slows the expansion of the universe; by contrast, dark energy serves to accelerate the universe's expansion.

3) **Shape of The Universe**

The shape or geometry of the universe includes both local geometry in the observable universe and global geometry, which we may or may not be able to measure. Shape can refer to curvature and topology. More formally, the subject in practice investigates which 3-manifold corresponds to the spatial section in commoving coordinates of the four-dimensional space-time of the universe. In terms of observation, the section of space -time that can be observed is the backward light cone (points within the cosmic light horizon, given time to reach a given observer). If the observable universe is smaller than the entire universe (in some models it is many orders of magnitude smaller), one cannot determine the global structure by observation: one is limited to a small patch. (**A lay man can easily understand the problem if he is led to inside a huge building blind folded and asked to comprehend the size and shape of the whole building.**)

What NASA Tells on Shape of The Universe

"Although our view of the universe is limited, our imaginations are not. Astronomers have indirect evidence that the universe of galaxies extends far beyond the region we can see. But no one knows if the whole universe is infinitely large — large beyond limit. According to the leading theories, other parts of the universe may look very different from our own — and may even have different laws of nature. We may never be able to find out for sure. But it is possible that clues to the answer lie in plain view, just waiting to be discovered!" (http://www.nasa.gov/audience/foreducators/58/features/F_How_Big_is_Our_Universe.html)

4) Multiverse Theory

Main articles: Multiverse, Many-worlds hypothesis, Bubble universe theory, and Parallel universe (fiction) (WIKEPEDIA)

Depiction of a multiverse of seven "bubble" universes, which are separate spacetime continua, each having different physical laws, physical constants, and perhaps even different numbers of dimensions or topologies.

Some speculative theories have proposed that this universe is but one of a set of disconnected universes, collectively denoted as the multiverse, altering the concept that the universe encompasses everything. By definition, there is no possible way for anything in one universe to affect another; if two "universes" could affect one another, they would be part of a single universe. Thus, although some fictional characters travel between parallel fictional "universes", this is, strictly speaking, an incorrect usage of the term universe. The disconnected universes are conceived as being physical, in the sense that each should have its own space and time, its own matter and energy, and its own physical laws — that also challenges the definition of parallelity as these universes don't exist synchronously (since they have their own time) or in a geometrically parallel way (since there's no interpretable relation between spatial positions of the different universes There are two scientific senses in which multiple universes are discussed. First, disconnected spacetime continua may exist; presumably, all forms of matter and energy are confined to one universe and cannot "tunnel" between them. An example of such a theory is the chaotic inflation model of the early universe Second, according to the many-worlds hypothesis, a parallel universe is born with every quantum measurement; the universe "forks" into parallel copies, each one corresponding to a different outcome of the quantum measurement. However, both senses of the term "multiverse" are speculative and may be considered unscientific; no known experimental test in one universe could reveal the existence or properties of another non-interacting universe.

Multiverse – The problems

The multiverse explanation is highly problematic. Perhaps the biggest difficulty is that <u>the existence of such parallel universes can be neither verified nor falsified</u>. The model is thus ad hoc and contrived. Second, given that the bio friendliness of the universe is in no way conducive to cosmic sustainability, no form of selection process or "cosmic evolution" can be invoked. Third, if the multiverse thesis is to commend itself as a plausible hypothesis, then a mechanism for generating such universes needs to be advanced. The concept of a 'bubble' of universes, each with their own fundamental constants and values, only throws the paradox back one step -- as one could easily ask who built the generator to give rise to this cosmic lottery.

What Is the Reason for Believing in Multiple Universes?

The argument in favour of multiple universes tends to go something like this:

How is it that a single universe came up in being with a very fine-tuned properties as discussed above so many cosmologists suggest that there are actually a vast number of universes, which can have different properties. Within that vast multiverse of universes, some subset of them (including our own) would contain properties that allow them to exist for relatively long periods of time, some subset of those (again, including our own universe) would have the properties that allow them to form complex chemicals and, ultimately, life.

String Theory and Multiple Universes

String theory has recently begun to support this idea, because the results make it clear that there are vast number of possible solutions to string theory - in other words, if string theory is correct then there are still many different ways to construct the universe.

In addition, since string theory presents the idea of extra dimensions, it also includes a structure to think about where these other universes could be located. Our universe, which includes 4 dimensions of spacetime, seems to exist in a universe that may contain as many as 11 total dimensions (often called *the bulk* by string theorists). There's no reason to think that the bulk couldn't contain other universes in addition to our own.

5) Dark Energy & Dark Matter

Dark Matter

We "see" visible matter because it is able to emit and reflect visible light. However, imagine matter that did not interact with light at all and was therefore, quite literally, invisible. This is what scientists today believe to be Dark Matter (DM). In fact, DM is most probably non-baryonic, meaning it does not interact with any electromagnetic radiation at all. Even though we cannot visually observe it, scientists are convinced that 70-90% of matter in The Universe is non-baryonic DM and that ordinary luminous matter constitutes only a small fraction of The Universe's mass density.

Evidence of Dark Matter

Finding physical evidence of DM is difficult because it cannot be directly detected with any optical equipment. Even though it does not interact with light, DM still interacts gravitationally, and this quality helps verify its presence. If DM does exist, there must be more gravity present in The Universe than visible matter alone can produce.

Evidence of this "extra" gravity includes:

- The strange *rotational velocities* of stars in galactic disks can only be explained if much more mass is present in each galaxy.
- The relative bulk motions of galaxies combined with restrictions from nucleosynthesis show that the majority of the Universe's matter must be non-baryonic dark matter.

- The *degree to which light is bent* by galaxies and clusters indicates that 90% of the Matter in the Universe is **missing.**
- The *density of the Universe* is just right to make its geometry flat. Moreover, *no viable theory of structure formation exists* that does not contain a minimum amount of dark matter.
- Dark matter can't be like ordinary matter, because it would have made too much deuterium in big-bang nucleosynthesis. When the universe was less than 3 minutes old, some protons and neutrons fused to make light elements, and cosmologists calculate that if there had been much more ordinary matter than we see, then the dense cauldron would have brewed up a lot more deuterium than is observed. See further detail here: (http://www.universeadventure.org/-final_frontier/dkmttr-whatis.htm)

Dark energy

Imagine you toss an apple straight up into the air. Due to gravity, one would expect the apple to come right back down to earth. But what if it doesn't? What if, due to some unseen force your apple continues going up, at an accelerated rate, no matter how much gravity pleads and begs for the apple to come back down. Could this really happen? Could there really be "anti-gravity?" On the scale of the Universe, there is; in the most basic sense, Dark Energy is akin to **negative gravity**. <u>Where gravity is attractive, Dark Energy is repulsive</u>. Dark Energy causes the Universe to expand at an increasing rate. For example, to a viewer on earth, gravity would attract a distant galaxy towards Earth, but Dark Energy would cause the galaxy to move away from the Earth. Similarly, neither force can be directly seen. We detect gravity by observing the effect between two masses. We detect Dark Energy by measuring the expansion of the Universe through the comparison of standard candles (Standard Candle is a celestial object whose intrinsic brightness is known or can be well estimated by some physical principle. Because we can see its observed brightness as well, we can determine its distance.)

If Dark Energy is causing the Universe to expand, where is it?

Dark energy is **everywhere**. Dark energy is thought to be an inherent property of space itself. However we don't notice dark energy mostly because it is an incredibly small amount of energy per volume. The effect is only seen acting on the universe as a whole, much like how we can feel a gust of wind, but cannot feel the individual particles in air.

The WMAP (Wilkinson Microwave Anisotropy Probe) spacecraft put the standard picture of cosmology on a firm footing by precisely measuring the spectrum of fluctuations in the microwave background, which fits a universe 13.7 billion years old, containing 4% ordinary matter, 22% dark matter, and 74% dark energy.

"Many people have come up with different theories for dark energy," a scientist said. "Unfortunately, the mystery remains, and in fact, **the nature of dark energy is now perhaps the most profound mystery in**

cosmology and astrophysics. It is considered the most outstanding problem in theoretical physics.

"The other great mystery concerning our universe is that it contains much more matter than can be accounted for in our visible stars. The missing mass is termed as dark matter, and despite many attempts at detecting dark matter, **the mystery of dark matter remains and even deepens**."

6) **Theory of Everything**

(http://www.netplaces.com/evidence-of-the-afterlife/-unraveling-string-theory/space-and-time-here-and-in-the-afterlife.htm)

There are two leading theories in physics that help explain most of the phenomena that is observed around humanity. The first is Einstein's theory of **general relativity**, which explains how gravity works, why planets go around the stars, why black holes and galaxies exist, and a lot of other astronomical phenomena. The second is **quantum mechanics**, which very accurately explains how particles like electrons and protons behave at subatomic levels, as well as the properties of light and other forms of radiation. However, one of the biggest unsolved problems in physics today is that these theories just don't reconcile. It simply cannot explain how relativity has impacts over particles at subatomic levels or how quantum mechanics interacts with gravity.

String theory is one of the speculations of a "theory of everything," which has been proposed as a solution to this problem. If proved true, it could be an overarching framework, consistent with both relativity and quantum physics. But its implications could go much beyond and it could even explain the existence of afterlife.

Key Aspects of String Theory

According to string theory, fundamental particles in nature, like photons, electrons, and quarks, are nothing but vibrations of extremely small strings. Just like a guitar string can create different musical notes when plucked, the tiny strings in string theory create different vibrations under different tensions, also known as **excitation modes**. Different kinds of vibrations represent different fundamental particles of nature.

An important difference from the guitar analogy is that in string theory, strings are not attached to anything and they float freely in space and time. An even more interesting characteristic of these strings is that they exist in ten dimensions. The first nine dimensions are in space and the tenth dimension is time. According to string theorists, six dimensions of space are unobservable, as they are either extremely small or they are "curled up" and cannot be detected with conventional experiments. Only the other three dimensions are big enough to be perceived as "real." **However, it is the hidden dimensions that define most of the properties of the world.**

M-Theory

String theory is a revolutionary new theory in quantum physics. String theory evolved into the M-theory and the existence of multiple dimensions as it gained wider acceptance and momentum among physicists. **M-theory is known as the "theory of everything."** It combines all string theories together. The M-theory requires mathematical tools that have not yet been totally accepted in order for it to be fully understood.

Could there be other dimensions to time? Could other frequencies exist that we cannot hear? Do other dimensions, also unseen, exist? Some physicists think so, but this leads to deeper questions such as the possibility of the existence of more than one universe.

British physicist and author Stephen Hawking originally believed that **M-theory** may be the "ultimate" theory, but later suggested that the search for understanding of mathematics and physics will never be complete. He said in his book **Stephen Hawking's Universe: The Cosmos Explained**, "My goal is simple. It is a complete understanding of the universe, **why it is as it is and why it exists at all."** Because string theory predicts phenomena we cannot presently measure, such as tiny strings of energy, extra dimensions, and multiple universes, some scientists reject it outright. Others find the mathematical puzzle of the M-theory proof in itself that it must be correct and expect M-theory and the existence of multiple universes and strings to eventually be validated.

To know New Possibilities in the realm of Physics visit this site:

http://www.netplaces.com/evidence-of-the-afterlife/unraveling-string-theory/m-theory-and-the-existence-of-multiple-dimensions.htm

The Large Hadron Collider (LHC)

To find a Higgs boson, a high-energy environment similar to that after the big bang has to be imitated, which is exactly what the LHC aims to do. (The Large Hadron Collider (LHC), built near Geneva, Switzerland, is the the world's largest and most powerful particle collider. The circular tunnel is 27 kilometers long (16.8 miles) and is about 600 feet under the ground. This massive machine has been designed to collide opposing proton beams at super high energy of 7 TeV. That's 7 trillion electron-volts) The LHC experiment can prove or disprove the existence of this elusive particle, which will be revolutionary for the field of physics.

The LHC particle collision experiments at such high energies that it is expected to shed light on the mysteries of the early and the current universe. Answers to many of the baffling physical questions and issues are expected, and some of the things scientists are looking for are:

- Proof of existence of Higgs boson and validation of the standard model and Higgs mechanism, which explains the origin of mass
- More information about the nature of the dark matter and dark energy, antiparticles, and other subatomic particles
- Evidence of existence of extra dimensions predicted by string theory

7) Unanswered Questions

If the Universe is expanding as the Big Bang theory tells, **into what it is expanding**?

There are many such unanswered questions. We do not know the true size of the universe, even whether it is infinite or not. Nor do we know its topology - whether space wraps around on itself or flat or spherical. We do not know what caused inflation, or whether it has created a plethora of parallel universes far from our own, as many inflationary theories imply.

And it is not clear why the universe favours matter over antimatter. Early in the big bang, when particles were being created, there must have been a strong bias towards matter, which the standard model of particle physics cannot explain. Otherwise matter and antimatter would have annihilated each other and there would been almost nothing left but radiation.

The fate of the universe depends on the unknown nature of dark energy and how it behaves in the future: galaxies might become isolated by acceleration, or all matter could be destroyed in a big rip, or the universe might collapse in a big crunch - perhaps re-expanding as a cyclic universe. The universe could even be swallowed by a giant wormhole.

And the true beginning, if there was one, is still unknown, because at the initial singularity all known physical theories break down. To understand the origin of the universe we will probably need a theory of quantum gravity.

Current status of Voyager 1

The ***Voyager 1*** spacecraft is a 722-kilogram (1,592 lb) robotic space probe of the outer Solar System and beyond, launched September 5, 1977. It still receives commands from, and transmits information to Earth, currently pursuing its extended mission to locate and study the boundaries of the Solar System, and beyond. Its original mission was to visit Jupiter and Saturn; and it was the first probe to provide detailed images of the moons of these planets.

Location and trajectories of Pioneer and Voyager spacecraft, as of April 4, 2007

As of 21 December 2009, *Voyager 1* was at a distance of 112.060 AU (approximately 16.49 billion kilometers, 10.22 billion miles, or 0.0017 light years) from the Sun, which makes it the most distant human-made object from Earth. At this distance, it is farther away from the Sun than any known natural solar system object, including Eris and 90377 Sedna, but excluding long-period comets.

At the above distance, light or radio waves, both of which are forms of electromagnetic radiation and propagate at 299,792.5 kilometers per second (the speed of light), take over 14.6 hours to reach the Earth from Voyager 1. As a basis for comparison, the Moon is about 1.4 light-seconds from Earth; the Sun is approximately 8.5 light-minutes away; Pluto is about 5.5 light-hours away the nearest star is 4.22 light-years away. **As of 9 October 2009, Voyager 1 was traveling at a speed of 17.078 kilometers per second relative to the Sun (61,600 km/h or 38,400 miles per hour),**

Voyager 1 is not heading towards any particular star, but in about 40,000 years it will pass within 1.6 light years of the star AC+79 3888 in the constellation Camelopardalis because with respect to the solar system *Voyager 1* is on a hyperbolic trajectory, i.e. its speed (17 km/s) is higher than the local escape velocity (11 km/sec). The speed is much less than the escape velocity with respect to the Milky Way ($\geqslant$ 525 km/s = 326 miles/sec). Thus it will not return to the inner solar system, but stay in the Milky Way. Along with Pioneer 10, Pioneer 11, Voyager 2, and the New Horizons, *Voyager 1* is an interstellar probe.

If *Voyager 1* were traveling in the direction of the nearest star, (Alpha Centauri, 4.36 light year distant) it would arrive there in about 75,000 years.

Entropy, a Measure of Order Degradation in the Universe

(The following writings are excerpts from a research paper on the above topic by Gelu BOURCEANU, published in *Journal for Interdisciplinary Research on Religion and Science*, No. 1, July 2007)

Among all the natural laws, there are no other two laws which can have so many implications in the evolution of cosmological, physical, chemical, biological, economic and social systems or in informatics, psychology and especially in religion as **Two laws of Thermodynamics.**

The first Law postulates equivalence of all forms of energy: mechanical, chemical, nuclear, electric, radiant, biological and thermic. This aspect involves the reversibility of transformation of energy from or into another energy form and vice versa. On the contrary, the second Law decrees that the transformation of an energy form into another and vice versa is achieved with **a certain degree of irreversibility**, the rest is lost as thermic energy (heat). **A measure of the irreversibility degree of any process is entropy.**

In 1865 Clausius formulates the two principles of thermodynamics through a cosmological enunciation.

I. The energy of the Universe is constant

II. The entropy of the Universe tends to maximum

The enunciation of the first principle represents an irrefutable truth. The validity of this principle was and has been reconfirmed by high energy physics. The enunciation of the second principle, as formulated above, implies an ending of the Universe because of the degradation of the ordered energy forms (chemical, nuclear, radiant, biological, etc.) into thermic energy, the only form of degraded energy. **Clausius draws the conclusion that the Universe will eventuate in thermic death.**

(I. Prigogine, *De la existență la devenire, [From being to becoming]*, Stiintifica Publishing House, Bucharest, 1992, p. 24 as quoted in Journal for Interdisciplinary Research on Religion and Science, No. 1, July 2007)

Entropy, Technology and Economy

The greatest part of the energy used by the human society, at least during the last one hundred years, is chemical energy stored in fossil fuel (coal, hydrocarbons) and nuclear fuel. The ordered chemical energy is delivered through combustion under the form of thermic energy (heat), the efficiency being100%. How can heat, a form of disordered energy, be changed into mechanical work, a form of ordered energy? Sadi Carnot gave the answer through the thermodynamic cycle bearing his name. **The real efficiency of transformation of thermic energy into mechanical energy is not more than 30%. The rest thermic energy is lost in the medium, leading to the increase of its entropy.**

There is not a (single) mechanical, physical, chemical, biochemical, or biological process which does not obey the law of entropy, or, in other words, which can develop without a partial degradation of the ordered energy into disordered energy. **A definition of entropy, in a wider meaning, is the following:** ***Entropy represents a measure of degradation of ordered energy into disordered energy within systems in function.***

The Final Note

Above is a very short glimpse of modern Cosmology prepared by us cautiously putting most of the statements of the scientists in their own parlance so that all current aspects could be covered briefly.

- **Going through this you must have felt that the scientists are just groping in darkness; no one theory is there that could be said to be certain with full conviction; there are only speculations and conjectures. However this introduction will help one to understand the Verses in the Quran related to this very important branch of science which has fascinated mankind all through the ages.**

A Very Short Glimpse Over Astronomical Data

Astronomy

Astronomy is the scientific study of celestial objects like stars, comets, planets and galaxies

The universe as we know it to be, is an amazing and astounding place, full of surprises. Amazing facts about earth or interesting facts about the solar system, just pale in comparison to the grandeur and vastness of the rest of the universe. Let us know some amazing facts about the world and the ocean of space time that we float in!

Astronomical Units

Distances in the solar system are often measured in astronomical units (abbreviated AU). An astronomical unit is the average distance between the Earth and the Sun:

$1\,AU = 1.496 \times 10^8\,km = 93$ million miles

Light-Years

To measure the distances between stars, astronomers often use light-years (abbreviated ly). A light-year is the distance that light travels in a vacuum in one year:

$1\,ly = 9.5 \times 10^{12}\,km = 63{,}240\,AU$

Jupiter is about 5.2 AU from the Sun and Pluto is about 39.5 AU from the Sun. The distance from the Sun to the center of the Milky Way is approximately 1.7×10^9 AU(26880 ly)

Parsecs

Many astronomers prefer to use parsecs (abbreviated pc) to measure distance to stars. This is because its definition is closely related to a method of measuring the distances between stars. A parsec is the distance at which 1 AU subtends and angle of 1 arcsec. 1 pc = 3.09×10^{13} km = 3.26 ly

Proxima Centauri is the nearest star to Earth (other than the Sun) and is 4.2 light-years away. This means light from Proxima Centauri takes 4.2 years to travel to Earth.

Speed of Light= 300,000 Km/sec

Jupiter Mars, Mercury,; Venus, Saturn, Uranus Neptune and, a dwarf planet, Pluto In addition, there are thousands of small bodies such as **asteroids** and **comets**. Most of the asteroids orbit in a region between the orbits of Mars and Jupiter, while the home of comets lies far beyond the orbit of Pluto, The four planets closest to the sun—Mercury, Venus, Earth, and Mars—are called the **terrestrial planets** because they have solid rocky surfaces. The four large planets beyond the orbit of Mars—Jupiter, Saturn, Uranus, and Neptune—are called **gas giants**. Tiny, distant, Pluto has a solid but icier surface than the terrestrial planets. Nearly every planet—and some of the moons—has an **atmosphere**. Earth's atmosphere is primarily nitrogen and oxygen. Venus has a thick atmosphere of carbon dioxide, with traces of poisonous gases such as sulfur dioxide. Mars's carbon dioxide atmosphere is extremely thin. Jupiter, Saturn, Uranus, and Neptune are primarily hydrogen and helium.

Moons, Rings, and Magnetospheres There are 140 known natural satellites, also called **moons**, in orbit around the various planets in our solar system, ranging from bodies larger than our own moon to small pieces of debris. From 1610 to 1977, Saturn was thought to be the only planet with

rings. We now know that Jupiter, Uranus, and Neptune also have ring systems, although Saturn's is by far the largest. Particles in these ring systems range in size from dust to boulders to house-size, and may be rocky and/or icy. (http://science.national-geographic.co.in/science/space/solar-system)

The Sun

The sun is a star which is around 4½ billion years old. Scientists have pointed out the sun is supposed to shine for another 5 billion years. 99.8% of the Solar system, is occupied by the sun, while Jupiter, which is the largest of the eight planets, occupies 0.2% of the solar system. Hence you can imagine, how small our earth seems in the solar system. <u>We need at least 109 Earths just to fit the disk of the sun, while we need around 1.2 million Earths to fill the interior of the sun</u>. The light from the sun travels over a distance of around 93 million miles (149 million Km) in order to reach the Earth in around 8.3 to 9 minutes. Speed of light= 300,000 Km/sec.

74% of the sun is made up of hydrogen, while 24% is made up of helium. Sun fuses 620 million metric tons of hydrogen each second The rest 2% contains small amounts of iron, oxygen and some other elements which are present in our solar system.

There are at least 200 billion stars in our universe and the sun is one of them. Of these 200 billion, only 6000 stars can be seen by the naked eyes of humans and the sun is one of them. But it would be wrong to think that the sun is the largest star in the universe. There are several stars, in front of which the sun would look like the earth does in front of the sun. The surface temperature of the sun is nearly around 10,000ºF (5500 ^{0}C) and the temperature of the center of the sun is around 27,000 ºF. The amount of energy produced by the sun is approximately 385 billion-billion megawatts out of which Earth receives around 95 billion megawatts.

Rotation of the sun: Different parts of the sun rotate at a different speed. The regions at the equator takes around 25 days for one rotation, the inside of the sun takes 27 days and the areas near the poles takes 36 days. This is possible because the sun is a gaseous body and not a solid body.

Revolution of the sun: The sun too revolves around the milky way on its own orbit and it takes 225,000,000 years(225million years) to complete one round around the milky way, while traveling at a speed of 800,000 km per hour. Read more at Buzzle: http://www.buzzle.com/articles/interesting-facts-about-the-sun.html

Planets

Mercury is the second smallest planet in the solar system and has no moon. It can get as hot as 800º C and cold as 300º C below zero. One year on Mercury is equal to 88 days on Earth.

Venus is the only planet that rotates from east to west. A year on this planet is equal to 225 days on Earth. Earth is nearly 93 million miles away from the Sun. It takes about 16 million horsepower to break the Earth's gravitational pull.

The planet Neptune was discovered more than150 years ago in 1846, and since then it has completed only one orbit around the Sun, as one Neptune year equals to 165 Earth years.

Pluto does not have a fixed orbit and its orbit comes in the middle of Neptune's orbit. Also, Pluto's size is very small which made scientists demote it to a dwarf planet status. Read more at Buzzle: http://www.buzzle.com/articles/fun-facts-about-astronomy.html

Galaxies

A **galaxy** is a massive, gravitationally bound system consisting of stars, stellar remnants, an interstellar medium of gas and dust, and dark matter,. Examples of galaxies range from dwarfs with as few as ten million (10^7) stars to giants with a hundred trillion (10^{14}) stars, each orbiting their galaxy's own center of mass. Galaxies contain varying numbers of star systems, star clusters and types of interstellar clouds. In between these objects is a sparse interstellar medium of gas, dust, and cosmic rays. Supermassive black holes reside at the center of most galaxies. They are thought to be the primary driver of active galactic nuclei found at the core of some galaxies. The Milky Way galaxy is known to harbor at least one such object.

Milky Way Galaxy

Milky Way galaxy in which our solar system resides is a disk about 100,000 light years in diameter and about 1000 light years thick. It has up to 200 billion stars like our Sun! There are estimated to be about 170 billion such galaxies in the universe. The nearest spiral galaxy to our milky way is the Andromeda galaxy, which is 2.6 million light years away. At the center of every galaxy, there resides a massive black hole. Even our Milky way galaxy has a massive black hole in its center.

There are probably more than 170 billion (1.7×10^{11}) galaxies in the observable universe. Most are 1,000 to 100,000 parsecs in diameter and usually separated by distances on the order of millions of parsecs (or megaparsecs). Intergalactic space (the space between galaxies) is filled with a tenuous gas of an average density less than one atom per cubic meter.

The majority of galaxies are organized into a hierarchy of associations known as groups and clusters, which, in turn usually form larger superclusters. At the largest scale, these associations are generally arranged into sheets and filaments, which are surrounded by immense voids. That supercluster of which our Milky way Galaxy is a part is called **Local Group** which is said to contain 47,000 galaxies stretched over a length of 110 million ly distance. a relatively small group of galaxies that has a diameter of approximately one megaparsec (3.26 million light year distance). The Milky Way and the Andromeda Galaxy are the two brightest galaxies within this group; many of the other member galaxies are dwarf companions of these two galaxies. The Local Group itself is a part of a cloud-like structure within the Virgo Supercluster. On December 12, 2012, astronomers, working with the Hubble Space Telescope, reported that the most distant known galaxy, UDFj-39546284, is approximately 13.42 billion light years from Earth.

Thus, we can assume that **Superclusters** are islands of galaxies in the vast ocean of the universe, they are in no way interacting with other superclusters (can we assume them to be different heavens as described by the Quran? We cannot say anything at this stage of our minimal knowledge.)

Black Holes

When a giant star dies and a black hole gets formed, all its mass gets squeezed into a single point. At this point, both space and time stops. It's very hard for us to imagine a place where mass has no volume and time does not pass, but that's what it is like at the center of a black hole.

Mathematically, a black hole is an object of zero size and infinite density (but finite mass)-a singularity. Singularity is the point at the center of a black hole. Within a certain distance of the singularity, the gravitational pull is so strong that nothing-not even light-can escape. That distance is called the **event horizon**.

Imagine an object with such an enormous concentration of mass in such a small radius that its **escape velocity** was greater than the velocity of light. Then, since nothing can go faster than light, nothing can escape the object's gravitational field. Thus, even a beam of light would be pulled back by gravity and would be unable to escape. But farther away, things do not get sucked in. Stars and planets at a safe distance will circle around the black hole, much like the motion of the planets around the Sun. The gravitational force on stars and planets orbiting a black hole is the same as when it was a star because gravity depends on how much mass there is, the black hole has the same mass as it was the star, it's just compressed. A **supermassive black hole** (SMBH) is the largest type of black hole, on the order of hundreds of thousands to billions of solar masses. Most—and possibly all—galaxies are inferred to contain a supermassive black hole at their centers.

Black holes are truly black from Thermodynamic point of view that is no wave is reflected from it. Light rays that get too close bend into, and are trapped by the intense gravity of the black hole. Trapped light rays will never escape. Since black holes do not shine, they are difficult to detect. Read more at Buzzle: http://www.buzzle.com/editorials/2-28-2005-66378.asp

Pulsar

A **pulsar** (*pulsating star*) is a highly magnetized, rotating neutron star that emits a beam of electromagnetic radiation. This radiation can only be observed when the beam of emission is pointing toward the Earth, much the way a lighthouse can only be seen when the light is pointed in the direction of an observer, and is responsible for the pulsed appearance of emission. Pulsars are rotating neutron stars with huge magnetic fields, which emit electromagnetic radiation. They are formed from the core of a star exploding in a supernova! A pulsar is like a light house. Just as the light house beam passes periodically in front of us, the pulsar pulses pass our earth every 1.4 milliseconds to 8.5 seconds. This is because they are rotating at phenomenal speeds, while they emit radiation Neutron stars are very dense, and have short, regular rotational periods. This produces a very precise interval between pulses that range from roughly milliseconds to seconds for an individual pulsar.

Quasar

A **quasi-stellar radio source** is a very energetic and distant active galactic nucleus. Quasars are extremely luminous and were first identified as being high redshift sources of electromagnetic energy, including radio waves and visible light, that were point-like, similar to stars, rather than extended sources similar to galaxies.

While the nature of these objects was controversial until as recently as the early 1980s, there is now a scientific consensus that a quasar is a compact region in the center of a massive galaxy, that surrounds its central supermassive black hole. They tend to inhabit the very centers of active, young galaxies, and are among the most luminous, powerful, and energetic objects known in the universe, emitting up to a thousand times the energy output of the Milky Way, which contains 200–400 billion stars. This radiation is emitted across the spectrum, almost equally, from X-rays to the far-infrared with a peak in the ultraviolet-optical bands, with some quasars also being strong sources of radio emission and of gamma-rays.

Supernova- An enormous and extremely bright explosion of a star at the end of its lifetime. Dying stars that grow too large may collapse in on themselves, or white dwarfs that get too heavy may trigger a thermonuclear explosion. The shock waves and expelled matter from supernovae are responsible for the birth of new stars.

What about the Observable Universe?

In star astronomy, the term observable Universe is used to refer to a part of the Universe - along with all the galaxies and other matter in it, which can be seen from the Earth at a given point of time. Irrespective of what the shape of actual Universe is, the observable Universe is always spherical in shape with its center at the place from where the observations are recorded. That being said, every point of the Universe has an observable Universe of its own and the chances of same overlapping with that of the Earth cannot be ruled out. In the Earth's observable Universe alone, there are as many as 170 billion galaxies.

At the end of the day, it is virtually impossible to ascertain the number of galaxies in the Universe as of today. In future, however, things may change considerably and we may (or may not) come across some method to answer this intricate question with an exact figure, instead of going with the estimates.

We are yet to go a long way in the field of space exploration, and as we make it to each milestone, more and more amazing facts about the Universe will come to light. One such milestone will be the launch of James Webb Space Telescope (JWST) - a planned infrared space observatory, as a part of the international collaboration between National Aeronautics and Space Administration (NASA), European Space Agency (ESA) and Canadian Space Agency (CSA) in near future.

- Now look back on the descriptions above on cosmological and astronomical data although very brief, it gives an impression of awe and amazement and as to how lowly and petty are we in face of the Universe. It is not for nothing that Allah describes in the Quran:

لَخَلْقُ السَّمٰوٰتِ وَالْاَرْضِ اَكْبَرُ مِنْ خَلْقِ النَّاسِ وَلٰكِنَّ اَكْثَرَ النَّاسِ لَا يَعْلَمُوْنَ۔

➢ [40:57] **Surely the creation of the heavens and the earth is a greater act than the creation of human beings. But most people do not know.**

(II) The Quran on Cosmology

[The Quran uses Arabic words, "Assamawat wal Ardh" literally meaning, "the heavens and the earth" for "the universe"; however at a few places it uses only "Assama" (singular of 'Assamawat') for the universe as in 41:11 and 2:29 ---To maintain the veracity of the Quranic statements and further so that any one may find it easy to check the meanings of Arabic words, we have taken care to put all verses in Arabic along with the translations in this chapter.]

The heavens have always attracted man in all ages, in many ways are they mentioned in various scriptures, the Quran does this also but with one distinction: it inspires and encourages men to contemplate over different aspects of the cosmology and most importantly it promises rewards in hereafter to those who devote their time in this work. In this regard the verses 191-192 of the third chapter Al-Imran are refreshing:

[Quran 3:190-191] "Verily, in the creation of the heavens and the earth, and in the succession of night and day, there are indeed messages for all who are endowed with insight and who remember God when they stand, and when they sit, and when they lie down on their sides, **and [thus] reflect on the creation of the heavens and the earth**: "O our Sustainer! Thou hast not created [aught of] this without meaning and purpose".

Unlike science books that describe scientific facts in terms of formulations and equations that look dry to laymen, the wording of the Quran in describing the scientific facts is matchless, it has a blending of logical as well as emotional impact which leaves its listener to stop for a moment and contemplate over the fact described but at the same time submitting himself to his Lord, so exhilarated that it moves barren eyes to tears and softens petrified hearts and fills one with ecstasy.

The Quran Refers Some Important Aspects of Cosmogony:

1. **The Big Bang**
2. **The gaseous state of the universe**
3. **The expansion of the universe**
4. **The big crunch**
5. **Inexplorable/ extraordinary vastness of the universe**
6. **Extra-terrestrial Life**
7. **Isotropic nature of the universe**
8. **Every Object in the universe is in motion, following their orbits**
9. **Sky of Our World is made beautiful but fortified**
10. **Creation of the Universe in 'SIX DAYS'**
11. **Significance of the Quranic word 'wama baynahuma'**
12. **Number and nature of the Heavens (seven, tibaqa, tarayeq)**

1. The Big Bang

أَوَلَمْ يَرَ الَّذِينَ كَفَرُوٓا أَنَّ السَّمٰوٰتِ وَالْأَرْضَ كَانَتَا رَتْقًا فَفَتَقْنٰهُمَا ۖ وَجَعَلْنَا مِنَ الْمَآءِ كُلَّ شَيْءٍ حَيٍّ ۖ أَفَلَا يُؤْمِنُونَ ﴿٣٠﴾

[Quran 21:30] Do not the Unbelievers see that the heavens and the earth were joined together (as one unit of creation), before we clove them asunder? We made from water every living thing. Will they not then believe?

In this verse, the Arabic words ***ratq*** and ***fataq*** are used. The word *ratq* can be translated into "**entity**" "**sewn to**" "**joined together**" or "**closed up**". The meaning of these translations all circulate around something that is mixed and that has a separate and distinct existence. The verb *fataq* is translated into "**We unstitched**" "**We clove them asunder**" "**We separated**" or "**We have opened them**". These meanings imply that something comes into being by an action of splitting or tearing apart. The sprouting of a seed from the soil is a good example of a similar illustration of the meaning of the verb *fataq*. (Verify the meanings of the above words in any Arabic-English Dictionary: Penrice, Mawrid or E W Lane)

These two words convey the complete sense of the 'Big Bang theory' described in the article attached.

2. The gaseous state of the universe

The Quran indicates in very clear words that the heaven and the Earth were all in gaseous state. This is exactly what the latest cosmologists say.

ثُمَّ اسْتَوٰٓى إِلَى السَّمَآءِ وَهِيَ دُخَانٌ

[Quran 41:11] Moreover He comprehended in His design the sky, and it had been (as) smoke.

3. The expansion of the universe

[Quran 51:47] "And the heaven We created with might, and indeed We are (its) expander."

The meaning of 'expansion' is drawn from the Arabic word in the Quran is: "***moosiaoon***" the root word for which is "wa-sa-aa", meaning 'to expand'.

4. The Big Crunch

[Quran 13:2] Allah is He Who raised the heavens without any pillars that ye can see; is firmly established on the throne (of authority); *He has subjected the sun and the moon (to his Law)! Each one runs (its course) for a term appointed.* He doth regulate all affairs, explaining the signs in detail, that you may believe with certainty in the meeting with your Lord.

[55:26] kullu man alaihaa faan

كُلُّ مَنْ عَلَيْهَا فَانٍ ﴿٢٦﴾

[Quran 55:26] All that lives on earth or in the heavens is bound to pass away:

وَلَا تَدْعُ مَعَ اللّٰهِ اِلٰهًا اٰخَرَ ۘ لَآ اِلٰهَ اِلَّا هُوَ ۚ كُلُّ شَيْءٍ هَالِكٌ اِلَّا وَجْهَهٗ ۭ لَهُ الْحُكْمُ
وَاِلَيْهِ تُرْجَعُوْنَ ﴿٨٨﴾

[Quran 28:88] And call not, besides Allah, on another god. There is no god but He. **Everything (that exists) will perish except His own Face.** To Him belongs the Command, and to Him will ye (all) be brought back.

يَوْمَ تُبَدَّلُ الْاَرْضُ غَيْرَ الْاَرْضِ وَالسَّمٰوٰتُ وَبَرَزُوْا لِلّٰهِ الْوَاحِدِ الْقَهَّارِ ﴿٤٨﴾

[Quran 14:48] One day the earth will be changed to a different earth, and so will be the heavens, and (men) will be marshalled forth, before Allah, the One, the Irresistible;

[Quran 81:1-3] "When the sun shall be folded up, when the stars shall scatter away when the mountains shall be set in motion". There are many such verses:77:8-10,81:1-3, 82:1-3, 84:1-5, 75:7-9

The Second Law of Thermodynamics Corroborates this Destroy of The Universe

The increase of entropy of the universe leads to decrease of the Available Energy of the universe—this is one of the recent facts established among modern physicists. We have dealt with this in this book elsewhere.

اَللّٰهُ الَّذِيْ رَفَعَ السَّمٰوٰتِ بِغَيْرِ عَمَدٍ تَرَوْنَهَا ثُمَّ اسْتَوٰى عَلَى الْعَرْشِ وَسَخَّرَ الشَّمْسَ وَالْقَمَرَ ؕ كُلٌّ يَّجْرِيْ لِاَجَلٍ مُّسَمًّى ؕ يُدَبِّرُ الْاَمْرَ يُفَصِّلُ الْاٰيٰتِ لَعَلَّكُمْ بِلِقَآءِ رَبِّكُمْ تُوْقِنُوْنَ ﴿٢﴾

[13:2] It is Allah Who has raised the heavens without any supports that you could see, and then He established Himself on the Throne (of Dominion). And He it is Who has made the sun and the moon subservient (to a law), each running its course till an appointed term. He governs the entire order of the universe and clearly explains the signs that you may be firmly convinced about meeting you.

خَلَقَ السَّمٰوٰتِ وَالْاَرْضَ بِالْحَقِّ ۚ يُكَوِّرُ الَّيْلَ عَلَى النَّهَارِ وَيُكَوِّرُ النَّهَارَ عَلَى الَّيْلِ
وَسَخَّرَ الشَّمْسَ وَالْقَمَرَ ۭ كُلٌّ يَّجْرِيْ لِاَجَلٍ مُّسَمًّى ۭ اَلَا هُوَ الْعَزِيْزُ الْغَفَّارُ ۝

[Quran 39:5] He it is who has created the heavens and the earth in accordance with [an inner] truth. He causes the night to flow into the day, and causes the day to flow into the night; and He has made the sun and the moon subservient [to His laws], **each running its course for a term set [by Him].** Is not He the Almighty, the All-Forgiving?

5. Inexplorable/Extraordinary Vastness of The Universe

It is impossible to explore the universe. Two reasons:

Scientific consideration: If we proceed to explore with whatever possible speed, we can never cross over the boundary of the all the time expanding universe, considering the fact that at the boundary, the farthest galaxies are receding with much greater velocity.

Practical consideration: There are limitations set by technical considerations as to the speed a man can sail his spacecraft with, life of the cells used, danger of cosmic radiations, danger of being sucked by high-gravity stars/galaxies/dark matter and most importantly the Time involved. Just consider the Voyger1 launched in Sep. 1977 has not yet crossed the Solar System outermost boundary even after 35 years; it is calculated that with current speed of it about 62,000 km/hr it will take 75,000 years to reach the nearest star from us 4.3 light years away, whereas we know today the Observable universe is 14 billion light years expanse, note the word billion, what you think, how many trillion or zillion years will it take! It is simply impossible because of the fact that the boundary of the universe is expanding with tremendously high speed.

Now see what the Quran on this topic:

يٰمَعْشَرَ الْجِنِّ وَالْاِنْسِ اِنِ اسْتَطَعْتُمْ اَنْ تَنْفُذُوْا مِنْ اَقْطَارِ السَّمٰوٰتِ وَالْاَرْضِ فَانْفُذُوْا ۭ لَا تَنْفُذُوْنَ اِلَّا بِسُلْطٰنٍ ۚ

[Quran 55:33] O assembly of Jinns and men! If you [think that you] can pass beyond the regions of the heavens and the earth, pass beyond them! [But] you cannot pass beyond them, save by a sanction [from God]!

6. Extra-Terrestrial Life

The Quran indicates various **signs** in the universe and brings about several descriptions connected to modern day science, some facts are so revealing that they have been discovered only in recent times and some are yet to be discovered,

For this last statement of mine, see how the Quran indicates the existence of EXTRA-TERRESTRIAL LIFE at various places: S.Talaq 65:12, S.Shura 42:29, S.Nahal 16:49, S.BaniIsrail 17:44, S.Noor 24:41, S.Hajj 22:18.

اَللّٰهُ الَّذِیْ خَلَقَ سَبْعَ سَمٰوٰتٍ وَّمِنَ الْاَرْضِ مِثْلَهُنَّ ؕ يَتَنَزَّلُ الْاَمْرُ بَيْنَهُنَّ لِتَعْلَمُوْۤا اَنَّ اللّٰهَ عَلٰی كُلِّ شَیْءٍ قَدِيْرٌ ۙ وَّاَنَّ اللّٰهَ قَدْ اَحَاطَ بِكُلِّ شَیْءٍ عِلْمًا ۟

[Quran 65:12] Allah is He Who created seven Firmaments and of the earth a similar number. Through the midst of them (all) descends His Command: that ye may know that Allah has power over all things, and that Allah comprehends all things in (His) Knowledge.

وَمِنْ اٰيٰتِهٖ خَلْقُ السَّمٰوٰتِ وَالْاَرْضِ وَمَا بَثَّ فِيْهِمَا مِنْ دَآبَّةٍ ؕ وَهُوَ عَلٰى جَمْعِهِمْ اِذَا يَشَآءُ قَدِيْرٌ ﴿٢٩﴾

[Quran 42:29] And among His signs is the [very] creation of the heavens and the earth, and of all the living creatures which He has caused to multiply throughout them: and [since He has created them,] He has [also] the power to gather them [unto Himself] whenever He wills.

[We have referred to this topic in the chapter," The Scientific Descriptions of the Quran"]

7. Isotropic Nature of The Universe

The Quran indicates that the whole Universe is a continuous entity; there is no cleavage, no fault.

الَّذِىْ خَلَقَ سَبْعَ سَمٰوٰتٍ طِبَاقًا ؕ مَا تَرٰى فِىْ خَلْقِ الرَّحْمٰنِ مِنْ تَفٰوُتٍ ؕ فَارْجِعِ الْبَصَرَ ۙ هَلْ تَرٰى مِنْ فُطُوْرٍ ﴿٣﴾

[Quran 67:3] He Who created the seven heavens one above another: No want of proportion wilt thou see in the Creation of (Allah) Most Gracious. So turn thy vision again: do you see any flaw/break/ cleavage?

This is why, all the Laws observed and formulated, here in our Earth are being well obeyed everywhere in the universe, this is proved by the fact that all the instruments, made here on Earth, based on certain laws are working well, when sent beyond Solar system ---- that means the same Laws are functioning there also.

8. Every Object in The Universe is in MOTION, Following its ORBIT

The Quran clearly states that all heavenly objects are in motion and that too in orbits.

وَالشَّمْسُ تَجْرِىْ لِمُسْتَقَرٍّ لَّهَا ۚ ذٰلِكَ تَقْدِيْرُ الْعَزِيْزِ الْعَلِيْمِ ﴿٣٨﴾

[Quran 36:38] They have a sign in the sun: it runs in an orbit of its own [and] that is laid down by the will of the Almighty, the All-Knowing;

All stars, the sun & moon, all are moving in certain orbits - the word orbit has been clearly used. S.Ambiya 21:

وَهُوَ الَّذِىْ خَلَقَ الَّيْلَ وَالنَّهَارَ وَالشَّمْسَ وَالْقَمَرَ ۚ كُلٌّ فِىْ فَلَكٍ يَّسْبَحُوْنَ ﴿٣٣﴾

[Quran 21:33] And He it is Who created the night and the day, and the sun and the moon. They float, each in an orbit.

The Quran mentions not only 'orbits' (falak) but it also mentions a very scientific word (yasbahoon, meaning floating or swimming).

This term 'swimming/floating' for movement of the celestial object is really a marvellous word indicating a very recent finding that the "space" between the celestial objects is not vacuum—but some medium is there—which we know, now, as very rarefied gases mainly Hydrogen and some INTERSTELLAR DUST. (see the detail in an another chapter: "What we observe in the Universe" and also explained below under the caption "Significance of the word "**wama bainahuma**")

9. Sky of Our World Made Beautiful But Fortified

[Quran 37:6] We have indeed decked the lower heaven with beauty (in) the stars,-

[Quran 67:5] And verily We have beatified the world's heaven with lamps (of stars).

[Quran 21:32] And We have made the heavens as a canopy well-guarded: yet do they turn away from the Signs which these things (point to)!

وَزَيَّنَّا السَّمَآءَ الدُّنْيَا بِمَصَابِيحَ ۖ وَحِفْظًا ۚ ذَٰلِكَ تَقْدِيرُ الْعَزِيزِ الْعَلِيمِ ﴿١٢﴾

[41:12] And We adorned the skies nearest to the earth with lights, <u>and made them secure: such is the Measuring</u> of the Almighty, the All-Knowing.

This is a very notable sentence--- it states three facts:

(*i*) the sky of our Earth is decked with glittering lamps (the nearest stars and planets, of different hue and colours),

(*ii*) our earth is well protected and fortified (as we know today, against many types of harmful radiations and cosmic waves),

(*iii*) that all these are well measured and designed in due proportion

10. Creation of The Universe in 'SIX DAYS'

إِنَّ رَبَّكُمُ اللَّهُ الَّذِي خَلَقَ السَّمَاوَاتِ وَالْأَرْضَ فِي سِتَّةِ أَيَّامٍ

[Quran 7:54] Your Guardian-Lord is Allah, **Who created the heavens and the earth in six days,**

Narrated 'Abdullah: I visited the Prophet during his ailments and he was suffering from a high fever. I said, "You have a high fever. Is it because you will have a double reward for it?" He said, "Yes, for no Muslim is afflicted with any harm but that Allah will remove his sins as the leaves of a tree fall down."

- The faith of one that he is being <u>tested</u> by God of his 'submission' to Him and that keeping patience over pains and problems will ensure reward in the life here-after, gives one strength to pass over the tides.

وَلَنَبْلُوَنَّكُمْ بِشَيْءٍ مِّنَ الْخَوْفِ وَالْجُوْعِ وَنَقْصٍ مِّنَ الْاَمْوَالِ وَالْاَنْفُسِ وَالثَّمَرٰتِ ؕ وَبَشِّرِ الصّٰبِرِيْنَ ﴿۱۵۵﴾

[Quran 2:155] Be sure We shall test you with something of fear and hunger, some loss in goods or lives or the fruits (of your toil), but give glad tidings to those who patiently persevere,

لِّيَبْلُوَكُمْ فِيْ مَاۤ اٰتٰىكُمْ ؕ

He might try you by means of what He has bestowed upon you [6:165]

فَاسْتَجَابَ لَهُمْ رَبُّهُمْ اَنِّيْ لَاۤ اُضِيْعُ عَمَلَ عَامِلٍ مِّنْكُمْ مِّنْ ذَكَرٍ اَوْ اُنْثٰى ۚ بَعْضُكُمْ مِّنْۢ بَعْضٍ ۚ فَالَّذِيْنَ هَاجَرُوْا وَ اُخْرِجُوْا مِنْ دِيَارِهِمْ وَاُوْذُوْا فِيْ سَبِيْلِيْ وَقٰتَلُوْا وَقُتِلُوْا لَاُكَفِّرَنَّ عَنْهُمْ سَيِّاٰتِهِمْ وَلَاُدْخِلَنَّهُمْ جَنّٰتٍ تَجْرِيْ مِنْ تَحْتِهَا الْاَنْهٰرُ ۚ ثَوَابًا مِّنْ عِنْدِ اللّٰهِ ؕ وَاللّٰهُ عِنْدَهٗ حُسْنُ الثَّوَابِ ﴿۱۹۵﴾

[3:195] And thus does their Sustainer answer their prayer: "I shall not lose sight of the labour of any of you who labours [in My way], be it man or woman: each of you is an issue of the other Hence, as for those who forsake the domain of

useful; had they indulged in unravelling the 'mystery of why' they would have become 'philosophers' and not 'engineers' and 'scientists'.

Similarly in the world of beliefs (aqaa-ed, eemaaniyaat), 'not –understanding' many of the mysteries do not deter us to pass a peaceful life with the help of those instruction which are clear and understandable to us.

An Enigma: Indulging in Open Follies Despite Being Logical and Rational?

If logic, intelligence and wisdom play vital role in the life of man and we see that how the man has progressed in all walks of life with its help then how is it that he is found to be indulged in quite open follies such as idolatry (in all its despised forms), breaking all sorts of prohibitions, committing all sorts of nuisance, knowing they are harmful to him? Why he does not apply logic here? Why his intelligence and wisdom of which he boasts so much fail here? The Quran answers these questions in several forms:

i) Man's own weakness of succumbing to his own inner whims and desire. (The Quran has mentioned three kinds of human self:

   (a) *'Ammarah'* : the self that urges man to evil;

   (b) *'Lawwamah'* : the self that feels repentant at doing wrong, thinking wrong and willing wrong and reproaches man for this; and the same is called conscience in modern terminology; and

   (c) *'Mutma'innah'*: the self that feels full satisfaction at following the right path and abandoning the wrong path)

ii) Biased to follow his forefather's path blindly, he considers putting his forefathers to logical tests as disrespect to them. But when they are told, "Follow what God has bestowed from on high," some answer, "Nay, we shall follow [only] that which we found our forefathers believing in and doing. Why, even if their forefathers did not use their reason at all, and were devoid of all guidance?" [Quran 2:170]

iii. *The lust for worldly assets* :

[Quran 3:14] "alluring unto man is the enjoyment of worldly desires through women, and children, and heaped-up treasures of gold and silver, and horses of high mark, and cattle, and lands. All this may be enjoyed in the life of this world - but the most beauteous of all goals is with God."

iv. *A slight twist in the logical argument* can make an evidently wrong thing look as right; thus idolatry has many arguments, though sheepish, in its favour.

v. *Lack of courage* : sometime one succumbs to outward pressure from the society, political power or current upheavals in face of him ---- and here all his logic, wisdom are suppressed.

vi. One more important factor is *the existence of Satan*. The Quran says that right from the day of creation of man Satan is after him to lead him astray. [Quran 2:208] O you who have attained to faith! Surrender yourselves wholly unto God, and follow not Satan's footsteps, for, verily, he is your open foe.

vii. The man of today may not find time out of his hectic busy schedules of daily life or at times he just ignores and shrugs off the call of his conscience to ponder on the signs in the nature---may be due to his false vanity of wisdom.

There may be many more such causes. There are various verses in the Quran depicting all the above factors and some more; here it is difficult, moreover, not needed at this place to go into such detail.

Conclusion

With the persistent effort to integrate faith with reason and spiritual with material, Islam constructed a coherent bond between science and morality in the East and the West wherever it spread. This reform could not have been successful if it hadn't been for the vehicle of the Quran that swept the world with its wisdom and application and promotion of intelligence and logic.

The human mind is not capable of grasping the Universe. We are like a little child entering a huge library. The walls are covered to the ceilings with books in many different tongues. The child knows that someone must have written these books. It does not know who or how. It does not understand the languages in which they are written. But the child notes a definite plan in the arrangement of the books - a mysterious order which it does not comprehend, but only dimly suspects. — Albert Einstein

6

The Quran — An Amazing Book

Which thing you call amazing?

Anything which comes within your experience lying beyond expectation and beyond intellect. For example - One does not expect from a man living in deserts who has never been to a sea, describing seafaring. See what a sailor tells to the famous Canadian priest Gary Miller. Miller wrote a book 'The Amazing Quran' after he embraced Islam, he writes in his book (now available in the Internet-- http://www.thetruecall.com/downloads/AmazingQuran.pdf):

Merchant Marine

"Some years ago, the story came to us in Toronto about a man who was in the merchant marine and made his living on the sea. A Muslim happened to give him a translation of the Quran to read. The merchant marine knew nothing about the history of Islam but he was interested in reading the Quran. When he finished reading it, he brought it back to the Muslim and asked, "This Muhammad (pbh), was he a sailor?" He was impressed as to how accurately the Quran describes a storm on a sea. When he was told, "No as a matter of fact, Muhammad (pbh) lived in the desert and never even saw a sea" that was enough for him. He embraced Islam on the spot.

Current of Soft Water Under Saline Water

Have you heard of Jacques Cousteau a French naval officer, explorer, ecologist, filmmaker, innovator, scientist, photographer and author who amazed the audience in a Science Congress by describing his findings that in the deep sea exists a barrier separating saline water with that of common soft water. There the famous author of "The Quran, the Bible and Science" Dr. Maurice Bucaille was present who endorsed the great oceanographer by informing that what he discovered today was already written in a Book 14 centuries back. (Some say that he was so impressed that he embraced Islam but later his secretary denied) (See the detail in Google).

Spiritual Resonance

In Physics there is a term ***'Resonance'***. It is defined as: "The increase in the amplitude of an oscillation of a system under the influence of a periodic force whose frequency is close to that of the system's natural frequency". In simple words it means if the frequency of any wave matches with the natural frequency of an object then that object picks up the frequency of the incoming wave and starts oscillating with the same. Something like this happens to the readers or listeners of the Quran. At times it so happens with the listeners that if he is well tuned with the reciter, tears roll down and the heart resounds.

Sometimes just a single verse of the Quran goes deep into the soul and opens up a new vista of meaning --- and just one verse may turn a new chapter in one's life. Here I relate some real stories---the first one is my personal experience and the second one is related with the famous Jew, Leopold Weiss of Vienna turned to Islam as Muhammad Asad, an extraordinary scholar of Islam (his translation of the Quran and other books "Road to Mecca" and "Islam at the Cross Roads" are available in the Net, refer: www.islamicity.com)

A Verse of the Quran: An Amulet for a Non-Muslim Brother

On return to hostel from library late night, during my research in IIT Delhi, a premier technical institute in India, I found smoke missing out from a room while the door was shut. After several anxious knocking it was opened, I found a young boy in a wrecked state while some papers and letters were burning in one corner. After much persuasion the boy related that he had received a shattering letter from his beloved that evening informing him that she had been compelled by her parents to marry somebody else. The boy became so desperate that he wished to finish his life. I consoled him in many ways and in the end I said, 'look, you are a non – Muslim and I don't know how much the Quran may appeal to you but I tell you there is one verse which may heal your wounds at this time of despair: I recited Surah Baqrah's verse no. 216: *"But it is possible that you dislike a thing which is good for you, and that you love a thing which is bad for you. But Allah knows, and you know not."* It acted like an arrow just to the target. I found and I still remember how the boy's facial expression changed. The next morning when I had not even finished my Fajar prayer, my door was knocked. There stood that boy, "Brother, can you give me that verse of the Quran in writing?" I gave him the translation of it; "oh, no, please give me that in Arabic and its transliteration - I will keep it with me forever as an amulet!"

A Verse of the Quran: A Life Saving Call

Another such inspiring story is narrated by the famous scholar of Islam, Muhammad (pbh) Asad (earlier a German Jew, Leopold Weiss) in his famous autobiography "Road to Mecca". While traversing the arid desert of Najd in Saudi Arabia he lost his way. Struggling long for survival in the wilderness and battered by thirst, hunger and weariness he became so desperate that he placed his gun upon his neck to terminate his life. He narrates that at that hour of time while he was just sinking into death, he felt as if someone was calling from far off distance a verse of the Quran: (2:155) *"Be sure we shall test you with something of fear and hunger, some loss in goods or lives or the fruits (of your toil), but give glad tidings to those who patiently persevere."* It was as if someone had awakened him, he withdrew his gun, but somehow the gun fired. The echo caught attention of a caravan passing by at a distance. (Read this interesting story in his book, available In the Internet: (http://www.islamicbulletin.com/services/all_ebooks_p1.aspx)

The Verses of the Quran Tested on Music Rhythm

I referred above a term of Physics "Resonance", in regard to the Quran, it is "Spiritual Resonance" which explains the rhyming of heart with the verse. A famous scholar Dr. Hamidullah who passed most of his life in Paris narrates yet another story, how a French Christian Musician turned Muslim who one day came to him shuddering with excitement and asked "Sir, is not the Quran a book of God?" "Why, what is the problem?" He said: "you know I am a musician; I was testing one passage of the Book on my instrument according to the musical rhythmic laws, at one point it is not conforming? Hamidullah asked him to recite that passage and located the point where he was not reciting correctly. That Musician went to a corner and kept trying with his instrument for a while, and came back smiling and said "sir, surely it is from God"!

Some excerpts from Gary Miller's book "The Amazing Quran" (http://www.thetruecall.com/downloads/-Amazing Quran.pdf)

It is highly recommended to read this book, I assure, you will find it interesting and informative:

Gary Miller (Abdul-Ahad Omar) shows how we can establish true faith by setting standards of truth. He illustrates a simple but effective method of finding out the right direction in our search for truth.

G.R. Miller is a mathematician and a theologian. He was active in Christian missionary work at a particular point of his life but he soon began to discover many inconsistencies in the Bible. In 1978, he happened to read the Quran expecting that it, too, would contain a mixture of truth and falsehood.

He discovered to his amazement that the message of the Quran was precisely the same as the essence of truth that he had distilled from the Bible. He became a Muslim and since then has been active in giving public presentations on Islam including radio and television appearances. He is also the author of several articles and publications about Islam. He writes:

"A few years ago, a group of men in Riyadh, Saudi Arabia collected all of the verses in the Quran which discuss *embryology* - the growth of the human being in the womb. They said, "Here is what the Quran says. Is it the truth?" In essence, they took the advice of the Quran: "Ask the men who know." They chose, as it happened, a non-Muslim who is a professor of embryology at the University of Toronto. His name is Keith Moore, and he is the author of textbooks on embryology - a world expert on the subject. They invited him to Riyadh and said, "This is what the Quran says about your subject. Is it true? What can you tell us?"

While he was in Riyadh, they gave him all the help that he needed in translation and all of the cooperation for which he asked. And he was so surprised at what he found that he changed his textbooks. In fact, in the second edition of one of his books, called Before We Are Born... in the section about the history of embryology, he included some material that was not in the first edition because of what he found in the Quran was ahead of its time and that those who believe in the Quran know what other people do not know.

Gary Miller Interviews Dr Keith Moore:

"I(Gary Miller) had the pleasure of interviewing Dr. Keith Moore for a television presentation, and we talked a great deal about this - it was illustrated by slides and so on.

He mentioned that some of the things that the Quran states about the growth of the human being were not known until thirty years ago. In fact, he said that one item in particular - the Quran's description of the human being as a "leech-like clot" ('alaqah) at one stage (Surahs al-Hajj 22:5; al-Mu'minun 23:14; and Ghafir 40:67) - was new to him; but **when he checked on it, he found that it was true, and so he added it to his book.** He said, "I never thought of that before," and he went to the zoology department and asked for a picture of a leech. When he found that it looked just like the human embryo, he decided to include both pictures in one of his textbooks. Although the aforementioned example of man researching information contained in the Quran deals with a non-Muslim, it is still valid because he is one of those who is knowledgeable in the subject being researched.

Had some layman claimed that what the Quran says about embryology is true, then one would not necessarily have to accept his word. However, because of the high position, respect, and esteem man gives scholars, one naturally assumes that if they research a subject and arrive at a conclusion based on that research, then the conclusion is valid.

Keith L. Moore (born 5 October, 1925 in Brantford, Ontario) is a professor emeritus in the division of anatomy, in the Faculty of Surgery, at the University of Toronto, Ontario, Canada. Moore is associate dean for Basic Medical Sciences in the university's Faculty of Medicine, and was Chair of Anatomy from 1976 to 1984. He is a founding member of the American Association of Clinical Anatomists (AACA), and was President of the AACA between 1989 and 1999

Moore has co-written (with Professor Arthur F. Dalley and Professor Anne M. R. Agur) *Clinically Oriented Anatomy,* an English-language anatomy textbook. He also co-wrote (with Professor Anne M. R. Agur and Professor Arthur F. Dalley) *Essential Clinical Anatomy.*

Dr. Moore also wrote a book on clinical embryology, and when he presented this information in Toronto, it caused quite a stir throughout Canada. It was on the front pages of some of the newspapers across Canada, and some of the headlines were quite funny. For instance, one headline read: "SURPRISING THING FOUND IN ANCIENT BOOK!". It seems obvious from this example that people do not clearly understand what it is all about. As a matter of fact, one newspaper reporter asked Professor Moore, *"Don't you think that maybe the Arabs might have known about these things - the description of the embryo, its appearance and how it changes and grows? Maybe there were not scientists, but maybe they did something crude dissections on their own - carved up people and examined these things."*

The professor immediately pointed out to him that he [i.e., the reporter] had missed a very important point - all of the slides of the embryo that had been shown and had been projected in the film had come from pictures taken through a microscope. He said, "It does not matter if someone had tried to discover embryology fourteen centuries ago, they could not have seen it!." *All of the descriptions in the Quran of the appearance of the embryo are of the item when it is still too small to see with the eye; therefore, one needs a microscope to see it.* Since such a device had only been around for little more than two hundred years, Dr. Moore taunted, "Maybe fourteen centuries ago someone secretly had a microscope and did this research, making no mistakes anywhere. Then he somehow taught Muhammad(pbh) and convinced him to put this information in his book. Then he destroyed his equipment and kept it a secret forever. Do you believe that? You really should not unless you bring some proof because it is such a ridiculous theory."

In fact, when he was asked "How do you explain this information in the Quran?" Dr. Moore's reply was, "It could only have been divinely revealed."! (http://www.quranandscience.com/human/135-dr-keith-moore-confirms-embryology-in-quran.html)

"It suffices for the purpose of this discussion to state that the Quran makes very clear and concise statements about various subjects while simultaneously advising the reader to verify the authenticity of these statements with research by scholars in those subjects. And as illustrated above the Quran has clearly emerged authentic. Undoubtedly, there is an attitude in the Quran which is not found anywhere else. It is interesting how when the Quran provides information, it often tells the reader, "You did not know this before." Indeed, there is no scripture that exists which makes that claim." (Excerpts from the book "The Amazing Quran")

7

Islamic Laws – Outdated, Barbaric or Useful

(I) An Important Prerequisite to Islamic Laws

❖ For any rules and regulations, there must be a conscious choice and intention in an individual's inner heart to follow those rules obediently and diligently. There is a famous saying "you can bend the neck but cannot bow the head."

In the formation of the Laws in secular systems, this aspect of human psychology has been ignored. The people must be 'prepared/framed' first to accept rather 'believe' faithfully in the Laws. To make the people Law abiding, they should be made ready to accept the authority and sovereignty of the Lawgiver.

❖ The prophet did this work very cautiously, wisely and

gradually. **He enthused in them three important 'beliefs':**

- **that Allah is all the time watching.**
- **That they are very willingly ready to follow the commands of the Prophet.**
- **That they are accountable for whatever they do -------- in open day light or in secret.**

This "framing of mind" was done in long 13 years of Makkan period and in the early period of Madinah and then only the penal and other Laws were promulgated and that too in gradual form. This is why people took the laws not as 'fearsome' or 'burdensome' but as tools for cleansing themselves and earning the pleasure of Allah. Within Islamic faith, the concepts of persuasion and incentives of rewards and admonition of punishments get transcended to the level of revelation from God to man. They invoke an effect that is far beyond the magnitude conceivable by secular sciences. Furthermore, the reward and punishment is carried beyond the imaginable limits of this world into the eternity of the Hereafter. Thus the concepts of penal and civil laws are totally different from those in vogue in secular systems and this brings forth the reason why the detractors of Islam are often swayed to conclude wrongly.

A practicing Muslim realizes that no material gain or loss equals God's pleasure or anger. The Quran tries to instil this belief in all its readers. In Islamic system of life until and unless the three beliefs mentioned above are not ingrained in its members the Islamic Laws will fail to show its fruitful results.

At this place I cite two examples:

- ❖ Examples of how wine flowed in the streets of Madinah (please read this in the article 'How Alcoholism was eradicated?')
- ❖ The stories of the punishment to death of two persons, one man Mai'z and another woman of name Ghamidiyah at the time of the Prophet are just amazing. These are two separate instances elaborately described in Hadees Books. They implored the Prophet to order punishment to them only to save themselves from the punishment in Akhirah (Hereafter). (Read these heart touching stories below in the sub-article: 'Zina—two famous cases')

These stories for a man of today make just amazed and to him they seem to be just unbelievable that such people ever lived on the surface of the earth.

Compare the achievement of the Prophet on this score with all the might and effort applied by the administration in the famous 'prohibitions' in 1930s in the US with dismal result.

(see Wikipedia, see the notes compiled from Wikipedia in my note 'prohibition & crime in US')

Alcoholism and Islam

(Extract from "Islam Provides Remedy to Alcoholism" By Siraj Islam Mufti)

[Dr. Siraj Mufti received several grants from the U.S. National Institutes of Health for his research on alcohol abuse. He is currently serving as an Islamic consultant to the Correctional Corporation of America in Arizona.

Previously he worked as a research professor at the University of Arizona and a chaplain with the U.S. Department of Justice.]

Islam is unique in its successful eradication of alcoholism in a people in whom excessive drinking was an established tradition and a psychological necessity in 7th century pre-Islamic Arabia. This unequalled phenomenon has continued in Muslim masses and therefore, its discussion is very pertinent in relation to our modern alcohol-saturated world.

The pre-Islamic Arabs consumed alcohol more than in any other society of their times. Their existence was centred on upholding their tribal honour. Arabic poetry, replete with songs glorifying excessive drinking as an insignia of manhood, would enthral them in times of tribal wars and display of manly romantic passions in times of peace. Drinking would provide escape from deep rooted personal insecurities and the instability of family life, *just as it does today.* The unstable family structure was due to general low esteem for women. Divorce was common; prostitution and promiscuity were rampant. Modern psychologists and psychoanalysts consider alcohol dependence the result of insecurities of childhood deprivation, emotional traumas and broken families – *traits that were as common in pre-Islamic families as they are now.*

Muslims in Madinah under the leadership of Prophet Muhammad(pbh) (*Peace be upon him*) served as one large experimental group where extraordinary revolutionary changes were taking place. ***The lessons learnt for developing willpower*** *with negligible relapses in the change wrought by Islam towards alcohol could be summed up as follows:*

A Well Organized Plan for Gradual Change

The Islamic prohibition on alcohol was a logical final step of a well organized plan executed over a period of 3 years, communicated by the Quran and put into practice by the Prophet. Thus the heavy and problem drinkers were gradually weaned off this habit.

(Maududi, the renowned exegetist of the Quran says that most of Sura 2 was revealed shortly after Muhammad (pbh)'s Hijrah (Emigration from Mecca to Medina) in AD 622. The following verse in Sura 2 shows that Muhammad (pbh) partially condemned drinking and gambling at that time. [Maududi, Tafheemul Quran vol. 1, p. 161, note 235]

[Quran 2:219] *They ask you [Prophet] about intoxicants and gambling: say, "There is great sin in both and some benefit for people: the sin is greater than the benefit*

[Quran 4:43] *You, who believe, do not come anywhere near the prayer if you are intoxicated, until you know what you are saying...*

Third Prohibition: final and absolute

Maududi says that Sura 5 was revealed in the timeframe of AD 628 and 629, so it is a late sura (Muhammad (pbh) died of a fever in AD 632). It lays down rules for a growing community after the Treaty of Hudaybiyah in AD 628 in which Muslims were promised a free and unmolested pilgrimage to Mecca a year later, which took place. So it was important for Muslims to prepare themselves and to give up all intoxicants. Hence, these two verses came down from Allah:

> [Quran 5:90] *You who believe, intoxicants and gambling, idolatrous practices, and [divining with] arrows are repugnant acts—Satan's doing: shun them so that you may prosper.* 91: *With intoxicants and gambling, Satan seeks only to incite enmity and hatred among you, and to stop you remembering God and prayer.* ***Will you not give them up****?*

Also, when the final revelation came down in Sura 5:90-91, Syed Qutb, another scholar from Egypt reports on the miraculous results in these words:

> *All the Muslims stopped drinking. Once the command was given, all wine containers were emptied and broken throughout Madinah. Indeed, those who were in the process of drinking did not swallow what was in their mouths when they were informed of the prohibition. It was, thus, a great triumph for the Quran and its approach.* [fi zilalil Quran vol. 3, p. 155]

An extraordinary exhibition

However, the most important factor was **the believers' whole-hearted readiness to give up drinking when the Divine command came: "Surely al-khamr (intoxicants; wine and alcoholic drinks) is forbidden."** This command was enough to stop drinking instantaneously, throw away any and all drinks and to break up or empty existing pots, skins full and other containers of fermented date, palm, honey and grape in every gathering and household until the streets of Madinah **flowed like streams of alcohol as a testimony to the greatest anti-alcohol movement ever witnessed by humankind. It was an extraordinary exhibition of willpower instilled by faith.**

Strong Motivation to Change

Sociologists agree that people will comply with new social norms when they are convinced of their truth and validity. The real intrinsic motivation that caused success of anti-alcohol campaign was Islam as a religion and way of life. Thus the persuasion to give up alcohol did not occur only in 3 years - but actually commenced 13 years earlier with the coming of Islam.

The Prophet first attacked the false beliefs and values of Arabs. These were the real sources of "ignorance" or *jahiliyyah* as the Quran calls them; drinking, gambling, adultery and other immoral acts were only the symptoms of this *jahiliyyah*.

Thus the Prophet devoted the first 13 years wholly to correct their belief system until the sense of accountability before God, fear of punishment in Hell and reward of Paradise became vivid realities in the minds of believers.

Once this understanding became part and parcel of their lives, their selfish sense of pride and their conflicts were substituted with the bonding of brotherhood or *Ummah*, their family structure revamped and strengthened along with eradication of all personal insecurities and social evils.

Incentives of Reward and Fear of Punishment

Within Islamic faith, the concepts of incentives of reward and punishment get transcended to the level of revelation from God to man. Thus they invoke an effect that is far beyond the magnitude conceivable by secular sciences.

Furthermore, the reward and punishment is carried beyond the un-imaginable limits of this world into the eternity of the Hereafter. A practicing Muslim realizes that no material gain or loss equals God's pleasure or anger. His immediate reward is apparent in psychological elation and personal fulfilment that accompanies the spiritual pleasure in complying with a Divine commandment.

Other Factors of Social Persuasion

Among other factors that Islam uses in its persuasion is consensus. Islam requires consensus in all matters concerning the family, society or state. Such group compliance must play a high role in exerting pressure within the family and society on the drinker to give up. The gradual process adopted for prohibition is also indicative of unanimous positive response obtained in such situations.

Another factor is the cohesion and brotherhood fortified by Islamic teachings and practices that nurture **care and consideration for those who falter**.

But by far the most important factor in these and all other cases must be the leadership role and *example set for it by those who ask for compliance. **The leadership of the Prophet and the example set by him inspired his followers then (and now) to emulate him in every aspect of their lives.***

Despite the Western cultural invasion, even in those who are weak in faith, this potential understanding of Islam is very much ingrained in their inherited psyche. Malik Badri, a well-known Islamic psychologist recalls his use of this "potential power of Islam as a force of persuasion and aversion" with much success for Muslims who drink.

Alongside this, Islam provides the consolation of repentance (*tawbah*) for the guilty. God is not only Merciful and Compassionate but also *Tawwaab*, Often Returning, no matter how often a man falters and sins but then repents sincerely, because He is Most Forgiving (*Ghaffaar*).

The experience of Muslim African-Americans: An Observation by James Baldwin

The experience of a vast Muslim African-American community signifies the validity of Islamic approach: that it is much more successful than all other modern Western endeavours. James Baldwin in his well-known little book, *The Fire Next Time*, testifies to the "miracle" that takes place in African-Americans, as the ***"harassed alcoholic and drug addicts suddenly change when they convert to Islam."*** He goes to say: "And now suddenly people who have never before been able to hear this message hear it, and believe it, and are changed. [Islam] has been able to do what generations of welfare workers and committees and resolutions and reports and housing projects and playgrounds have failed to do:

To heal and redeem drunkards and junkies, to convert people who have come out of prisons and keep them out, to make men chaste and women virtuous, and to invest both male and female with the pride and serenity that hang about them like unfailing light".

This sudden change in the lifestyle seems inexplicable; take the example of sister-in-law of the ex-Prime minister of Britain Tony Blair, Lauren Booth.

Booth, a journalist and former reality TV contestant, decided to convert immediately after her return to Britain (from Iran). She has now stopped eating pork, reads the

Quran daily, attends a mosque and wears a headscarf when she goes out. She has also not ruled out the possibility of wearing a burka in the future. In an interview she said:

"I also haven't had a drink in 45 days, the longest period in 25 years,' she said. 'The strange thing is that since I decided to convert I haven't wanted to touch alcohol, and I was someone who craved a glass of wine or two at the end of a day."

Two Famous Cases of "Zina" At the Time of the Prophet

Zina (fornication= the unlawful sexual union between a man and a woman who are not married to each other.)

The most important case is that of Ma'iz bin Malik Aslami, which has been related by a large number of reporters on the authority of many Companions of the Holy Prophet (Allah's peace be upon him) and almost all books of Traditions contain details with regard to it. Ma'iz was an orphan boy from the clan of Aslam who had been brought up by Hazzal bin Nu'aim. He committed zina with a freed slave-girl. Hazzal said to him, "Go to the Holy Prophet and inform him of your sin; may be he prays for your forgiveness." Ma'iz went before the Holy Prophet in the Mosque and said, "I have committed zina; **please purify me**" The Holy Prophet turned his face away from him and said, "Woe be to you, go back and pray to Allah for forgiveness." But the boy again appeared before the Holy Prophet and said the same thing and the Holy Prophet again turned his face away. The boy then repeated his offence for the third time and the Holy Prophet again turned his face away. Hadrat Abu Bakr warned the boy that if he confessed the crime for the fourth time, the Holy

Prophet would get him stoned. But the boy persisted and repeated the same thing again. At this the Holy Prophet turned to him and said: "You might have only kissed or embraced or caressed her, or you might have looked at her with lust and you thought it was an act of Zina." The boy said, "No." The Holy Prophet asked, "Did you lie with her in the same bed?" The boy replied in the affirmative. The Holy Prophet again asked: "Did you have sexual intercourse with her? The boy again replied in the affirmative. The Holy Prophet then inquired in the most explicit Arabic expression specifically used for this act. Such a naked expression had never before been heard nor was ever heard afterwards from him. Had it not been the question of the life of an individual, the Holy Prophet would never have uttered such words. But the boy again replied in the affirmative to this explicit question. The Holy Prophet then asked: "Did you commit the act in such a manner that your male organ disappeared in her female part'?" The boy answered, "Yes." Again he was asked whether the act was as a rope goes into a well. The boy again answered in the affirmative. Again he was asked whether he really understood what zina meant, and the boy said, "Yes, I have committed the same act with her illegitimately which a husband commits legitimately with his wife." The Holy Prophet asked: "Are 'you married?" He said, "Yes". Again the Holy Prophet asked whether he had taken any wine. He said, "No", and one of the Companions smelt his mouth and continued that he had not. After this the Holy Prophet inquired of his neighbors whether he was suffering from insanity. They replied that he had not exhibited any sign of insanity. Then the Holy Prophet said to Hazzal: *"Had you kept it secret, it would have been better for you."* Then he ordered Ma'iz to be stoned to death and he was stoned to death outside the city. When they began to throw stones at him, Ma'iz tried to escape, and said, "O people, take me back to the Holy Prophet. The people of my clan deluded me, assuring that the Holy Prophet would not condemn me to death. "But they did not let him escape. Afterwards when this incident was reported to the Holy Prophet, he said: "Why did you not let him off? Had you brought him to me, he might have repented. And Allah might have accepted his repentance."

The second incident is of Ghamidiyyah, who was a woman from the clan of Ghamid, a branch of Juhainah tribe. She also confessed four times that she had committed zina and had become pregnant as a result thereof. At her first confession, the Holy Prophet said: "Woe be to you, go back and ask forgiveness of Allah and repent." But she said, "O Messenger of Allah, do you want to put me off like Ma'iz? I am pregnant as a result of zina. "As there existed pregnancy along with the confession, the Holy Prophet did not cross examine her in detail as he did in the case of Ma'iz. He said to her, "Well, if you do not accept my counsel, go back and come to me after the birth of the child." After delivery had taken place, she came along with the child and said, "**Please purify me now**." The Holy Prophet said: "Go and suckle your child, and come to me after the suckling is over." She again came after the weaning of the child and brought a piece of bread with her. She fed the child with the piece of bread before the Holy Prophet and said, "O Messenger of Allah, now the child has been weaned and has started taking bread." At this the Holy Prophet entrusted the child to a person to bring it up and ordered the stoning of the woman.

An Extra Note

According to Jabir bin 'Abdullah Ansari, as cited in Bukhari, when Ma'iz bin Malik was stoned to death, the Holy Prophet said good words about him and himself led his funeral prayer. A Tradition from Buraidah, as cited in Muslim, (another authentic book of the Prophet's sayings) states that the Holy Prophet said: "Pray for the forgiveness of Ma'iz bin Malik: **he has offered such repentance that if it were to be distributed over a whole community, it would suffice for the forgiveness of its entire people.**" In the same Tradition it has been mentioned that when Ghaimidiyyah died due to stoning, her funeral prayer was led by the Holy Prophet. When Khalid bin Walid talked ill of her, the Holy Prophet said: "Khalid, hold your tongue! I swear by Him Who controls my life that her repentance was such that even if a cruel tax-collector had offered such a repentance, he would have been forgiven." According to Abu Hurairah, as cited in Abu Da'ud, after the stoning of Ma'iz one day when the Holy Prophet was walking along, he heard two men talking ill of Ma'iz. When he had gone a few paces further, he saw the dead body of a donkey. He stopped there and asked the two men: "Come on and eat something out of it." They said, "O Prophet of Allah, who can eat a dead donkey?" The Holy Prophet replied: "Talking ill of your own brother was much worse than eating a dead donkey."

This sympathetic consideration of the Prophet leads one to conclude that in the sight of Islamic laws it is the 'crime' that is despised not the one who commits it.

(Those interested to know the detailed rulings in regard to 'Zina'/adultery/fornication are advised to see an elaborate and very informative discussion in the explanatory note of the first verse of S, Noor, chapter24 of the Quran in http://www.quranenglish.com/tafheem_quran/024.html "The Meaning of the Quran" by A A Maududi---- it can be said without any fear of rebuttal that such an analytical study on this topic is not available in any 'tafsir' (exegesis) of the Quran, old or new.)

"Zina" in Modern Era

In the West, the institution of marriage has significantly declined and nearly half of the marriages end up in divorce. The family has broken down resulting in much tension and the disintegration of other institutions in society and the rate of crime has steadily risen to epidemic proportion. The root 'cause' of all these is ***zina*** (fornication= the unlawful sexual union between a man and a woman who are not married to each other.) *Zina* is the greatest breach of one of the most important 'trust' that a man and a woman can ever have and it leads to disastrous consequences such as breakdown of family ties, depression, domestic violence, child abuse, rape and "the AIDS epidemic as a result of promiscuous sexual activity in direct contravention of Divine law". That's why there are now voices raised in the West by many sane persons to restore family values in order to reduce the crime rate and to maintain social order. *Zina* is the most deadly of all social crimes and "Islam puts an end to all those factors that 'allure' a man to *zina* or provide occasions for it"

Do Not Go Near Adultery

The Quran condemns *zina* not with the words "*La Tazanu*" (Do not commit adultery), as in the Pentateuch "Thou shall not commit adultery", but with the words *"La Taqrabuzzina"* (Do not go near adultery---take note that it is not said" don't commit adultery" but it is forbidden even to go near to it)...thus blocking all possible 'paths' leading to that act". That is why in Islamic societies, there is the segregation of the sexes and the Quran orders both men and' women to *"lower their gaze" (24:30-1)* and for women to wear the *Hijab* so that *"they may be recognised and not molested"* (33:59) as it is better for the *purification* of the hearts of both the sexes *(33:53).*

To eliminate the root cause of *zina,* Islam also takes other large scale precautionary and prohibitory measures such as developing God-consciousness, repugnance to sin and the belief in accountability, in every stage of education and it also encourages "early marriage and provides aid from the Public Treasury for those who wish to get married yet cannot afford to do so". Islamic societies, for this reason, will also not tolerate lures, mixed parties, pornography and the like which is likely to arouse the passion and disturb family relations because after all, according to the Quran, *"Man is created weak" (4:28).*

Islam also very strongly condemns false *imputation of zina on another person (qadhf)* as the Quran declares: *"As for those who slander chaste women and produce not four reliable witnesses, then stripe them with eighty lashes and never accept their testimony thereafter" (24:4).* Thus slander of this kind is dealt with severely as it seriously affects and damages self-confidence and strains family relations. Islam is never prepared to accept the kind of gossip that are so frequently found in the *tabloid papers* and the scandal - mongers are punished severely with eighty stripes.

For fornication between unmarried couples the penalty is 100 lashes and for adultery between married couples the penalty is stoning to death (*rajm*). Even then the *haad* punishment is not prescribed for the mere commission of *zina*, but other definitional elements of the crime has to be satisfied; only that kind of adultery is punishable by stoning which is committed intentionally by a free person who is both mature and sane, the accused must be committed to a marriage and has had intercourse with his lawful spouse, the accused must have committed *zina* voluntarily without compulsion and the act of *zina* must be attested by four honest, reliable and trustworthy witnesses who must have all seen the act of penepration and all four witnesses must be 'unanimous' in every stage of the act including minute details.

Such is the strict legal technicalities that has to be understood before the *haad* of stoning is carried out on adulterers and these facts are not highlighted by the West when condemning the punishments for *zina*. All the above mentioned conditions have to be met, before the *haad* is imposed which is very hard to do. Especially the question of witnesses is the most difficult aspect of all - the necessity of a minimum of four witnesses, as opposed to other *haad* offences where two are sufficient, who must be a devout person.

(II) Islamic Laws – Outdated? Barbaric? or Useful?

Skillfully manipulated display of the imagery of a whip cracking on a naked back of a Nigerian woman and a veil enshrouding a woman's face in Afghanistan have led many to believe that *Shariah*, the divine code of Muslim conduct, is in reality no more than a set of principles and practices that are primitive, unrefined and barbaric. As Khurram Murad states, **"What to mankind is the thing of mercy has been very subtly projected as a relic from the dark ages".**

The theme of this essay involves some common misconceptions and false charges levelled against the Islamic law in general and its penal policy in particular. Many volumes have been written by Islamic scholars to rebut and refute these allegations. In a short essay like this it is difficult to discuss all aspects in full, I will try to dispel some doubts at least. (In writing this chapter I am indebted to Abdullah Mohammad and A.A.Maududi.)

"No Separation of Church and State"

To understand Islamic Law one must first understand the assumptions of Islam and the basic tenets of the religion. The meaning of the word Islam is "submission or surrender to Allah's (God's) will." Therefore, Muslims must first and foremost obey and submit to Allah's will.

In Islam the Law giver is Allah, sovereignty rests only in Allah. *In fact, even the Messenger himself was not allowed to do anything in framing a law but only to convey the Message.* He was not given the authority to make a contribution of his own in framing a law.

Allah says in the Quran: "And if he had forged a false saying concerning Us, We surely would have seized him by his right hand, and then certainly would have cut off his life artery."

However the Prophet was allowed to put the Law in practice in the most adaptable way suitable to mankind; moreover the faithful were commanded to follow the

Prophet's way in day to day affairs. The Quran says:

> "Obey Allah and obey the messenger, and beware! if ye turn away, then know that the duty of Our messenger is only plain conveyance [of the message]." [5:92]

A Muslim must observe the Quranic Injunctions as well as the authentic traditions of the Prophet (called, Sunnah) in his all walks of life, mundane or spritual; in his worships in the mosque as well as in his dealings in the business.The Islamic Law is a unique amalgam of spritual and worldly affairs; thus a pure worldly affair such as a business transaction done in accordance with the commands of Allah and His Messenger carries, promises of reward (sawaaab) in the life hereafter or admonition of punishment if done otherwise.

The Sources of Islamic Law

Islamic law is based upon four main sources:

The Quran

Muslims believe the Quran to be the direct words of Allah, as revealed to and transmitted by the Prophet Muhammad (pbh). All sources of Islamic law must be in essential agreement with the Quran, the most fundamental source of Islamic knowledge. When the Quran itself does not speak directly, explicitly or in detail on a certain subject, only then Muslims turn to alternative sources of Islamic law. In that case the second source to be considered is: the Sunnah.

The Sunnah

Sunnah is the traditions or known practices of the Prophet

Muhammad (pbh), many of which have been recorded in the volumes of Hadith literature. The resources include many things that he said, did, or agreed to - and he lived his life according to the Quran, putting the Quran into practice in his own life. During his lifetime, the Prophet's family and companions observed him and shared with others exactly what they had seen in his words and behaviours - i.e. how he performed ablutions, how he prayed, and how he performed many other acts of worship, how he fought wars how he ordered punishment to those who committed criminal acts. Often people asked the Prophet directly for rulings on various matters, and he would pronounce his judgment. All of these details were passed on and recorded, to be referred to in future legal rulings. Many issues concerning personal conduct, community and family relations, political matters, etc. were addressed during the time of the Prophet, decided by him, and recorded. The Sunnah can thus clarify details of what is stated generally in the Quran. *The overwhelming majority of Muslims consider the sunnah to be essential supplements to and clarifications of the* Quran. In Islamic jurisprudence, the Quran contains many rules for the behavior expected of Muslims but there are no specific Quranic rules on many religious and practical matters. Muslims believe that they can look at the way of life, or sunnah, of Muhammad (pbh) and his companions to discover what to follow and what to avoid.

Ijma' (consensus)

The *ijma'*, or consensus amongst Muslim jurists on a particular legal issue, constitutes the third source of Islamic law. Muslim jurists present many verses of the Quran that legitimize *ijma'* as a source of legislation. Muhammad(pbh) himself said:

- "My followers will never agree (collectively) upon an error or what is wrong",
- "God's hand is with the entire community".

In history, it has been the most important factor in defining the meaning of the other sources and thus in formulating the doctrine and practice of the Muslim community. This is so because *ijma'* represents the unanimous agreement of Muslims on a regulation or law at any given time. There are various views on *ijma'* among Muslims. Some jurists consider *ijma'* as a source, in matters of legislation, as important as the Quran and Sunnah whereas others consider *ijma'* as source of secondary importance, and a source that is, unlike the Quran and Sunnah, not free from error.

Qiyas (Analogy)

In cases when something needs a legal ruling, but has not been clearly addressed in the other sources, judges may use analogy, reasoning, and legal precedent to decide new case law. This is often the case when a general principle can be applied to new situations. *Qiyas* is the process of legal deduction according to which the jurist, confronted with an unprecedented case, *bases his argument on the logic used in the* Quran *and* Sunnah. *Qiyas* must not be based on arbitrary judgment, but rather be firmly rooted in the primary sources.

According to Hadith, Muhammad (pbh) said: **"Where there is no revealed injunction, I will judge amongst you according to reason."** Further, he extended the right to reason to others. Finally, *qiyas* is sanctioned by the ijma, or consensus, amongst the Prophet's Companions. Thus, if the cause of an injunction can be deduced from the primary sources, then analogical deduction can be applied to cases with similar causes. For example, wine is prohibited in Islam because of its intoxicating property. Thus *qiyas* leads to the conclusion that all intoxicants are forbidden.

Ijtihad

Scholars narrate a hadith that the Prophet, while sending his companion, Mu'adh to Yemen, as a governor there, asked him as to on what he would base his judgements. "In accordance with the Book of Allah," replied Mu'adh, "But what if you don't find it there?" inquired the Prophet. "According to the Sunnah of the Apostle of Allah," replied Mu'adh. "But what if you don't find it there too?" asked the Prophet again. ***'I will exert my own opinion'***, replied Mu'adh. In affirmation, the Prophet put his hand on Mu'adh's chest and said: "Thank God for assisting His Apostle with what he loves." They have narrated other traditions on the subject to the effect that either the Prophet directly commanded his Companions to exercise ijtihad in case they could not find a rule in the Book and the Sunnah, or to the effect that he approved of the practice of his Companions that practised ijtihad. To the Sunnis, this is something definite, confirmed by consensus (*ijma'*).

It is maintained that if a solution to a problem cannot be found from the primary sources, then *aql* or reason should be given free rein to deduce a proper response from the primary sources. The process, whereby rational efforts are made by the jurist to arrive at an appropriate ruling, when applied is called *ijtihad* (literally meaning "exerting oneself"). Some jurists maintain *that qiyas is a specific type of ijtihad. The Sunni Shafi' school of thought, however, holds that both qiyas and ijtihad are the same.*

In the history of Islamic jurisprudence it is found that gradually, with the decline of political power and in academics , ijtihad was replaced by ***taqlid*** *(the acceptance of doctrines developed previously).* Later in Sunni history, however, there were notable instances of jurists using reason to re-derive law from the first principles. One was Ibn Taymiyya (d. 728/1328), another was Ibn Rushd (d. 595/1198).

Sharia law, is in simple terms Islamic Law: the moral code and religious law of Islam. Sharia deals with many topics addressed by secular law, including crime, politics and economics, as well as personal matters such as hygiene, diet, prayer, and fasting and even man-woman relationship. Though interpretations of sharia vary between cultures, in its strictest definition it is considered the infallible law of God—as opposed to the human interpretation of the law.

Penal Laws

In fact there are arguments to suggest that Islamic punishments are only applicable and enforceable in a just and proper Islamic state where the socio-economic and political systems are fully operating according to *Shari'ah. In an Islamic state, punishment follows a long series of prohibitory and reformatory steps where all efforts are made to eliminate all the root 'causes' of crime and to create a healthy crime-free environment.* ***Even then punishment is not meted out for all breaches of the Shari'ah but only certain specifically defined crimes with certain strict conditions.***

Islam, being cognizant of human conditions, provides for this when it divides its penal penalties in three categories.

Hudood

The first and most severe type of punishments are known as the *hudood* (singular *hadd*) meaning a thing which restrains or prevents since a punishment "prevents a man from doing crimes". However, it is a strictly defined penalty which is mentioned in the Quran or the Hadith and it includes adultery, fornication, false allegations against someone's chastity (*qadhf*), drunkenness, armed robbery, sedition and apostasy._*But it must be noted that Hudood can function well only when all other systems are being applied in true and full Spirit)*

Qisas

The second category of punishment, known as *qisas* (equitable retribution), is inflicted for deliberate killing or wounding of a person. Unlike *hadd*, the penalty could be waived by the victim or his heir in lieu of blood-money (*diya*), but for unintentional homicide or wounding there is no retribution and only compensation is paid. The Quran teaches that:

> *"And for you in equitable retribution there is Life, 0 people of understanding, that you may ward off evil"*
> [Quran 2: 179]

Ta'zeer

The third category of punishment is known as *ta'zeer* (discretionary punishment) and it is "a sentence or punishment whose measure is not fixed by the *Shari'ah*" neither as to the offence nor the penalty. It helps to meet varying circumstances eg. whipping, though other alternatives such as a warning, fines and imprisonment could be given, but the quantum of punishment for *ta'zeer* is generally much below that of *hadd*.

The Islamic penal policy is not to create opportunities for crime and then to punish the culprit, but it aims at eliminating the very root cause of crime. There is a saying "prevention is the best cure" and if we can eliminate alcohol from society, then we can eliminate or at least substantially reduce the rate of general crimes. That is why "in true Islamic societies there is virtually no drunkenness with its associated catalogue of crimes" such as homicide, physical assault, domestic violence, reckless driving, vandalism and rape. "Islam punishes before there is the chance for a serious crime to be committed" and thereby it stops public nuisance and safeguards people's lives, honour, intellect and property. Alcoholism is a widespread disease and no human solutions are apparent in hand.

'Islamic law is out dated'?

Out-dated implies old-fashioned and obsolete, even impracticable, something that has lost its moral and ethical values and is not worthy of use in the given time. Let us examine the human beings. Is the 'man' out-dated today? *Has his needs, desires, nature of lust for food, sex and all such instincts have changed ?? - the 'MAN' as a whole is the same*

Allah knows well what are man's shortcomings and how they may be corrected. So Shariah as applicable today as it was in past *Shari'ah* is not old to forsake it for the latest modern trend. The *Shari'ah* emanates from Allah, the All Wise who, being well aware of human conditions, has revealed a law *(5:48)* that is "perfectly universal and applicable to all nations" for all times. "It is not a system of law to be judged and evaluated as 'good' or 'bad' in accordance with the changing views of the population or the policies of the state" and therefore the *Shari'ah* is radically different from "the ordinary law in which the legislative authority is free to explain and comment on the law introduced by it which it can freely amend, cancel or withdraw".

Shari'ah vis-á-vis Man-made Laws

If the aim of the law is to control unacceptable human behaviour and to reduce the rate of crime, then there has to be an element of permanence so that it may be easily recognised by the citizens who after all, are the ones who are bound to follow the law (English law teaches that 'ignorance of law is no defence'). But man-made laws change all the time according to changing "social attitudes" so much so that actions that were once regarded as 'detestable' and 'heinous' crimes (such as abortion, suicide, prostitution, homosexuality and adultery in England) are now regarded as 'legal' and normal under the same laws! Such is the nature of human laws which cannot fully comprehend human nature or predict the future and is constantly changing. T*he man-made laws have miserably failed and the rate of crime has reached epidemic proportion.* Allah knew that MAN, inclined to wrong-doings will detest strict punishments, in the Quran, He says

> *"It may happen that you hate a thing which is in fact 'good' for you and it may happen that you love a thing which is in fact 'bad' for you but Allah knows and you do'nt."* [Quran2:216]

Important remarks

- The *Shari'ah* encompasses and governs every aspect of life and any of its specific provisions, including the penal system, *must be seen in its totality* where the moral, socio-economic, political and educational systems are in force and it must not be seen in isolation. ***If the penal system is only one of the branches of law, which is dependent on other institutions in society,*** then it is totally unfair to look at some of the rare punishments of Islam to judge the merit or de-merit of the whole legal and social and political systems. Thus the punishment of theft is to be applied only if system of zakat and charity are distributed well and punishment for adultery to be enforced only when all rules and regulations regarding *Hijab* and purdah are well observed.

- The alleged severity of the Islamic punishments is not really what the West is concerned about, but the 'moral values' of Islam as then they will be barred from 'real ENJOYMENT of life' such as wine and adultery ,the two things, they are used to nay, they are immersed in.

- There is no distinction between the secular and the *sacred* in Islam and it does not recognise the Biblical maxim "Render unto Caesar the things that are Caesar's, and render unto God the things that are God's" [*Mark 12:17*]. Here in Islam both are intermingled, intertwined, interdependent.

Extra Notes:

1 – What is a "FATWA"

A fatwa is an Islamic religious ruling, a scholarly opinion on a matter of Islamic law.

A fatwa is issued by a recognized religious authority in Islam. But since there is no hierarchical priesthood or anything of the sort in Islam, a fatwa is not necessarily "binding" on the faithful. The people who pronounce these rulings are supposed to be knowledgeable, and base their rulings in knowledge and wisdom. They need to supply the evidence from Islamic sources (as mentioned above) for their opinions, and it is not uncommon for scholars to come to different conclusions regarding the same issue.

In general Muslims look at the Fatwa and judge on the basis of the reputation of the person giving it, the evidence given to support it, and then decide whether to follow it or not. When there are conflicting opinions issued by different scholars, they compare the evidence and then choose the opinion to which their conscience guides them.

2 – Terms Used in the Quran are Comprehensive

[5:90] O! YOU who have attained to faith! ***Khamr*** (Intoxicants), and games of chance, and idolatrous practices, and the divining of the future are but a loathsome evil of Satan's doing:' shun it, then, so that you might attain to a happy state!

In the above verse pronouncing the forbiddance of alcohol, the word خمر is used. There are many other words which could have been used here to refer to wine and alcohol such as نبيذ or شراب. But there is great wisdom in using the word 'Khamr' here. Literal meaning of the word خمر is *'the thing which covers the head/mind'*, it is from the same root word as خمار which is a cloth used by women to cover the head. Thus the word *Khamr* is used to refer to things which befog the mind. There is also the hadith of

Prophet Muhammad (pbh) declaring all intoxicating things to be 'khamr'. Ibn 'Umar reported Allah's Messenger (peace be upon him) as saying: Every intoxicant is Khamr and every intoxicant is forbidden. (Muslim)

Therefore all drinks or food substances which intoxicate the mind would come under 'khamr' and are forbidden. This shows the great wisdom of Islamic laws and their universality. In the era of Prophet Muhammad(pbh) (s) there were no narcotics, but in our times drugs have become a major problem. Therefore hashish, opium, cocaine, morphine, marijuana and all such substances which befog the mind would also come under 'khamr' This is to ensure the safety and wellbeing of individuals and society as a whole as the disastrous impact of alcohol and drugs is well acknowledged.

- ❖ If the Islamic Law was out-dated, it would not be able to deal with new substances, but would only be applicable in its own time. However, the fact is that since the Islamic laws comes from Allah who has full knowledge of the past present and the future therefore all the laws are so updated that they were fully applicable in the past, are still applicable in the present and will be fully applicable in the future.
- ❖ If in the future any new substance is discovered or created which also has an intoxicating effect, it would also come under 'khamr' and would thus be forbidden.

8

Man-Woman Relationship

The Quran on Man-Woman Relationship

> **"And among His Signs is this, that He created for you wives from among yourselves, that you may find repose in them, and He has put between you affection and mercy. Verily, in that are indeed signs for a people who reflect."** [Quran 30:21]

The Noble Messenger of Allah (peace be upon him) is reported to have said:

> **"The most perfect of the believers is the best of you in character, and the best of you are those among you who are best to their wives."** [Hadith-Al-Tirmidhi]

The duty of every husband to be loving, affectionate and caring to his spouse. Nobody is

perfect and we should always try to overlook the faults of our spouse. The Messenger of Allah (pbh) is reported to have said that "If he dislikes something in her character, he should be pleased with some other trait of hers." [Hadith-Muslim]

Man-Woman: 'Pair' or 'Identical'

It is to be noted that Allah created everything, animate or inanimate, in pairs. (See these verses:

[Quran 51:49] And of everything We have created pairs: That ye may receive instructions.

[Quran 78:8] And We have created you in pairs;

[Quran 36:36] Glory to Allah, Who created in pairs all things that the earth produces, as well as their own (human) kind and (other) things of which they have no knowledge.

Man and Woman are created in pairs; from engineering point of view, each part of a pair will have many similar elements but in some elements they have to be dissimilar: it all depends upon the purpose of the pair for which it is made. If two parts are exactly similar, identical, in all respects then these two parts can never make a 'pair' and hence the purpose for which it is made can never be achieved. This is a simple idea but in modern times this simple logic has been ignored in case of Man-Woman-pair: people are coaxed to believe that the two parts of the 'pair' are identical and hence 'functions' of both parts of the 'pair' must be same. It is one of the many 'open follies' of modern times. It is also going against all the laws operating in the Nature and when one operates against Nature it yields tragic consequences!

It is a reality that men and women are not identical. There definitely exists a difference between them. The difference lies in not only in anatomy and physiology but also in psychology of each. This 'difference' leads them to play different roles in a society. Indeed, it is due to having disregarded the separate roles of men and women that Europe, America and other western countries are witnessing the complications and conflicts in their society. Broken families, abandoned children, single parents, morally psychologically deprived children, are all a direct result of the artificial concoction of 'gender equality'. What was designed to be a harmonious pair, has been reduced to two equal counterparts, fighting for equality and dominance, with the children bearing the brunt of the fight and the woman often becoming a mental wreck in the process because in actuality she is weaker physically and psychologically.

Farce Claim

Why they clamour for Gender Equality; are the genital parts and reproductive systems of man and woman the same? Does man in anyway share with woman the pain and labour in bearing and rearing children? The advocators of women liberation are only fooling themselves. Which professional sports team in the entire world has half males and half females? Which army in the world has exactly the same number of women as men fighting in the front line of the battlefield? Which country has its army chief a woman? Have we ever wondered why there never was a boxing or wrestling match where a man contested a woman? Why is it considered chivalrous for a man to protect a woman and not vice versa? The list of examples can go on...

Evils bred by Gender Equality

Let us take a cursory glance at some of the evils that the folly of gender equality has bred:

1. Instead of improving the quality of life for woman, it has only turned life into a misery for her because of the added responsibilities of sharing man in his outdoor activities, in all walks of life; (whereas by nature of her gender she has to bear children - the children by nature need ***her*** lap for caring and feeding). This extended the working hours for her, taking care of home as well as 'outdoor activity' (which in many cases included laborious works worthy of being done only by men). Alas! She took this added responsibility in the name of 'Liberation'. Man succeeded in trapping her but it is an irony that she let herself be fooled gladly.

   Broken marriages: Countless marriages have broken down or are on the verge of breaking down. While there are many reasons for the escalating rate of divorce, a major contributing factor is the unnatural situation brought about by the notion of gender equality. One can easily comprehend the situation in a family where children come to home from schools where mother is not there to take care of them; mother and father come late in evening, each tired and carrying tension in their heads of their jobs; children by instinct of nature hope care from mother and she responds despite her fatigue and sometimes additional ailments (of menstruation or pregnancy - alas! how cruel this 'liberation' is to her.)

2. Delinquent children: Since both parents no longer have any time for their children, they have no direction, system or values in life.

3. Women's dress, outfit and interaction with the men:

   Why a woman is lured to put on dresses wherein she is exposed to the men? The modern women may deny the fact and claim these dresses as their own choice out of their own free will etc. but the truth remains unchanged, that, it is only to quench the immodest desires of the male. Not convinced? Well, go to any night club in any country in the West and see the men in fully dressed to suit the shivering cold outside while ladies in scanty dress bearing the cold. Why?

4. Double-edged sword

   The women's modern dress, alluring, enticing and sometimes ludicrous make-up and free interaction with men have acted as double-edged-sword.Has it really brought any good for women? The women may aptly feel good about themselves for a while, but what does it mean for every other woman? Women who look upon these images usually become anxious, jealous, unsure and critical of themselves, or all of these things. Many men who view them will become aroused, or even unhappy, less satisfied with the partners they already have. What does this lead to?

Impact of World War I & II on the society

Last century was an era of extraordinary changes in different fields of society. Technological developments brought about new devices and appliances available to women which eased her in domestic works and changed the lifestyle. The two World Wars wreaked havoc on women; they were compelled to step out of homes to earn in absence of their men. Also after the War there was a shortage of men in fields and factories; this paved the way for intermixing of sexes. New contraceptive methods available within reach of any one, very young to old, added fuel to fire. This led to promiscuity and extra-marital relationship to a proportion never witnessed in the history. An important point to be observed: the concept of morality in the West was very loose as they had divorced religion (Christianity) fully or partially after the Renaissance in Europe. (At this place it is inappropriate to remark that Biblical injunctions in regard to marriage, divorce and family affairs were inadequate to raise a society on solid background which could sustain the onslaughts of devastating wars and technological changes. We will indicate these at places later on)

Going through the history of feminist movements in the West and the burdens women had to bear after World War I and particularly after WW II one can understand the causes which led the women from one extreme of oppression to the other. It is the need of the hour to come to the middle path as enshrined in the Quran. (See the detail in: en.wikipedia.org/wiki/**Women's_liberation_movement,**-novaonline.nvcc.edu/.../**womensliberation/womens-liberation** www.marxists.org/subject/**women/move-ment/index**. htmhttp://www.glbtq.com/social-sciences/womens_liberation_ movement,2.html)

The Call of the Quran

Hijab

Hijab, or headscarf, is one of the most noticeable and misunderstood badges of Muslim women. But there's much more to the Islamic dress code for women than the *Hijab*. It's a total package that deals with clothing, behavior, demeanor, modesty and more importantly keeping away from nudity. For some *Hijab* means pairing a headscarf with Western-style clothes. For others it means wearing loose robes as well. Still others add a niqab, or face veil, to their ensembles.

What do Islam and the Quran exactly say about modest clothing for women? For men? What does Islamic dress exactly entail?

The word "*Hijab*" comes from the Arabic "hajaba" which means to conceal or hide from view. In general terms, it refers to Islamic modest dressing for women. But it has come to signify the headscarf, which is the covering many Muslim women use to hide their hair, neck, and often bosom.

Islamic Dress for Women

Islam has no fixed uniform of dress for Muslim women or men. But there are two requirements, which come from the Quran and *hadith* (verified sayings of the Prophet Muhammad(pbh)): First, a woman's body should be covered such that only her face, hands, and feet are revealed. For men the area to be covered is from navel to below the knee. Secondly, the clothing must be loose enough so that it does not accentuate her figure. Other parameters (as stated in *hadiths*) are that women shouldn't dress so as to look like men, women shouldn't dress in a way similar to those who don't believe in God, and the clothing should be modest, neither ragged nor overly fancy, should not be transparent. It is important to remember that Islam teaches Muslims that the concept of modest dress doesn't just mean covering the body, but it also has to do with behavior, manners, speech, and public appearance. Modesty is a total package, with dress being one part of it.

Mandated by the Quran?

A common misconception is there that *Hijab* is a social custom 'invented' by mullahs and is not mandated by the Quran; this is far from truth. The Quran and the Traditions of the Prophet are very clear on this account. The instructions in the Quran regarding ***Hijab, Modesty,*** **Nudity** and social manners are given mainly in two chapters Surah Noor 24 verses27-31 and Surah Ahzaab 33:59 Surah Aaraf 7:19-26-27.

Nudity –a weapon of Satan

In Surah Aaraf 7: verse 19 onward is described how Adam and Eve both were deceived by Satan and their dresses were pulled off as the first penalty to following the Satan; in verses 26 and 27 Allah commands thus:

[7:26] **0 Children of Adam! Indeed We have sent down to you a garment which covers your shame and provides protection and adornment. But the finest of all is the garment of piety. That is one of the signs of Allah so that they may take heed (7:27) Children of Adam! Let not Satan deceive you in the manner he deceived your parents out of Paradise, pulling off from them their clothing to reveal to them their shame. He and his host surely see you from whence you do not see them. We have made satans the guardians of those who do not believe.**

(see the explanatory note below on these two verses by A. Maududi : http://islamicstudies.info/taf-heem.php?sura=7&verse=26&to=31):

These verses bring into focus some important points.

First, that the need to cover oneself is not an artificial urge in man; rather it is an important dictate of human nature. Unlike animals, God did not provide man with the protective covering that He provided to animals. God rather endowed man with the natural instincts of modesty and bashfulness. Moreover, the private parts of the body are not only, related to sex, but also constitute 'sawat' that is, something the exposure of which is felt to be shameful. Also, God did not provide man with a natural covering in response to man's modesty and bashfulness, but has inspired in him see (verse 26) the urge to cover himself. This is in order that man might use his reason to understand the requirements of his nature, use the resources made available by God, and provide himself a dress.

Second, man instinctively knows that the moral purpose behind the use of dress takes precedence over the physical purpose. Hence the idea that man should resort to dress in order to cover his private parts precedes the mention of dress as a means of providing protection and adornment to the human body. In this connection man is altogether different from animals, With regard to the latter; the natural covering that has been granted serves to protect them from the inclemency of weather and also to beautify their bodies. However, that natural covering is altogether unrelated to the purpose of concealing their sexual organs. The exposure of those organs is not a matter of shame for them and hence their nature is altogether devoid of the urge to cover them. However, as men fell prey to Satanic influences, they developed a false and unhealthy notion about the function of dress. They were led to believe that the function of dress for human beings is no different from that for animals, viz., to protect them from the inclemency of weather and to make them look attractive. As for concealing the private parts of the body, the importance of that function has been belittled. For, men have been misled into believing that their private parts are, in fact, like other organs of their body. As in the case of animals, there is little need for human beings to conceal their sex organs.

Third, the Quran emphasizes that it is not enough for the dress

i. to cover the private parts and

ii. to provide protection and

iii. adornment to the human body.

iv. Man's dress ought to be the **dress of piety**.

This means that a man's dress ought to conceal his private parts. It should also render a man reasonably presentable - the dress being neither too shabby and cheap nor overly expensive and extravagant relative to his financial standing. Nor should dress smack of pride or hauteur, or reflect that pathological mental state in which men prefer characteristically feminine dresses and vice versa: or that the people belonging to one nation mimic people of other nations so as to resemble them, thereby becoming a living emblem of collective humiliation and abasement. The Quranic ideal can only be achieved by those who truly believe in the Prophets and sincerely try to follow God's Guidance. For as soon as man decides to reject God's

Guidance, Satan assumes his patronage and by one means or another manages to lead him into error after error.

Hijab and modesty are mentioned in the Quran:

[24:30] **(O Prophet), enjoin believing men to cast down their looks and guard their private parts. That is purer for them. Surely Allah is well aware of all what they do.**

[24:31] **And enjoin believing women to cast down their looks and guard their private parts and not reveal their adornment except that which is revealed of itself, and to draw their veils over their bosoms (and to extend their head coverings (khimars) to cover their bosoms (jaybs), and not to reveal their adornment save to their husbands, or their fathers, or the fathers of their husbands, or of their own sons, or the sons of their husbands, (list of relatives continues)**

(see http://islamicstudies.info/tafheem.php?sura=24&verse=27&to=34) See the explanatory notes, marked above, full detail in this site—below is a summary:

Lowering the Gaze

The Arabic word 'ghadd' used in the above verse means to reduce, shorten or lower down something. Accordingly, 'ghaddbasar' is generally translated as lowering the gaze or keeping it lowered. But the command of 'ghaddbasar' does not imply that the gaze should always be kept lowered. It only means to imply that one should restrain his gaze and avoid fixing the look. That is, if it is not desirable to see a thing, one should turn the eyes away and avoid havit.ng a direct visual contact. The restriction of a restrained gaze is applicable only in a limited sphere. The context in which the words occur shows that this restriction applies to the men's gazing at women, or casting looks at the 'satar' (explained below) of the other persons, or fixing the eyes at indecent scenes.

The details of this divine commandment as explained in the Sunnah of the Prophet (peace be upon him) are given below:

It is not lawful for a man to cast a full gaze at the other women except at his own wife or the mahram (a person with whom wedlock is not permissible) women of his family. The chance look is pardonable but not the second look which one casts when one feels the lure of the object. The Prophet (peace be upon him) has termed such gazing and glancing as wickedness of the eyes. He has said that man commits adultery with all his sensory organs. The evil look at the other woman is the adultery of the eyes; lustful talk is the adultery of the tongue; relishing the other woman's voice is adultery of the ears; and touching her body with the hand or walking for an unlawful purpose is adultery of the hands and feet. After these preliminaries the sexual organs either bring the act of adultery to completion or leave it incomplete. [Bukhari, Muslim, Abu Daud]

According to a tradition related by Buraidah, the Prophet (peace be upon him) instructed Ali: O Ali, do not cast a second look after the first look. The first look is pardonable but not the second one. [Tirmizi;, Ahmad, Abu Daud]. Jarir bin Abdullah Bajali says that he asked the Prophet, What should I do if I happen to cast a chance look? The Prophet (pbh) replied: Turn your eyes away or lower your gaze. [Muslim, Ahmad, Tirmizi, Abu Daud, Nasai]. Abdullah bin Masud quotes the Prophet (peace be upon him) as having said: Allah says that the gaze is one of the poisonous arrows of Satan. Whoever forsakes it, out of His fear, he will be rewarded with a faith whose sweetness he will relish in his own heart. [Tabarani]. According to a tradition related by Abu Umamah, the Prophet (peace be upon him) said: If a Muslim happens to glance at the charms of a woman and then turns his eyes away, Allah will bless his worship and devotion and will make it all the more sweet. [Musnad Ahmad]

Exceptions

There are certain exceptions to the command of lowering the gaze or restraining the look. These exceptions relate to occasions when it is really necessary to see a woman, for instance, when a man intends to marry her. It is not only permissible to see the woman in such a case but even commendable. Mughirah bin Shubah has stated: I wanted to marry in a certain family. The Holy Prophet asked me whether I had seen the girl or not. When 1 replied in the negative, he said: Have a look at her; this will enhance harmonious relationship between you two. [Ahmad, Tirmizi, Nasai, Ibn Majah, Darimi]

Guard Your Private Parts

They are to abstain from illicit sexual gratification and from exposing their satar before others. For males, the satar is the part of the body from the navel to the knee, and it is not permissible to expose that part of the body intentionally before anybody except one's own wife. [Daraqutni, Baihaqi]

Jarhad Aslami states that once he was sitting in the company of the Prophet (peace be upon him) with his thigh exposed. The Prophet (peace be upon him) said: Do you not know that the thigh has to be kept concealed. [Tirmizi, Abu Daud, Muatta]

Ali reports that the Prophet (peace be upon him) said: Do not expose your thigh. [Abu Daud, Ibn Majah]

Not only is the satar to be kept concealed before others but even when alone. The Prophet has warned: Beware, never remain naked, for with you are those (that is, the angels of goodness and mercy), who never leave you alone except when you ease yourself or you go to your wives. So feel shy of them and give them due respect. [Tirmizi]

Satar - Parts of Body Required to be Covered

That is, they should abstain from illicit gratification of their sex desire as well as from exposing their satar before others. Though the commandments for men in this respect are the same as for women, the boundaries of satar for women are different from those prescribed for men. Moreover, the female satar with respect to men is different from that with respect to women. The female satar with respect to men is the entire body, excluding only the hand and the face, which should not be exposed before any other man, not even the brother and father, except the husband. The woman is not allowed to wear a thin or a tight fitting dress which might reveal the skin or the outlines of the body. According to a tradition from Aishah, once her sister Asma came before the Prophet (peace be upon him) in a thin dress. The Prophet (peace be upon him) immediately turned his face away and said: O Asma, when a woman has attained her maturity, it is not permissible that any part of her body should be exposed except the face and the hand. [Abu Daud]

The only relaxation permitted in this connection is that a woman can uncover only that much of her body before her close relatives (for example, her brother, father, etc.) as is absolutely necessary for attending to the household duties. For instance, she can roll up her sleeves while kneading the flour, or tuck up her trousers while washing the floor.

Hijab is Beneficial to any Society Muslim or non-Muslim

Hijab Instructions as enshrined in the Quran and Sunnah and its observance in society is beneficial to women (Muslim or non-Muslim alike) in many aspects:

1. They can protect both their social worth and inner values much better, and guard themselves against just being an object on display. (This is evident in all advertisements of any item even remotely concerned with women: billboard ads, cartoons, movies, music videos, print ads, etc., that portray women and girls in sensually.)

2. A woman's social behaviour, which is based on Islamic ethics, would set her husband's mind at rest; such a man would not be attracted to other women. On the contrary, a man whose wife is not concerned with Islamic *Hijab* and who displays her beauty to other men or socializes with them would seriously remain upset; such a husband would always suffer from distress and pessimism and his love for his family may gradually fade away.

3. Observing Islamic *Hijab* has its marked benefit that the loafers and oglers would cease to tease. *Hijab* also prevents young boys from getting aroused.

4. If all women observed the regulation of Islamic *Hijab*, then they could rest assured that their husbands, when not at home would not encounter a lewd woman who might draw his attention away from the family.

5. The relation between man and woman is aptly summed up in the verse quoted at the head of this article 30:21 and lastly in the following verse: 4:34 Men are the protectors and maintainers of women, because Allah has given the one more (strength) than the other, and because they support them from their means. Therefore the righteous women are devoutly obedient, and guard in (the husband's) absence what Allah would have them guard.

Polygamy

At the outset it should be clearly understood that Islam did not introduce polygamy. Unrestricted polygamy was practiced in most human societies throughout the world in every age. It is the Quran that regulated polygamy by limiting the number of wives and establishing responsibility in its practice and introducing certain restrictions as we will indicate below.

The Bible did not condemn polygamy. To the contrary, the Old Testament and Rabbinic writings frequently attest to the legality of polygamy. King Solomon is said to have had 700 wives and 300 concubines [1 Kings 11:3] Also, King David is said to have had many wives and concubines [2 Samuel 5:13]. The Old Testament does have some injunctions on how to distribute the property of a man among his sons from different wives [Deuteronomy. 22:7]. The only restriction on polygamy is a ban on taking a wife's sister as a rival wife [Leviticus. 18: 18]. The Talmud advises a maximum of four wives (Leonard J. Swidler, Women in Judaism: the Status of Women in Formative Judaism (Metuchen, N. J: Scarecrow Press, 1976-p 144)

Similarly in early Hindu society unrestricted polygamy was rampant and it is described in the scriptures elaborately.

Quranic Injunctions

> "If ye fear that ye shall not be able to deal justly with the orphans, marry women of your choice, two, or three, or four; but if ye fear that ye shall not be able to deal justly (with them), then only one, or that which your right hands possess. That will be more suitable, to prevent you from doing injustice." [Surah Nisa 4: 3]

It is seen clearly in the verse that marrying more than one woman 2, 3 and finally 4 is not an order that has to be carried out like fardh or wajib (compulsory) but it is just a permission. However, this permission depends on dealing justly among the wives. It is stated that being content with one wife is the closest and rightest way to justice; it is ordered that a person who fears that he won't be able to deal justly has to be content with one wife.

Conditions of Marrying More Than One Woman

Islam set forth some conditions for marrying more than one woman. Those conditions are as follows:

1. Limitation of the number

Islam put a limitation to the limitless marriages of men during the period of pre-Islamic era (Jahiliyyah : Ignorance). After Allah sent down that verse put a limit of four wives at a time, those who had more than four wives divorced the extra ones.

2. To deal justly among the wives

This is limited with the human capability; it includes being just in food, clothes, housing, interest and treatment. However, justice does not include issues like liking, inclination of the heart and love, because they cannot be controlled. It is forbidden to incline to one of the wives extremely and deprive the others from love. It is stated in a verse:

> "Ye are never able to do justice between wives even if it is your ardent desire: but turn not away (from a woman) altogether, so as to leave her (as it were) hanging (in the air)." [Surah Nisa, 4:129]

When the two verses above are evaluated, we can draw the conclusion that polygamy is not an essential rule but a permission that can be used when extraordinary conditions are present.

3. To be able to maintain the family

In Islam, it is necessary for a man who wants to marry one woman or more to be able to meet the eating, drinking, clothing and housing expenses of her or them. The Prophet (pbh) said the following: O young men! Those among you who can support a wife should marry" [Bukhari, Sawm, 10, Nikah, 2, 3, 19; Muslim, Nikah, 1,3]

The Reasons Why Islam Permits Polygamy

In Islam monogamy is essential and polygamy is exceptional. Let it be noted that celibacy is very much disliked by the Quran and the Prophet; there is no asceticism in Islam.24:32 "and [you ought to] marry the single from among you (whether men or women) as well as such of your male and female slaves as are fit [for marriage]. If they [whom you intend to marry] are poor, [let this not deter you;] God will grant them sufficiency out of His bounty - for God is infinite [in His mercy], all-knowing".

The Prophet (pbh) said the following: O young men! Those among you who can support a wife **should marry,** for that will help him to lower his gaze and guard his modesty" [Bukhari, Sawm, 10, Nikah, 2, 3, 19; Muslim, Nikah, 1,3] The importance of the institution or marriage receives its greatest emphasis from the following Hadith of the Prophet, "Marriage is my sunnah (my way of life). Whosoever keeps away from it, is not from me." [Bukhari]

General Reasons:

Unbalanced Sex Ratio : the consequence of the WW I & II

In some regions the male population decreases and female population may increase above normal. During the time of wars it is more frequent. As a matter of fact, after the World War I in Germany, there were four or six women for one man. Then German women advocated that men should marry more than one woman. In such a situation polygamy serves to protect women from prostitution, to provide them with a warm home and to guard fatherless children.

After the second world war, there were 7,300,000 more women than men in Germany (3.3 million of them were widows). There were 100 men aged 20 to 30 for every 167 women in that age group. (Ute Frevert, *Women in German History: from Bourgeois Emancipation to Sexual Liberation* (New York: Berg Publishers, 1988) pp. 263-264).Many of these women needed a man not only as a companion but also as a provider for the household in a time of unprecedented misery and hardship. The soldiers of the victorious Allied Armies exploited these women's vulnerability. Many young girls and widows had liaisons with members of the occupying forces. Many American and British soldiers paid for their pleasures in cigarettes, chocolate, and bread. Children were overjoyed at the gifts these strangers brought. A 10 year-old boy on hearing of such gifts from other children wished from all his heart for an 'Englishman' for his mother so that she need not go hungry any longer. (Ute Frevert, *Women in German History: from Bourgeois Emancipation to Sexual Liberation* (New York: Berg Publishers, 1988) pp. 257-258

In the U. S. there are, at least, eight million more women than men. In a country like Guinea there are 122 females for every 100 males. In Tanzania, there are 95.1 males per 100 females Eugene Hillman, Polygamy Reconsidered: *African Plural Marriage and the Christian Churches* (New, York. Orbis Books, 1975).

What Should a Society do Towards Such Unbalanced Sex Ratios?

There are various solutions, some might suggest celibacy (a very unnatural solution), others would prefer female infanticide (which does still happen in some societies in the world today!) Others may think the only outlet is that the society should tolerate all manners of sexual permissiveness: prostitution, sex out of wedlock, homosexuality, etc. Sometimes it may be necessary to marry more than one woman to increase the population in some regions; for instance, the death of most of the population in war.

An Extra Note by a famous scholar Dr. Bilal Philips (http://www.islamswomen.com/marriage/islams_position_on_polygamy.php)

- Monogamy of the West inherited from Greece and Rome where men were restricted by law to one wife but were free to have as many mistresses among the majority slave population as they wished. In the West today, most married men have extramarital relations with mistresses, girlfriends and prostitutes. Consequently the Western claim to monogamy is false.

- Monogamy illogical. If a man wishes to have a second wife whom he takes care of and whose children carry his name and he provides for he is considered a criminal, bigamist, who may be sentenced to years in jail. However, it is considered legal if he has numerous mistresses and illegitimate children.

- Men by nature are created polygamous because of a need in human society. There is normally a surplus of women in most human societies.1 The surplus is a result of men dying in wars, violent crimes and women outliving men.2 The upsurge in homosexuality further increases the problem. If systems do not cater to the need of surplus women it will result in corruption in society. Example, Germany after World War II, when suggestions to legalize polygamy were rejected by the Church. Resulting in the legalization of prostitution. Now German prostitutes are considered as workers like any other profession. They receive health benefits and pay taxes like any other citizen. Furthermore, the rate of marriage has been steadily declining as each succeeding generation finds the institution of marriage more and more irrelevant.

- Institutional polygamy prevents the spread of diseases like Herpes and AIDS. Such venereal diseases spread in promiscuous societies where extra-marital affairs abound.

- **Polygamy protects the interests of women and children in society. Men, in Western society make the laws. They prefer to keep polygamy illegal because it absolves them of responsibility. Legalized polygamy would require them to spend on their additional wives and their offspring. Monogamy allows them to enjoy extra-marital affairs without economic consequence.**

- Only a minority will practice polygamy in Muslim society. In spite of polygamy being legal in Muslim countries, only 10-15% of Muslims in these countries practice polygamy. Although the majority of men would like to have more than one wife, they cannot afford the expense of maintaining more than one family. Even those who are financially capable of looking after additional families are often reluctant due to the psychological burdens of handling more than one wife.

- Feminists may object to this male right by insisting <u>that women should also be able to practice polygamy</u>. However, a woman marrying four husbands would only increase the problem of surplus women. Furthermore, No child will like to carry more than one name of fathers in his/her tag; how the mother will identify that a particular child is born by the semen of which husband. (Furthermore woman by nature is not polygamous. From medical point of view also it is not advisable as interaction of different men's semen at one place is likely to induce many diseases including STI, sexually transmitted infections.)

- The question which remains is, "If God is good and wishes good for His creatures, why did he legislate something which would be harmful to most women?" Divine legislation looks at the society as a whole seeking to maximize benefit. If a certain legislation benefits the majority of the society and causes some emotional harm to a minority, the general welfare of society is given precedence.

[There are many other topics related to man-woman relationship such as 'marriage & divorce', 'inheritance' – for brevity we are not going to describe these but one must know that the Quran being a practical book does contain many injunctions regarding family affairs.]

9

Wars and Fightings as Described in the Quran

(I) Quran on War, Fighting, Persecution & Jihad

What for one Fights?

There are many obvious reasons but broadly we may categorize as : either one fights to oppress on other or one fights to resist it. It is a fact no one can deny that 'fighting' as such is in the nature of man. This is why all religious scriptures talk about it and give injunctions to its adherents; we could quote from all major world scriptures, but we will limit to the Quran now.

At the very outset we find that the Quran gives utmost importance to the human life: [Quran 5:32]

"Because of this did We ordain unto the children of Israel that if anyone slays a human being-unless it be [in punishment] for

murder or for spreading corruption on earth-it shall be as though he had slain all mankind; whereas, if anyone saves a life, it shall be as though he had saved the lives of all mankind."

This is the preaching of the Holy Quran, if someone kills even a single innocent human being he/she will be punished by Allah on the Day of Judgment for a punishment of that equivalent to killing the entire mankind and he will be sent into the Hell fire.

Before we delve into this subject of fighting we must understand the nature or essence of the Quran.

- Islam is not a religion in usual sense; its proper name is 'DEEN' (comprehensive way of life). It encompasses all spheres of life, its guidance is not limited to only 'worship' and certain all universally accepted virtues but gives injunctions to be applied in the fields of battles and floors of the political forums - all walks of life. The Quran uses a word 'ibaadat' for 'worship'; the root of this word is 'abd' (عـــــــبد) which means 'slave' - slave of Allah; a slave is not a part time slave rather full time, obeying Allah and surrendering to Him whole sole.

- There is another essence of the Quran that must not be over looked: The Quran not only recommends for preaching the 'good' trying to change the hearts but at times *invokes its reader to 'enforce' the 'good'* and not only recommends to preach to remove the 'evils' but *'to eradicate' the evils wherever possible with force.*

- So the point is that Islam being complete <u>'Way of life'</u> (*deen*, in the terminology of the Quran) has given guidance with regards to the way Muslims should defend themselves, the way an Islamic state should handle internal rebellion, the way the Islamic state should expand its influence and authority and most of them permit fighting in the given circumstances.

The reality is that all nations, if occupied by a colonial state or an oppressor would, rather must defend themselves. The history is replete with such fighting; the presence of the injunctions of the Quran in this regard should not thus surprise anyone, on the contrary its absence would have made this Book an impractical book.

- Fighting is a social necessity if one's freedom is at stake. It is vital that people under persecution should fight to defend themselves, to gain their rights. Thus the Quran asks Mohammed and his followers to fight for their **freedom**. *[Quran 2:251] And thereupon, by God's leave, they routed them. And David slew Goliath; and God bestowed upon him dominion, and wisdom, and imparted to him the knowledge of whatever He willed.* ***And if God had not enabled people to defend themselves against one another, corruption would surely overwhelm the earth:*** *but God is limitless in His bounty unto all the worlds.*

- [Quran 3:104] "And from among you there must be a party who invite people to all that is good and ***enjoin the doing of all that is right and forbid the doing of all that is wrong***. It is they who will attain true success".

- It is in the nature of man that he does not like to be preached for doing 'good' and does not like to be forbidden of doing wrong and never likes to be admonished from committing oppression and surely an oppressor never likes that his hands be held back by some one: *here comes in fighting*. The Quran gives utmost emphasis on this and the Prophet's commandments in this regard are very clear.

[Quran 4:75] *And how could you refuse to fight in the cause of God and of the utterly helpless men and women and children who are crying, "O our Sustainer! Lead us forth [to freedom] out of this land whose people are oppressors, and raise for us, out of Thy grace, a protector, and raise for us, out of Thy grace, one who will bring us succour!"*.

➢ One important 'Hadees' of the Prophet:
"I swear by Allah in whose power is my life, you shall have to enforce good and curb evil and arrest the hand of the evil –doer and force him to do right or the inevitable consequences of the law of nature will be manifested in this fashion that the curse of the evil-doers will infiltrate yours hearts and you shall also become contemptible like them".

Sahih Al-Bukhari Hadith - 3.66

"Whoever is killed while protecting his property then he is a martyr."

➢ *One cannot understand rather one will surely be misled by the Quranic injunctions in regard to fighting in the way of Allah unless he keeps in mind the above facts mentioned and one thing more :*

The back ground of the verses when and where they were revealed.

Any unbiased person can easily see in the life history of the Prophet that he along with his followers was persecuted in

Makkah for 13 long years to the point that they were forced to eat grass and leaves of trees apart from being killed several of them. They were evicted from their houses, they were forced to flee the place of their birth, their forefathers were living for generations, and they were haunted even to Madinah and were compelled to come to battle field more than once. They were at times betrayed by hypocrites and disbelievers. This makes it necessary to know the background to understand the verses revealed in such situations.

The Quran is not a book to be recited only, and chanted in monasteries, it is a practical book teaching man: when to submit to oppression and when to raise arms for fighting against it.

(II) Wars and Fightings as Described in the Quran

In terms of modern warfare, 'wars' is a misnomer for the battles Muhammad(pbh) and his followers fought. In truth they can hardly be called battles: they were mere skirmishes. An analysis of the figures of the dead in the conflicts between 622 (the period when the Muslims migrated to Madinah) and 632 (when the Prophet died) shows that in all, no more than 500 people died in both sides. Compare this with many battles fought in the Middle Ages when thousands perished and in the modern wars when millions are devoured with just one bomb.

War in Islam as regulated by the Quran and *hadith* has been subject to many distortions by Western scholars and even by some Muslim writers. These are due either to misconceptions or by deliberately using quotations taken out of context only to misinterpret these.

The topic encompasses a vast field of research; we focus here only on the Quran as to what are its directives, leaving aside the battles the Prophet fought in his life time, and the reasons behind each battle. For ease of understanding we subdivide the discussion in three sections:

- Basic ideas of the Quran in regard to fighting, peace, and freedom
- Growth of wars and encounters stage by stage
- Understanding why 'fighting' was ordained.

Basic Ideas of the Quran in Regard to Fighting, Peace, and Freedom:

The entire Quran, taken as a complete text, gives a message of hope, faith, and peace. The overwhelming message is that peace is to be prevailed through faith in God, and justice among fellow human beings. At the time the Quran was revealed (7th century A.D.), inter-tribal violence and vengeance was commonplace, as a matter of survival, one had to defend against aggression from all sides. Nevertheless, the Quran repeatedly urges forgiveness and restraint, and warns believers not to "transgress" or become "oppressors". Some examples:

Sanctity of life

[Quran 5:32] Because of this did We ordain unto the children of Israel that if anyone slays a human being-unless it be [in punishment] for murder or for spreading corruption on earth-it shall be as though he had slain all mankind; whereas, if anyone saves a life, it shall be as though he had saved the lives of all mankind. And, indeed, there came unto them Our apostles with all evidence of the truth: yet, behold, notwithstanding all this, many of them go on committing all manner of excesses on earth.

Justice –in any case

[Quran 4:135] Oh you who believe! Stand out firmly for justice, as witnesses to God, **even against yourselves, or your rents, or your kin, and whether it be against rich or poor,** for God can best protect both. Follow not the cravings of your hearts, lest you swerve, and if you distort justice or decline to do justice, verily God is well acquainted with all that you do.

Oppressor to be blamed

[Quran 42:40] **The** recompense for an injury is an injury equal thereto (in degree): but if a person forgives and makes reconciliation, his reward is due from Allah, for ((Allah)) loveth not those who do wrong.

[Quran 42:41] Yet indeed, as for any who defend themselves after having been wronged - no blame whatever attaches to them:

[Quran 42:42] blame attaches but to those who oppress [other] people and behave outrageously on earth, offending against all right: for them there is grievous suffering in store!

[Quran 42:43] However, if one is patient in adversity and forgives - this, behold, is indeed something to set one's heart upon!

Finally goodness is to prevail

- Goodness and evil are not equal. Repel evil with what is better. Then that person, with whom there was hatred, may become your intimate friend! And no one will be granted such goodness except those who exercise patience and self-restraint, none but people of the greatest good fortune. [Quran 41:34-35]

[Quran 60:8] As for such [of the unbelievers] who do not fight against you on account of [your] faith, and neither drive you forth from your homelands, God does not forbid you to show them kindness and to behave towards them with full equity: for, verily, God loves those who act equitably.

[Quran 8:61] *"If they resort to peace, so shall you, and put your trust in GOD. He is the Hearer, the Omniscient."*

[Quran 4:90] *"...... Therefore, if they leave you alone, refrain from fighting you, and offer you peace, then GOD gives you no excuse to fight them."*

No compulsion to accept a religion

Islam, the religion of nature and nature's God, is clear, self-evident, and easy to understand. The Quran instructs us clearly that *God did not wish people to become believers by way of force and compulsion, but only by way of study, reflection, and contemplation*. **Therefore, to force others into Islam would be an insult to the Quran**.

The method of beautiful preaching and reasoned argument is the basic rule Prophet Muhammad (pbh) and his companions used to spread Islam. We cite the following verse:

[Quran 16:125] *Call to the way of your Lord with wisdom and good teaching. Argue with them in the most courteous way,* for your Lord knows best who has strayed from His way and who is rightly guided.

[Quran 2:256] **There is no compulsion in religion**; true guidance has become distinct from error, so whoever rejects false gods and believes in God has grasped the firmest hand-hold, one that will never break. God is all hearing and all knowing.

[Quran 81:27-28] This is a message for all people; for those who wish to take the straight path.

[Quran 88:21] Therefore you give admonition, for you are one to (only) admonish.

[Quran 88:22] You cannot not compel them [to believe].

Elsewhere the Prophets are called as 'Warnes'

[Quran 6:48] And We send [Our] message-bearers only as heralds of glad tidings and as warners: hence, all who believe and live righteously -no fear need they have, and neither shall they grieve; (the word 'warning' used here should not confuse one to mean worldly punishments but what it means here and elsewhere in the Quran is in the sense of accountability. *Warning is given to all mankind that they will be held accountable on The Day of Judgment of the proper use of whatever possessions they were given by God in this world and whether they followed their Prophets or not?)*

Therefore, religious freedom is paramount in Islam because God can only be truly worshipped by people who freely choose Him.

Fighting at Times Becomes a Necessity

"The fighting", even though by its nature is disliked by the human soul because of the liability, of being killed, or being taken as a captive, or being injured, with the wasting of the wealth, the damaging of the industries, the destruction of the country, the spreading of fear and awe in the souls and the (possibility) of being exiled from one's homeland, Allah has made ready an immensely good reward that cannot be imagined by a human soul to those who stand up and fight the evil doers and save the oppressed.

Pardon and forgiveness on the individual level is highly recommended in the Quran. As quoted above (41:34-35) it is said that good and evil deeds are not alike, men are inspired to *"Requite evil with good, and he who is your enemy will become your dearest friend"*). Also see 45:14. But when it comes to the places of worship being subjected to destruction and when hopeless, old men, women and children are persecuted and when unbelievers try to force believers to renounce their religion, the Quran considers it total dereliction of the duty for the Muslim state not to oppose such oppression and defend what is right.

Growth of Wars and Encounters Stage by Stage:

In Makkah, the Muslims suffered for several years under the worst kinds of harassment, persecuted for the sake of the creed in which they found reassurance and terrorized with regard to their property and personal safety. For all these reasons they were compelled to emigrate. They left their dwellings in Makkah and settled in Madinah, patiently submitting to God's orders and gladly accepting His authority.

The Muslims at first were forbidden to fight against their oppressors and the Prophet used to hold them back, saying, "I have not been ordered to fight." Finally, in Madinah, the following verses were revealed giving the Muslims permission to defend themselves:

[Quran 22:39] To those against whom war is made, permission is given (to fight), because they are wronged; and verily, Allah is most powerful for their aid

[Quran 22:40] (They are) those who have been expelled from their homes in defiance of right, - (for no cause) except that they say, "Our Lord is Allah.. Did not Allah check one set of people by means of another, there would surely have been pulled down monasteries, churches, synagogues, and mosques, in which the name of Allah is commemorated in abundant measure. Allah will certainly aid those who aid His (cause); - for verily Allah is full of Strength, Exalted in Might, (able to enforce His Will).

It is about defending one's self, property and freedom against aggression that targets them. This is emphasized in so many verses throughout the Quran.

The right of self-defense is recognized in the **Universal Declaration of Human Rights, Article 12:**

"No one shall be subjected to arbitrary interference with his privacy, family, home or correspondence, nor to attacks upon his honor and reputation. Everyone has the right to the protection of the law against such interference or attacks."

But is fighting in The Quran only defensive in nature? No, had it been so, it would be a lopsided view of the real world where **at times fighting becomes necessary as 'offensive' or 'preemptive'.**

It is the most beautiful part of the Quran that it does not talk 'unrealistic' things, does not conceal its intention ,does not talk 'in consonant with the thinking' of the masses to gain false appeasement rather talks hard facts of life however abhorrent at first it may appear but which prove to be beneficial to the humankind at last.

The Prophet once said: I swear by Allah in Whose power is my life, you shall have to enforce good and curb evil and arrest the hand of the evildoer and force him to do right or the inevitable consequences of the law of nature will be manifested in this fashion that curse of the evil- doers will infiltrate your hearts and you shall also become contemptible like them.

The same point is highlighted in the following verse:

[Quran 4:75] And how could you refuse to fight in the cause of God and of the utterly helpless men and women and children who are crying, "O our Sustainer! Lead us forth [to freedom] out of this land whose people are oppressors, and raise for us, out of Thy grace, a protector, and raise for us, out of Thy grace, one who will bring us succour!"

Understanding Why 'Fighting' was Ordained

'Jihad' defined

"Jihad is one of the most misunderstood and abused aspects of Islam. There are some Muslims who exploit and misuse this concept for their own political objectives. There are many non-Muslims who misunderstand it. There are some other non-Muslims who misinterpret it to discredit Islam and Muslims.

The word 'Jihad' is derived from the Arabic word *jahd* which means fatigue or from the word *juhd* which means 'effort' or 'struggle'. A *mujahid* is the one who strives and exerts efforts to the extent which makes him feel fatigued. Jihad means exerting effort to achieve a desired thing or 'to prevent an undesired one'. Jihad can be observed through any means and in any field whether material or moral. *Among the types of Jihad are struggling against one's desires, Satan, poverty, illiteracy, and disease, and fighting all evil forces in the world*. The effort may come in fighting the evil in your own heart, or in standing up to a dictator. Military effort is included as an option, but as a last resort and surely not "to spread Islam by the sword" as the stereotype would have one believe.

There are many religious texts that refer to these types of Jihad. One of the forms of Jihad is defending life, property or honour. Those who die while engaging in Jihad are considered to be martyrs, as confirmed by Prophetic Hadiths. Jihad is also done to avert aggression on home countries and on all that is held sacred, or in order to face those who try to hinder the march of the call of truth."

The Quran describes *Jihad* as a system of checks and balances, as a way that Allah set up to "check one people by means of another." When one person or group transgresses their limits and violate the rights of others, Muslims have the right and at times are bound by the duty to "check" them and bring them back into line. There are several verses of the Quran that describe jihad in this manner. One example:

[Quran 2:251] And if Allah had not repelled some men by others the earth would have been corrupted. But Allah is a Lord of Kindness to (His) creatures.

Islam never asks to begin unprovoked aggression from its own side; Muslims are commanded in the Quran not to begin hostilities, embark on any act of aggression, violate the rights of others, or harm the innocent. Even hurting or destroying animals or trees is forbidden. War is waged only to defend the religious community against oppression and persecution, because the Quran says that "persecution is worse than slaughter" and "let there be no hostility except to those who practice oppression" [Quran 2:190-193].

[Quran 2:217] They ask thee concerning fighting in the Prohibited Month. Say: "Fighting therein is a grave (offence); but graver is it in the sight of Allah to prevent access to the path of Allah, to deny Him, to prevent access to the Sacred Mosque, and drive out its members." **Violence and oppression are worse than slaughter.** Nor will they cease fighting you until they turn you back from your faith if they can. And if any of you turn back from their faith and die in unbelief, their works will bear no fruit in this life and in the Hereafter; they will be companions of the Fire and will abide therein.

Holy War—is it Jihad?

'Holy War' is used by some and is taken as equivalent to 'Jihad'---this is totally wrong; this word is quite foreign to the Quran, nowhere it is found in the Quran or Hadees and its translation as 'harb muqaddisa' is alien in Arabic.

'Jihad fi sabilillah' what it is?

Jihad is not merely 'struggle' but struggle in the cause of Allah or in the way of Allah: ***"jihad fi sabilillah"*** **(struggle in the way of Allah)**

This phrase misled some people into believing that 'jihad in the way of Allah' means forcible conversion of the people to the faith of Islam, for the people with narrow thinking could interpret expression '**in the way of Allah**' in no other and wider sense. But in the terminology of Islam this expression carries much wider sense. *All that is done for the collective well–being of mankind without any material consideration and solely to win the favour of Allah, is regarded in Islam as something done 'in the way of Allah'* : for example if you give away something for charity with a motive of gaining some moral or material consideration in this world, it would not be regarded as an 'act in the way of Allah'. Instead if your intention is to win the pleasure of Allah by helping someone poor, it would be deemed to be an act 'in the way of Allah'. This is why many of the fighting carried out by Muslim warriors with an intention of expanding their own regimes can never be called as 'jihad fi sabilillah'. Hence the term in the way of Allah exclusively applies only to such deeds as are undertaken with perfect sincerity, without any considerations of material and worldly gain for one's own self.

[Quran 61:11] - You are to believe in God and His Apostle, and to strive hard in God's cause with your possessions and your lives: this is for your own good - if you but knew it!

- Thus 'Jihad' in Islam is not merely a 'struggle', it is instead a 'struggle for the 'cause of Allah'. The cause of Allah is essential for the term of 'jihad' in Islam.
- Here it should be clarified that the intention of some one or some group enthusiastic of 'imposing Islamic faith by force' on others not only makes such struggle far out of 'the way of Allah' but on the contrary it draws wrath of Allah.

[Quran 26:151-152] "And obey not the dictates of the transgressors who spread mischief on the earth and reform nothing."

[Quran 18:28] "And obey not one whose heart we have made heedless of our remembrance, who follows his own lust, and goes to extremes in the conduct of his affairs".

[Quran 27:34] "Verily, whenever kings enter a country they corrupt it, and turn the noblest of its people into the most abject. And this is the way they [always] behave?

[Quran 2:205] But whenever he prevails, he goes about the earth spreading corruption and destroying [man's] harvests and progeny: and God does not love corruption.

And in this background jihad becomes an act of obligation to one who proclaims total submission to Allah. It is essential to arrest such transgressors who spread corruption in the earth.

Jihad as an Obligation

[Quran 2:193] And fight them on until there is no more violence or oppression, and there prevail justice and faith in Allah. but if they cease, Let there be no hostility except to those who practise oppression.

Note : In the above verse fighting is ordered to be waged till the oppression is finished and it is to be further noticed that this fighting is to be stopped as soon as the oppressor surrenders.

[Quran 8:73] With all this, [remember that] those who are bent on denying the truth are allies of one another; and unless you act likewise [unless you help one another likewise], oppression will reign on earth, and great disorder.

[Quran 9:33] He it is Who has sent forth His Apostle with the [task of spreading] guidance and the religion of truth, to the end that He may cause it to prevail over all [false] religion--however detestable this may be to those who ascribe divinity to aught beside God.

It becomes an obligation for defending religious freedom (Quran 22:39-41), for self-defence (Quran 2:190) and defending those people who are oppressed: men, women and children who cry for help (Quran 4:75). It is the duty of the Muslims to help the oppressed, except against a people with whom the Muslims have a treaty (Quran 8:72). These are the only valid justifications for war we find in the Quran.

The Prophet had no Standing Army

It is to be noted that the Prophet had no regular army, he had to "urge on the believers" (Quran 4:64) at times of need to come out to the field. The Quran - and the *hadith* at greater length - urge on the Muslims , the common folk, in the strongest way: by showing the justice of their cause, exposing the bad conduct of the enemy, and promising great rewards in the afterlife for those who are prepared to sacrifice their lives and property in such a good cause because it is a great service to mankind as ultimately 'the fighting' had to pave the way for 'rule of law'.

Extra Notes:

Islam could not have had the huge appeal it did if Muslims' first response was to kill "infidels." Within one hundred years of the Prophet's death, Islam spread from Spain in the West to the borders of India and China in the East. Scholars of repute have presented various factors for such phenomenal rise of a creed. **Was Islam's initial spread through military might? Had it been under the 'shadow of the sword' the people enmasse would have turned back to their original faiths as soon as the political-military power of the Muslims declined; but the history is witness to not a single instance of mass apostasy anywhere.**

However, Muslim rulers usually insured that local populations could practice their own religions and have their own institutions, provided they accepted Muslim rule and paid their taxes. Muslims ruled places like the Indian subcontinent for 900 centuries and in Spain for about 700 centuries but did not convert the population by force or by allurement. In fact, India and Spain remained majority

Hindu or Christian respectively under the Muslim rule. **Now compare this with what happened after the fall of Muslims in Spain:**

In the Catholic Reconquista of Muslim Spain, Muslim and Spanish Jews were generally ordered to convert to Christianity, be expelled, or die.

When the Spanish Jews fled the Catholics, where did they go? They sought refuge with the Ottoman Muslims in Istanbul. This was in the 15th century. To this day, there is a Jewish quarter in Istanbul where the people still speak Spanish, descendants of the Spanish Jews who found a home with the Muslims!

In this article we intend to present only what the Quran tells its readers about fighting, the situations where it permits fighting and the circumstances where it forbids it; we are not here to show the violence committed either by the followers of the Quran in blatant disregard to its teachings or by the followers of other religions. History is replete with such instances. Neither we intend here to respond to the argument of Huttington that Muslims are bent to fighting, they fight with others or keep fighting among themselves. Such statement is not expected from a man like him of high repute; he very easily ignored the violence committed by the Crusaders, the infighting among the various sects of Christianity in medieval ages and the two World Wars fought among themselves in recent times.

10

The Quranic Directives in Politics

Derived from two ancient Greek words *demos* (the people) and *kratos* (strength), Democracy is a political system in which the supreme power lies in a body of citizens who can elect people to represent them. Then, the numerical majority of the elected representatives can make laws, rules or decisions binding on the whole group. While making laws and rules, these elected representatives do not have any objective standards, unprejudiced touchstones, absolute criteria or bounds of any permanent values to take into account. The difference between such a system and the Islamic System is that the law-making in the latter is based upon the objective standards and the absolute criteria given in the Quran and do not go against the permanent values enshrined therein.

Before anyone becomes a believer in such a system, he has full choice whether he wants to become a believer or not

[18:29]. There is no compulsion whatsoever upon him to become a member of the Muslim community [2:256]. But once he becomes a member of the Muslim community, he is obligated to abide by its Laws. The authority would make sure that he does so. He cannot be left with that he abides by some laws that he likes and violates others that he dislikes. No community, no nation and no country would allow that.

The Last Messenger of Allah established a system of life in which He used to rule or judge people according to the Book revealed to him [5:48-49, 4:105, 6:114]. And this was not new only to him. In fact, all the previous Messengers of Allah also established systems of life during their time whereby they ruled or judged according to the Books revealed to them [5:44-47, 2:213]. Indeed, any one who does not rule or judge according to Allah's Revelation is *Kaafir (denier of truth)* [5:44], *Zalim (evil doers)* [5:45] and *Fasiq(transgressor)* [5:47], according to the Quran. The principle of ruling or judging by the Book is the foundation of an Islamic System. No system can be called *Islamic* unless all the judgments and rulings therein are according to the Book, Al-Quran, the last of the Revealed Books that is the Watcher over all the old Scriptures and guards the Truth in them [5:48].

In an Islamic System, all the so-called rulers or judges are obligated to rule and judge as per Allah's Rule and Judgment(al-hukm). *Al-Hukm* (it means the *Judgment or the Rule or the Command* as per context) belongs to none but Allah alone [6:57, 6:62, 12:40, 12:67, 28:70, 28:80, 40:12, 42:10]

Sunnah or the Tradition of the Prophet is not part of *Al-Hukm,* since Allah does not take any partners in His *Hukm* [18:26]. *However, in Sunnah of the Prophet, guidance may be* *sought for ways and methods to implement Al-Hukm, or formulate bye-laws based upon Al-Hukm.*_But the *ways* to implement or enforce *Al-Hukm* as well as *bye-laws* based upon it, are not as unchangeable as is *Al-Hukm* itself. The *ways* and *by-laws* may be altered according to the suitability of time and circumstances but *Al-Hukm(the Command of Allah)* itself cannot be changed in any circumstances.

Allah's Laws and Commands, in the Quran, cannot implement or enforce themselves upon people, on their own. Moreover, each individual may interpret these Commands in his own way and abide by them according to his own right. So, for practical demonstration there is a need of guidance from the Prophet as Central Authority and his obedience [***Aatee-ur-Rasool***].

Muhammad(pbh) was mortal and could not live forever [3:144]. But this did not mean the end of the Islamic System. The Central Authority, after his death, would transfer from him to his *Khalifa,* the Successor. Moreover, as the expanse of the Islamic System will increase, it becomes impossible for the single human Authority to be present at all places and for at all times to come to make judgments, rulings or implement or enforce the Law. So there is a need for sub-authorities or subordinates, hence, the obedience to *Ol-il-Amr (those charged with authority among you).*

All above points are well summarised in a famous verse of <u>Surah Nisa 4:59</u>

[Quran 4:59] Believers! Obey Allah and obey the Messenger, and those from among you who are invested with authority; and then if you were to dispute among yourselves about anything refer it to Allah and the Messenger *, if you indeed believe in Allah and the Last Day; that is better and more commendable in the end.

(See the explanatory notes on this verse as follows; for more detail : http://www.islamicstudies.info-/tafheem.php?sura=4&verse=57&to=70#s4_n90)

❖ (**this verse is the cornerstone of the entire religious, social and political structure of Islam, and the very first clause of the constitution of an Islamic state**. *It lays down the following principles as permanent guidelines:*

1. In the Islamic order of life, **God alone is the focus of loyalty and obedience**. A Muslim is the servant of God before anything else, and obedience and loyalty to God constitute the centre and axis of both the individual and collective life of a Muslim. Other claims to loyalty and obedience are acceptable only insofar as they remain secondary and subservient, and do not compete with those owed to God. All loyalties which may tend to challenge the primacy of man's loyalty to God must be rejected. This has been expressed by the Prophet (peace be on him) in the following words: 'There may be no obedience to any creature in disobedience to the Creator.' [Muslim, 'Iman', 37; Ahmad b. Hanbal, Musnad, vol. 3, p. 472]

2. Another basic principle of the Islamic order of life is **obedience to the Prophet** (peace be on him). No Prophet, of course, is entitled to obedience in his own right. Obedience to Prophets, however, is the only practical way of obeying God, since they are the only authentic means by which He communicates His injunctions and ordinances to men. Hence, we can obey God only if we obey a Prophet. Independent

obedience to God is not acceptable, and to turn one's back on the Prophets amounts to rebellion against God. The following tradition from the Prophet (peace be on him) explains this: 'Whoever obeyed me, indeed obeyed God; and whoever disobeyed me, indeed disobeyed God.' (Bukhari, 'Jihad', 109; 'I'tisam', 2; Muslim, 'Amarah', 32, 33; Nasa'i, 'Bay'ah', 27; etc.) We shall see this explained in more detail a little further on in the Quran.

3. In the Islamic order of *life Muslims are further required to obey fellow Muslims in authority. This obedience follows, and is subordinate to, obedience to God and the Prophet (peace be on him).* Those invested with authority (ulu al-amr) include all those entrusted with directing Muslims in matters of common concern. *Hence, persons 'invested with authority' include the intellectual and political leaders of the community, as well as administrative officials, judges of the courts, tribal chiefs and regional representatives.* In all these capacities, those 'invested with authority' are entitled to obedience, and it is improper for Muslims to cause dislocation in their collective life by engaging in strife and conflict with them. This obedience is contingent, however, on two conditions: first, that these men should be believers; and second, that they should themselves be obedient to God and the Prophet (peace be on him). These two conditions are not only clearly mentioned in this verse they have also been elucidated at length by the Prophet (peace be on him) and can be found in the Hadith. Let us consider, for example, the following traditions: A Muslim is obliged to heed and to obey an order whether he likes it or not, as long as he is not

> ordered to carry out an act of disobedience to God. When ordered to carry out an act of disobedience-to God he need neither heed nor obey.

What to do when the rulers are bad

There is no obedience in sin; obedience is only in what is good (ma'ruf). (For these traditions see Bukhari, 'Ahkam', 4; 'Jihad', 108; Muslim, 'Amarah', 39; Tirmidhi, 'Jihad', 29; Ibn Majah, 'Jihad', 40; Ahmad b. Hanbal, Musnad, vol. 2, pp. 17 and 142 - Ed.). There will be rulers over you, some of whose actions you will consider good and others abominable. Who even disapproves of their abominable acts will be acquitted of all blame, and whoever resents them he too will remain secure (from all blame); not so one who approves and follows them in their abominable acts. They (i.e. the Companions) asked: 'Should we not fight against them?' The Prophet (peace be on him) said: 'No, not as long as they continue to pray.' (See Bukhari, 'Jihad',). This means that their abandonment of Prayer will be a clear sign of their having forsaken obedience to God and the Prophet (peace be on him). Thereafter it becomes proper to fight against them. In another tradition the Prophet (peace be on him) says:

> Your worst leaders are those whom you hate and who hate you; whom you curse and who curse you. We asked: 'O Messenger of God! Should we not rise against them?' The Prophet (peace be on him) said: 'No, not as long as they establish Prayer *among you:* not as long as they establish Prayer among you.' [See Muslim, 'Amarah', 65, 66; Tirmidhi, 'Fitan', 77; Darimi, 'Riqaq, 78; Ahmad b. Hanbal, Musnad, vol. 6, pp. 24, 28]

In this tradition the position is further clarified. The earlier tradition could have created the impression that it was not permissible to revolt against rulers as long as they observed their Prayers privately. But the latter tradition makes it clear that what is really meant by 'praying' <u>is the establishment of the system of congregational Prayers in the collective life of Muslims</u>. This means that it is by no means sufficient that the rulers merely continue observing their Prayers: it is also necessary that the system run by them should at least be concerned with the establishment of Prayer. This concern with Prayer is a definite indication that a government is essentially an Islamic one. But if no concern for establishing Prayer is noticed, it shows that the government has drifted far away from Islam making it permissible to overthrow it. The same principle is also enunciated by the Prophet (peace be on him) in another tradition, in which the narrator says:

'The Prophet (peace be on him) also made us pledge not to rise against our rulers unless we see them involved in open disbelief, so that we have definite evidence against them to lay before God' (Bukhari and Muslim).

4. *In an Islamic order the injunctions of God and the way of the Prophet (peace be on him) constitute the basic law and paramount authority in all matters. Whenever there is any dispute among Muslims or between the rulers and the ruled the matter should be referred to the Quran and the Sunnah, and all concerned should accept with sincerity whatever judgement results.*

➢ *I*n fact, willingness to take the Book of God and the Sunnah of His Messenger as the common point of reference, and to treat the judgement of the Quran and the Sunnah as the last word on all matters, is a central characteristic which distinguishes an Islamic system from un-Islamic ones. Some people question the principle that we should refer everything to the Book of God and the Sunnah of the Prophet (peace be on him). They wonder how we can possibly do so when there are numerous practical questions involved, for example, rules and regulations relating to municipal administration, the management of railways and postal services and so on which are not treated at all in these sources. This doubt arises, however, from a misapprehension about Islam. The basic difference between a Muslim and a non-Muslim is that whereas the latter feels free to do as he wishes, the basic characteristic of a Muslim is that he always looks to God and to His Prophet for guidance, and where such guidance is available, a Muslim is bound by it.

- ***On the other hand, it is also quite important to remember that when no specific guidance is available, a Muslim is free to exercise his discretion because the silence of the Law indicates that God Himself has deliberately granted man the freedom to make his decision.***

An another equally important verse is as follows:

[Quran 4:60] (O Messenger!) Have you not seen those who claim to believe in the Book which has been revealed to you and in the Books revealed before you, and yet desire to submit their disputes to the judgement of *taghut* (the Satanic/evil authorities who decide independently of the Law of Allah), whereas they had been asked to reject it. And

Satan seeks to make them drift far away from the right way.

(See: http://www.islamicstudies.info-/tafheem.php?sura=4 &verse=57&to=70#s4_n90)

(***Taghut*** *clearly signifies here a sovereign who judges things according to criteria other than the law of God.* It also stands for a legal and judicial system which acknowledges neither the sovereignty of God nor the paramount authority of the Book of God. This verse categorically proclaims that to refer disputes to the judgement of a court of law which is essentially taghut contravenes the dictates of a believer's faith. In fact, true faith in God and His Book necessarily requires that a man should refuse to recognize the legitimacy of such courts. According to the Quran, belief in God necessitates repudiation of the authority of taghut. To try to submit both to God and to taghut at the same time is hypocrisy.)

Following are verses of the Quran which depict some important aspects of the Quranic directives in regard to politics :

1. Sovereignty is vested in God

Do you not know that to Allah belongs the dominion of the heavens and the earth? And besides Him you have neither patron nor helper. To Allah belongs the dominion of the heavens and the earth; and Allah has power over all things. Surah Al-i'Imran (3:189)

"If not Him, you worship nothing but names which you have named,- you and your fathers,- for which *Allah has sent down no authority: the command is for none but Allah: He has commanded that you worship none but Him: that is the right religion, but most men understand not...* Surah Yusuf(12:40) *Is it not His to create and to govern? Blessed be Allah, the Cherisher and Sustainer of the worlds*

2. **It is binding on the believers to "follow" the commands of Allah and His messenger**

The answer of the Believers, when summoned to Allah and His Messenger, in order that He may judge between them, is no other than this: they say, "*We hear and we obey*": it is such as these that will attain felicity. It is such as obey Allah and His Messenger, and fear Allah and do right, that will win (in the end).

> It is not fitting for a Believer, man or woman, when a matter has been decided by Allah and His Messenger to have any option about their decision: if any one disobeys Allah and His Messenger, he is indeed on a clearly wrong Path. Surah Al-Ahzab [33:36]

> O David! We did indeed make you a vice-regent on earth: so judge you between men in truth (and justice): Nor follow you the lusts (of your heart), for they will mislead you from the Path of Allah: for those who wander astray from the Path of Allah, is a Penalty Grievous, for that they forget the Day of Account. Surah Sad [38:26]

3. **Make a Consultative Body**

And consult them in affairs (of moment). Then, when you have taken a decision put your trust in Allah. For Allah loves those who put their trust (in Him)

[42:38] Those who hearken to their Lord, and establish regular Prayer; **who (conduct) their affairs by mutual Consultation;** who spend out of what We bestow on them for Sustenance; Who (conduct) their affairs by mutual Consultation; who spend out of what We bestow on them for Sustenance;

4. **Qualities of a Ruler, and obeying his rule**

Their Prophet said to them: "Allah has appointed Talut as king over you." They said: "How can he exercise authority over us when we are better fitted than he to exercise authority, and he is not even gifted, with wealth in abundance?" He said: "Allah has Chosen him above you, and **has gifted him abundantly with knowledge and bodily prowess**: Allah Granteth His authority to whom He pleaseth. Allah careth for all, and He knoweth all things." Surah Al-Baqara [2:247]

5. **Appoint a Leader and follow him**

O ye who believe! Obey Allah, and obey the Messenger, and those charged with authority among you. If ye differ in anything among yourselves, refer it to Allah and His Messenger, if ye do believe in Allah and the Last Day: That is best, and most suitable for final determination.

Here lies the difference between the modern concept of democracy and that of Islam: the opinion of the majority is not final, it must be under the framework of the commands of Allah and directives of the prophet. Allah warns in the following verses:

[6:116] (O Muhammad(pbh)!) If you obey the majority of those who live on earth, they will lead you away from Allah's path. They only follow idle fancies, indulging in conjecture.

❖ (One need not follow the way of life of the majority, for the majority tend to follow their conjectures and fancies rather than sound knowledge. Their beliefs, their ideas and concepts, their philosophies of life, the guiding principles of their conduct, their laws - all these are founded on conjecture. On the contrary, the way of life which pleases God, was revealed by Him and hence is based on true knowledge rather than conjecture. Instead of trying to discover the way of life of the majority, a seeker after truth should, therefore, persevere in the way prescribed by God, even if he finds himself to be a solitary traveller.) (from Tafheemul Quran-see http://www.islamicstudies.-info/tafheem.php? sura=6&verse=111&to=121)

Thus have We revealed it to be a judgment of authority in Arabic. Wert you to follow their (vain) desires after the knowledge which has reached you, then wouldst you find neither protector nor defender against Allah. Surah Ar-Ra'd [13:37]

6. Opinion of majority must be in framing of rules

O Ye who believe! Put not yourselves forward before Allah and His Messenger; but fear Allah: for Allah is He Who hears and knows all things. S. Al-Hujurat [49:1]

7. Warning if they don't obey the Commandments

If anyone desires a religion other than Islam (submission to Allah), never will it be accepted of him; and in the Hereafter He will be in the ranks of those who have lost (All spiritual good).

> S.Al-i'Imran(3:85)And hold fast, all together, by the rope which Allah (stretches out for you), and be not divided among yourselves; and remember with gratitude Allahś favour on you; for ye were enemies and He joined your hearts in love, so that by His Grace, ye became brethren; and ye were on the brink of the pit of Fire, and He saved you from it. Thus does Allah make His Signs clear to you: That ye may be guided. S. i'Imran [3:103]

But those who disobey Allah and His Messenger and transgress His limits will be admitted to a Fire, to abide therein: And they shall have a humiliating punishment. S.An-Nisaa [4:14]

Those are limits set by Allah: those who obey Allah and His Messenger will be admitted to Gardens with rivers flowing beneath, to abide therein (for ever) and that will be the supreme achievement. S.An-Nisaa [4:13]

Have you not turned Your vision to those who have been given a portion of the Book? They are invited to the Book of Allah, to settle their dispute, but a party of them Turn back and decline (The arbitration). Surah Al-i'Imran [3:23]

O Mankind! The Messenger has come to you in truth from Allah: believe in him: It is best for you.

But if ye reject Faith, to Allah belong all things in the heavens and on earth: And Allah is All-knowing, All-wise. Surah An-Nisaa [4:170]

O mankind! Verily there has come to you a convincing proof from your Lord: For We have sent unto you a light (that is) manifest. *Let the people of the Gospel judge by what Allah has revealed therein. If any do fail to judge by (the light of) what Allah has revealed, they are (no better than) those who rebel.*

8. All prophets and particularly Muhammad(pbh) was tasked to *establish the RULE of Allah*

It is He Who has sent His Messenger with Guidance and the Religion of Truth, to proclaim it over all religion: and enough is Allah for a Witness. S. Al-Fatah [48:28]

Follow you the inspiration sent unto you, and be patient and constant, till Allah do decide: for He is the best to decide. S.Yunus [10:109]

We sent a foretime our messengers with Clear Signs and sent down with them the Book and the Balance (of Right and Wrong), that men may stand forth in justice; and We sent down Iron, in which is (material for) mighty war, as well as many benefits for mankind, that Allah may test who it is that will help, Unseen, Him and His messengers: For Allah is Full of Strength, Exalted in Might (and able to enforce His Will). Surah Al-Hadid [57:25]

O mankind! verily there has come to you a convincing proof from your Lord: For We have sent unto you a light (that is) manifest.

11

The Quran on Economics

The Directives of the Quran in Economics

Every ideology has its basic underlying philosophy: Capitalism emphasises the individual 'free will', Communism equates the value of man with his productive capacity, and Modern Philosophy stresses the relativity of everything. **The underlying philosophical notion of Islam is *BALANCE* (adl—this is Arabic word meaning justice, balance not going to any extreme).** This principle can be applied to all spheres of human experience. The over-rating of material advancement has suppressed spiritual advancement; as a consequence, uncontrolled pollution has disturbed ecological equilibrium; greed has produced a world of contrasts through an unfair distribution of resources; the world's leading nations' careless comfort-loving has caused 'consumerism' to an extent of exploitation. The absence of "adl" has led the world to the brink of economic disaster and brought war to the doorsteps of many nations.

The basis of the ideal economic system is in the Quran. As in most things, the Quran gives the fundamental principles and leaves the details to be filled in by human beings according to the need of the society. However, at no stage of their experience should human beings transgress the fundamental limits set up by the Creator.

Need of Moral Concept

As we have indicated in the article 'An important prerequisite for Islamic the intention and belief of man is very important in implementation of any law, more so to the economic and penal laws. Hiding money, hoarding goods, embezzlement of money etc. have their roots deep-seated in the hearts of men-----you make whatever rules, however good, if there is no fear of Allah, no fear of being accountable in the hereafter, these evils cannot be eradicated. Have a look on the laws and 'recommendations' of the Quran in regard to economics, they are more of moral nature than cognizable by worldly authorities. Muslims are reminded to recognize that wealth, earnings, and material goods are the property of God, and that we are merely His trustees. The principles of Islam aim at establishing a just society wherein everyone will behave responsibly and honestly. The fundamental principles of the Islamic economic system are as follows:

Individual Life

Addressing two classes of people: the exceedingly rich and the desperately poor. Firstly, an appeal was made to the wealthy class to arrange for the provision of sustenance to the poor and needy. They were warned that failure to do so would result in 'distressful wrath' from Allah (69:34-5; 76:8-10).

Sadaqaat (Alms)

One should take up and fulfil the needs of every poor person, helping others over family and close ones if it applies (2:215; 30:38).

Social Reforms

Do not devour others' property wrongfully (2: 188; 4:29). Since religious leaders devour others' property, do not give them anything; thus encourage them to work to earn their living (9:34).

Protect the property of the orphans (4:6; 6:153; 17:34). If women earn something, then men cannot unjustifiably take it for themselves. A woman keeps whatever she earns and a man keeps whatever he earns (4:32). All matters pertaining to finance should be kept on written record. (2:282-Interestingly, this is the longest verse of the Quran, a detailed directive in transacting business.)

If a debtor is penniless give him or her time until it is easier to repay the loan, and if he/she is not in a position to pay back the loan, then it should be nullified (2:280). One must prepare a will for the distribution of bequeathed property (2: 180; 5: 106) If it happens that the deceased did not set up a will or if the will does not fully account for all of his/her property, then the estate should be distributed as per the directives outlined in the Quran (4:7). These directives ensure that the property is distributed fairly

Collective Administration

Since the Prophet was the first Head of the Islamic State, it was his responsibility to see to the collection of the

Sadaqaat (9: I 03), and to distribute the collections for the welfare of society as described in Sura AI Taubah (9:60).

The beneficiaries of this expenditure are (and were):

1. the poor,
2. those who cannot earn for any reason,
3. those employed to administer the Sadaqaat,
4. those who wish to join the Divine order but cannot for financial reasons,
5. refugees of oppression,
6. those in debt, those who fight in the cause of Allah, and
7. stranded travelers.

Accumulation of Wealth

The Quran has emphatically stated that accumulating and boarding wealth is a heinous crime. This wealth will ultimately fuel the fire of Hell -and the hoarders will be branded and burnt from it:

(9:34-35: **And there are those who amass gold and silver and do not spend it in the Way of Allah. Announce to them the tidings of a painful chastisement [9:35] on a Day when they shall be heated up in the Fire of Hell, and their foreheads and their sides and their backs shall be branded with it, (and they shall be told): "This is the treasure which you hoarded for yourselves. Taste, then, the punishment for what you have hoarded."** But as for all who lay up treasures of gold and silver and do not spend them for the sake of Gods - give them the tiding of grievous suffering [in the life to come]. These flames will engulf the hearts of such people (104:2-7). Despite their efforts to escape from it, it will pull them and destroy everything like the flow of lava from a volcano (70:5-18).

The Quran also emphasizes that the flow of wealth should not be restricted to the rich class alone. It should be circulated throughout the body of society, as blood circulates through the human body (59:7: ***so that it (wealth)may not merely circulate between the rich among you.*** So accept whatever the Messenger gives you, and refrain from whatever he forbids you. And fear Allah: verily Allah is Most Stern in retribution.)

Riba (Capital Interest)

It is like a war against the Quranic System

After issuing many severe warnings against accumulating wealth, the Quran issued a commandment that totally uprooted the motive for continuing the practice. Money that is made from money rather than by labour is termed as riba in the Quran. The Quran has clearly stated that riba is unlawful (haram) and a serious crime; indeed it is regarded as a rebellion against the Islamic System. The Holy Quran has warned those who establish a capitalist (riba) system (in spite of the Quran's warning) that they will face war from God's side (2:275-79)

(2:278) Believers! Have fear of Allah and give up all outstanding interest if you do truly believe. (2:279) But if you fail to do so, then be warned of war from Allah and His Messenger. If you repent even now, you have the right of the return of your capital; neither will you do wrong nor will you be wronged. (2:280) But if the debtor is in straitened circumstance, let him have respite until the time of ease; and whatever you remit by way of charity is better for you, if only you know.

It has categorically stated: that any situation in which someone invests money with the intent of getting more than the original investment also falls under the definition of riba (30:34). In present day terminology we know this as commercial interest, and it includes sleeping partners in business, crop-sharing tenancies and leasing properties. The Quran provides a fundamental Principle to avoid riba, and this is that people must be paid for labor and not for their capital. Essentially it is written that under the system of riba, there is no doubt that the wealth of some individuals will increase but in the long term the result will be that the wealth of the majority will decline to a point of economic disaster. The affluent members of society, in wrongfully plundering the fruits of others' labor, not only become incapable of working for themselves, but end up with a lack of social conscience (i.e. they do not concern themselves with the plight of other less fortunate people). The rest of the people meanwhile become increasingly destitute, having been deprived of the fruits of their own labor; and as a result, they start with having hatred against the affluent group and seek vengeance (a symptom of class struggle)-and in the end everyone pays the price (3: 130: ***Believers! Do not swallow interest, doubled and redoubled, and be mindful of Allah so that you may attain true success***.)

Zakat

> "And they have been commanded no more than this: to worship Allah, offering Him sincere devotion, being true in faith. To establish regular prayer, and to give zakat. And that is the religion right and straight" [Quran 98:5]

Every Muslim who owns wealth, more than a certain amount to meet his or her needs, must pay a fixed rate of Zakat to those in need. Zakat is a means of narrowing the gap between the rich and the poor, and to make sure that everyone's needs are met.

❖ "**Your riches and your children may be but a trial**. Whereas Allah, with Him is the highest reward. So fear Allah as much as you can, listen and obey, and **spend in charity for the benefit of your own souls. And those saved from the selfishness of their own souls, they are the ones that achieve prosperity**" [Quran 64:15-16]

❖ The Prophet Muhammad(pbh) once said that "nobody's assets are reduced by charity."

[30:39] The usury that is practiced to increase some people's wealth, does not gain anything with Allah. But if you invest in ***zakat***, seeking Allah's countenance, these are the ones who receive their reward manifold.

Both ***zakat*** and usury involve the investment of capital in order to seek material gains. But whereas ***zakat*** is a method of investment approved by Allah, usury is condemned. The above verse indicates the cardinal principle that the material gains resulting from the practice of usury gain nothing with Allah, whereas the gains, resulting from the practice of ***zakat***, receive 'Allah's blessing'.

[22:41] Those who, if We give them power in the land, establish worship and invest in zakat and enjoin kindness and forbid iniquity. And Allah's is the sequel of events.

Verse 22:78 further confirms this Ordinance.

[22:78] [...]So establish worship, invest in ***zakat***, and hold fast to Allah. He is your protecting Friend. A blessed Patron and a blessed Helper!

Here is a list of references which deal with ***zakat*** directly: 2:43,83,110,177,277; 4:162; 5:12; 7:156; 9:5,11,18,71; 21:73; 22:41,78; 24:37,56; 27:3; 31:4; 33:33; 41:7.

Zakat* prevents hoarding of money and causes the wealth to grow so that people can earn their living instead of depending on charity**. Another way of looking at ***zakat is that if the spare cash is simply given away in charity then, in the long run, the person may not be able to give in charity but may himself become dependent on charity, due to his circumstances changing. However, if ***zakat*** is used as an investment for growth then one can still live a modest life, and help the society in creating employment, so that the people do not need to depend on charity. At the same time the question of hoarding is removed.

- The concepts of welfare and pension were introduced in early Islamic law as forms of Zakat (charity), one of the Five Pillars of Islam, during the time of the Rashidun caliph Umar in the 7th century. This practiced continued well into the era of the Abbasid Caliphate, as seen under Al-Ma'mun's rule in the 8th century, for example. The taxes (including *Zakat* and Jizya) collected in the treasury of an Islamic government were used to provide income for the needy, including the poor, elderly, orphans, widows, and the disabled. According to the Islamic jurist Al-Ghazali (Algazel, 1058–1111), the government was also expected to stockpile food supplies in every region in case a disaster or famine occurred. The Caliphate is thus considered the world's first major welfare state. (Crone, Patricia (2005), *Medieval Islamic Political Thought*, Edinburgh University Press, pp. 308–9,)

- Some argue early Islamic theory and practice formed a "coherent" economic system with "a blueprint for a new order in society, in which all participants would be treated more fairly". Michael Bonner, for example, has written that an "economy of poverty" prevailed in Islam until the 13th and 14th centuries. Under this system God's guidance made sure the flow of money and goods was "purified" by being channeled from those who had much of it to those who had little by encouraging zakat (charity) and discouraging riba (usury/interest) on loans. Bonner maintains the prophet also helped poor traders by allowing only tents, not permanent buildings in the market of Medina, and not charging fees and rents there. (Michael Bonner, "Poverty and Economics in the Quran", *Journal of Interdisciplinary History,* xxxv:3 (Winter, 2005), 391–406) (as quoted in Wikepedia: Islamic Economics in the World)

Business Dealings (*Baiy*) and Trading (*Tejarat*)

Business dealings and trading are two different practices as indicated in the following verses: ***baiy*** literally: "bargaining" or "selling" or "buying and selling" (bay) - a metonym for anything that might bring worldly gain. (24:37) Such people as remember Allah while trading or making ***baiy*** [...the verse continues]

The nearest concept of ***baiy*** in this verse is business dealing which pertains to the dealings with money where the exchange of commodity is not involved. Outwardly, it would look similar to the practice of usury. However, it has a subtle and vital difference. When we understand this, the wording of following verse becomes clear.

> [2:275] ...They say ***baiy*** is just like usury: whereas Allah permits ***baiy*** and forbids usury...

As an example, a model of money lending based on ***baiy*** would be that profits and losses would be shared equitably. Alternatively, to repay the loan in such a way that it retained its original purchasing power. There could be no question of repaying in devalued money. In contrast, money lending based on usury, where money is lent at an agreed rate of interest, would be independent of whether the borrower makes a profit or loss out of the money lent.

Verse 2:282 below clarifies ***baiy*** as essentially a practice of mutual agreement designed to last over a period of time, which therefore, must be signed and witnessed. Trading on the other hand may be long term or across the table, where a commodity is exchanged for money. It excludes the practice of money dealing, without involvement of commodities.

> [2:282] O ye who believe! When ye contract a debt for a fixed term, record it in writing[...] And call to witness, from among your men, two witnesses[...] (there is much emphasis on recording the contract in writing----this is a very practical suggestion given by the Quran— Interestingly this this is the longest verse of the Quran)

General Guidance in Regard to Economics

People are only Trustees not Owners

People in general are instructed by the Quran that the assets of the world in general are the assets of Allah, people are just the custodians for a transitory period.

[57:10] -- And why should you not spend freely in the cause of God, seeing that God's [alone] is the heritage of the heavens and the earth?

Worldly Assets

It is emphasized that the worldly assets are lucrative and alluring but a true Muslim should be aware that the real assets are stored for them in the hereafter.

- ❖ [3:14] ----ALLURING unto man is the enjoyment of worldly desires through women, and children, and heaped-up treasures of gold and silver, and horses of high mark, and cattle, and lands. All this may be enjoyed in the life of this world - but the most beauteous of all goals is with God. –

- ❖ [18:46] --- Wealth and children are an adornment of this world's life: but good deeds, the fruit whereof endures forever, are of far greater merit in thy Sustainer's sight, and a far better source of hope.

- ❖ It is told to the Muslims that the best expenditure is that expended in the cause of Allah----this point is so much emphasized that **it is said to be a loan to Allah which He would repay it in the hereafter manifold**. 57:11 -- WHO IS IT that will offer up unto God a goodly loan, which He will amply repay. For, such [as do so] shall have a noble reward - 51:19 --- "and [would assign] in all that they possessed a due share unto such as might ask [for help] and such as might suffer privation".----here it is said that the needy have a due share in the wealth of the rich.

❖ Gold----what is the Islamic directive about it?

Gold has been a valuable and highly sought-after precious metal for coinage, jewelry, and other arts since long before the beginning of recorded history. Gold standards have been the most common basis for monetary policies throughout human history, being widely supplanted by fiat currency only in the late 20th century. (Fiat money is money that derives its value from government regulation or law. The term fiat currency is used when the fiat money is used as the main currency of the country. The Nixon Shock of 1971 ended the direct convertibility of the United States dollar to gold. Since then all reserve currencies have been fiat currencies, including the U.S. dollar and the Euro.) The world consumption of new gold produced is about 50% in jewelry, 40% in investments, and 10% in industry. <u>It has been used as a tribute to idols presented with reverence by devotees;</u> (India is the world's largest single consumer of gold, as Indians buy about 25% of the world's gold, purchasing approximately 800 tonnes of gold every year, mostly for jewelry. India is also the largest importer of gold; in 2008, India imported around 400 tons of gold. Indian households hold 18,000 tons of gold which represents 11 per cent of the global stock and worth more than $950 billion.)

The Quran and the Prophet on gold and hoardings:

- [9:34-35] --- "... As for those who hoard treasures of gold and silver and do not spend them for the sake of Allah--warn them of grievous suffering [in the life to come]" --- "on the Day when that [hoarded wealth] shall be heated in the fire of hell and their foreheads and their sides and their backs branded therewith, [those sinners shall be told:] "These are the treasures which you have laid up for yourselves! Taste, then, [the evil of] your hoarded treasures!"

Al-Tirmidhi Hadith (Hadith 574)

Abdullah told of two women, wearing gold bangles on their wrists, coming to Allah's Messenger (peace be upon him), who asked them whether they paid **zakat** on them. On their replying that they did not, he asked them whether they wanted Allah to put two bangles of fire on them, and when they replied that they did not, he told them to pay the zakat due on them.

Al-Tirmidhi Hadith (Hadith 1152)

The Prophet (peace be upon him) said, "Gold and silk are permitted to the females among my people but prohibited to the males."

Sahih Muslim Hadith (Hadith 982)

Allah's Messenger (peace be upon him) saw a person wearing a gold signet ring in his hand. He (the Prophet) pulled it off and threw it away, saying: One of you is wishing live coal from Hell, and putting it on his hand. It was said to the person after Allah's Messenger (peace be upon him) had left: Take your signet ring (of gold) and derive benefit out of it, whereupon he said: No, by Allah, I would never take it when Allah's Messenger (peace be upon him) has thrown it away.

Sahih Al-Bukhari Hadith (Hadith 8.646)

Allah's Apostle had a gold ring made for himself, and he used to wear it with the stone towards the inner part of his hand. Consequently, the people had similar rings made for themselves. Afterwards the Prophet; sat on the pulpit and took it off, saying, "I used to wear this ring and keep its stone towards the palm of my hand." He then threw it away and said, "By Allah, I will never wear it." Therefore all the people threw away their rings as well.

Sahih Al-Bukhari Hadith (Hadith 8.452)

Allah Apostle said, "If I had gold equal to the mountain of Uhud, it would not please me that anything of it should remain with me after three nights (i.e., I would spend all of it in Allah's Cause) except what I would keep for repaying debts."

Sahih Al-Bukhari Hadith (Hadith 5.541)

When we conquered Khaibar, we gained neither gold nor silver as booty, but we gained cows, camels, goods and gardens. Then we departed with Allah's Apostle to the valley of Al-Qira, and at that time Allah's Apostle had a slave called Mid'am who had been presented to him by one of Banu Ad-Dibbab. While the slave was dismounting the saddle of Allah's Apostle an arrow the thrower of which was unknown, came and hit him. The people said, "Congratulations to him for the martyrdom." Allah's Apostle said, "No, by Him in Whose Hand my soul is, the sheet (of cloth) which he had taken (illegally) on the day of Khaibar from the booty before the distribution of the booty, has become a flame of Fire burning him." On hearing that, a man brought one or two leather straps of shoes to the Prophet and said, "These are things I took (illegally)." On that Allah's Apostle said, "This is a strap, or these are two straps of Fire."

Sahih Al-Bukhari Hadith (Hadith 7.754)

The Prophet forbade the wearing of a gold ring.

> **It is forbidden to gain property or wealth by fraud, deceit, theft, or other falsehoods.** "...Give just measure and weight, and do not withhold from people the things that are their due. And do not do mischief on the earth after it has been set in order. That will be best for you, if you have faith" [Quran 7:85]

Sahih Al-Bukhari Hadith (Hadith 3.633)

That there was a dispute between him and some people (about a piece of land). When he told 'Aisha about it, she said, "O Abu Salama! Avoid taking the land unjustly, for **the Prophet said, 'Whoever usurps even one span of the land of somebody, his neck will be encircled with it down the seven earths."**

(The above excerpts are taken from http://www.alim.org /library/hadith/)

It is particularly hateful for a guardian to take from an orphan's property. "To orphans restore their property (when they reach their age). Do not substitute your worthless things for their good ones, and do not devour their property by mixing it up with your own. For this is indeed a great sin" [Quran 4:2]

Forbidden are earnings from <u>gambling, lotteries, and the production, sale, and distribution of alcohol</u>

- Quran-5: 90-91-92: you who believe! Intoxicants and gambling, sacrificing to stones, and divination by arrows are an abomination of Satan's handiwork. Shun such abomination, that you may prosper" By means of intoxicants and games of chance Satan seeks only to sow enmity and hatred among you, and to turn you away from the remembrance of God and from prayer. Will you not, then, desist?' Hence, pay heed unto God, and pay heed unto the Apostle, and be ever on your guard [against evil]; and if you turn away, then know that Our Apostle's only duty is a clear delivery of the message [entrusted to him].

It is Unlawful to Hoard Food and Other Basic Necessities

Everyone should take what they need and no more. "And let those who covetously withhold of the gifts which Allah has given them of His Grace, think that it is good for them. No, it will be the worse for them. Soon it will be tied to their necks like a twisted collar, on the Day of Judgment. To Allah belongs the heritage of the heavens and the earth, and Allah is well-acquainted with all that you do" (Quran

3:180). The whole chapter Takasur no.102 is devoted to this theme: The craving for ever-greater worldly gains and to excel others in that regard keeps you occupied The craving for ever-greater worldly gains and to excel others in that regard keeps you occupied until you reach your graves. Nay, you will soon come to know. nay, again, you shall soon come to know. -----Then, on that Day, you will be called to account for all the bounties you enjoyed..

Al-Muwatta Hadith (Hadith 31.56)

- Yahya related to me from Malik that he had heard that Umar ibn al-Khattab said, “There is no hoarding in our market, and men who have excess gold in their hands should not buy up one of Allah’s provisions which he has sent to our courtyard and then hoard it up against us. Someone who brings imported goods through great fatigue to himself in the summer and winter, that person is the guest of Umar. Let him sell what Allah wills and keep what Allah wills.”

A Muslim should be Responsible in Spending Money

- Extravagance and waste are strongly discouraged. “[The Servants of Allah are] Those who, when they spend, are not extravagant and not stingy, but hold a just balance between those extremes” (Quran 25:67). “O Children of Adam! Wear your beautiful apparel at every time and place of prayer. Eat and drink, <u>but waste not by excess, for Allah loves not the wasters”</u> [Quran 7:31]

People are encouraged to give constantly in charity.

"Your riches and your children may be but a trial. Whereas Allah, with Him is the highest reward. So fear Allah as much as you can, listen and obey, and spend in charity for the benefit of your own souls. And those saved from the selfishness of their own souls, they are the ones that achieve prosperity" [Quran 64:15-16]

- The Prophet Muhammad(pbh) once said that "nobody's assets are reduced by charity."

Conclusion

Today, most modern economies are based on interest to such an extent that it is difficult to imagine any economic activity where interest was not involved directly or indirectly. Many Muslims have attempted to resolve this contradiction between what the Quran demands and the principles of a modern economy, but as yet no viable system has been developed. The so-called Islamic countries which shook off the yoke of colonialism have remained intellectually and economically controlled externally by the West and internally by despots, who had more interest in saving their grip over the people than striving for their Welfare. The conclusion one comes to after such a long and singular failure on the part of such countries is that any suggested economic system cannot be implemented and tested without the prior establishment of a true Islamic Welfare State.

12

The Quran & Muhammad – the two are entwined

(I) Brief Life Sketch of the Prophet

[Unlike the founders of many religions, the final prophet of Islam is a real documented and historical figure. He lived in the full light of history, and the minutest details of his life are known to us. Not only do Muslims have the complete text of Allah's words that were revealed to Muhammad (pbh), but they have also preserved his sayings and teachings in what is called "hadith" literature].

Prophet Muhammad(pbh) was born in 570 CE in Makkah, as an orphan. His father, Abdullah, died several weeks before his birth. Under the guardianship of Abu Talib, his uncle, Muhammad(pbh) began to earn a living as a businessman and a trader. At the age of twelve, he accompanied Abu Talib with a merchant caravan as far as Syria. Muhammad(pbh) was popularly known as 'al-Ameen' for his unimpeachable character by the Makkans and outsiders alike. The title Al-Ameen means the Honest, the Reliable and the Trustworthy, and it signified the highest standard of moral and public life.

A Call in the Wilderness

For three years after the first revelations, Muhammad(pbh) remained a secluded person, coming to terms with God's message. The first group of people who were converted to a belief in his preaching were his wife Khadijah, his ten year old cousin Ali ibn AbiTalib, Zayd ibn Haritha, (the ex-slave but now his adopted son) and his friend Abu Bakr. At the heart of Makkah was the sacred *kaaba*, or enclosure, to which all Arab pagans came during the months of truce. The control of commerce and the pagan pilgrims belonged to the rulers of Makkah, the Quraysh. Muhammad(pbh) was quite aware that the nobility of Makkah would not approve of his *new religion* only because it would jeopardise their vested economic interests as well as undermine their political privileges.

The Gathering Clouds

He began to urge his hearers to worship one God alone, to repudiate their idols and be ready themselves for the day of Judgment. At first he was not taken seriously and was even ridiculed. Gradually, however, he converted a few nobles of the Quraysh, some middle class people, and a number of slaves and poor people. They were people who were most dissatisfied with the changing morals and social climate of Makkah. For them the Prophet's message promised a vital alternative. The Quran's message was so impressive for them that they were willing to give up the home town and migrate to Abyssinia (an African state, west of Arab land, across the Red Sea). These people were willing to leave their families and clans to take up life together in a foreign land. For them the bonds of common belief were stronger than the bonds of blood.

The role of Chieftains of Makkah

The chieftains of Makkah became agitated because they thought that Muhammad(pbh) was bent upon shaking the foundations of their faith and trying to foster a pioneer band of companions who would in future challenge their power structure. The thirteen long years saw different phases: simple denouncement, insults to harassment to economic boycott resulting in extreme hunger to the extent that he and his followers had to eat grass and leaves sometimes. Several of the followers, who did not have tribal or family protection as Muhammad(pbh) himself did, were martyred in the course of time.

The Migration to Madinah

By 622 Muhammad(pbh) came to realise that to protect himself and his followers from the unending persecution and to overcome the resistance of the Quraysh, migration was the only alternative left to him. He and his followers immigrated to Madina, 250 miles in the north of Makkah. According to some records, the emigration took place in two groups, one after the other, with an interval of about two months. The first group consisted of fifteen people and the second one, hundred. For the small band of dedicated followers this migration seemed to be entering into a bleak future but strangely enough it proved to be opening a new era in the human history, that is why, Islamic Calendar counts it as the starting date (10 September 622CE) (CE stands for Christian Era, this abbreviation is preferable to A.D. which means *in the year of our Lord*)

The Quran as Guide and Comforter

In Madina the Quranic revelation played a greater role in binding together the immigrants from Makkah with the natives of Madinah who were called (*Ansar*,helpers) to form one political and religious group to be called the *Umma (Ummah)*, still the word used for the Muslim community at large. The revelation kept reminding them, "Be not infirm and be not grieved, you shall have the upper hand" (Sura 3:139). It was a kind of the slogan, "We shall overcome". Their duty was to listen to Allah and his apostle and obey, *Atiullahwaatiurrasul*, obey Allah and obey the Prophet (Sura 3:132) as obedience to Allah is not possible without following the Prophet diligently as he is the only model for practicing the Quranic injunctions.

There were several Jewish tribes living in and around Madina. There were some Christian communities in Arabia in places like Najran. To attract them to Islam the Quran presented its point of view of Jesus. The majority of both, the Jews and Christians turned hostile to Muhammad(pbh) but it was the Jews of Madinah and neighboring locality that turned out to be of a major concern. Many of the Jews in Madina conspired with the Makkans against Muhammad(pbh) and the little band of Muslim. In this conspiracy they were joined by the hypocrites, the Madinan Arabs, who had not sincerely accepted Islam (Sura 31:7; 63:1-4; 2:8-16). As a consequence of skirmishes, most of the Jews were banished from Madinah.

A New Society Formed

Muhammad(pbh) in the light of the Quran worked to create a community, sometime called *Ummah,* based on shared religious beliefs, ceremonies, ethics and laws - a community which was bound to transcend the traditional social structure based on families, clans, and tribes and unite disparate groups into a 'New Society'. Numerous rituals and social codes were set up. These included the five pillars of faith, *Shahadah, Salat, Saum, Zakat,* and *Hajj (declaring Faith, prayer five times, Fasting for one month in a year, Zakat, doling out a portion of one's wealth to the poor and needy and Hajj, the pilgrimage to Makkah.* The Quran demarcated the social norms of the new community. Indeed its teaching on family laws were the crux of a social revolution. The family ideal was protected by a clear definition of its collective duties. The Quran urged respect for women's modesty and privacy. Women were now able to hold property in their own names. Daughters were no more to be killed or buried alive (Sura 2:221; 4:7;11,24 etc.). Apart from family laws and morals, the Quran dealt with many other kinds of communal and social problems. Norms for business transactions were laid down, injunctions to deal justly, honour contracts, give true witness and not to take usurious interest.

Madinah: The crucible of the Revolution (622 - 632 CE)

The Makkans were not at rest after the migration of the Muslims from there. They could foresee that if Islam flourished in Madinah it would stand as a challenging force to them. They decided to invade Madinah. It was then that permission to fight against the wrong doers was granted to Muslims. At the battle of *Badr* (624 CE), Muhammad(pbh) defeated a larger Makkan force, decimated Makkah's leadership and won tremendous prestige everywhere in Arabia (Sura 3:13;123; 8:7-13). To take revenge the Makkans attacked Madina next year, at the battle of *Uhud* (625 CE) and then the battle of *Khandaq*, the Trench (627 CE) but with not much success (Sura 3:121-128, 152-155; Sura 33:9-27).

The Arab tribes by then realised that the Makkans they had supported were not going to last long. Most of them withdrew their support from Makkah. The buoyance and the zeal of the believers were at the highest ebb. In the end, Muhammad(pbh) brought his native city of Makkah under his total control. In a lapse of just two years after the battle of the Trench Muhammad(pbh) completed his triumph over Makkah. He returned victorious to the city whose leaders had virtually exiled him only eight years earlier. Makkan leaders surrendered the city (Sura 48:1-2). *Ka'ba* was cleansed of idols and became the centre of the Islamic activities.

In the following two years deputation from all parts of Arabia came and embraced Islam (Sura 110:1-3). The time came for Muhammad(pbh) to depart and the revelation ceased at his death in 632. The final utterance of the Quran amounts to the words: "This day I perfected your religion for you, completed my favour upon you, and have chosen for you Islam as your religion" (Sura 5:3).

- Even a cursory glance over his life history impresses one to believe that right from the day he was appointed the Messenger by Allah till his last day, he was never in a state of rest. For the entire span of twenty three years he had been undergoing turmoil and facing wars from outside and handling social and economic problems from within.

- Prophet Muhammad(pbh) lived a most simple, humble, austere and modest life. He and his family sometimes went without cooked meal several days at a stretch, feeding only on dates, dried bread and water. During the day he was the busiest man, as he performing his duties in varied roles all at once as head of the state, chief justice, commander-in-chief, arbitrator, instructor and family man. He was the most devoted man at night. <u>He used to spend one- to two-thirds of every night in prayer and meditation.</u>Some orientalists and his detractors of the Prophet present him to be fond of luxury and opulence; this is far from the truth, a total lie, an attempt at devaluating him. The Prophet's possession consisted of mats, blankets, jugs and such simple things even when he was the virtual ruler of Arabia. He left nothing to be inherited except a white mule, a few swords and a piece of land that he had given out as a gift during his life time. Among his last words were: "We the community of Prophets are not inherited. Whatever we leave is for charity."

- Islam enjoins us to have belief in all prophets and revealed scriptures (original, non-corrupted) as part of the Articles of Faith. Muhammad(pbh) is greatly revered as the model of Quranic principles. **Muslims mention his name by adding <u>"peace be upon him (pbh, in abbreviation),"</u> a phrase used with the name of all prophets.**

- All sincere Muslims try to follow the Quran and the Prophet's traditions to minute details. The account of every aspect of his life has been preserved (numerous daily accounts including his family life). Prophet Muhammad(pbh) has served as an example for all Muslims in all period's ancient and modern times. He will remain a model guide for all humanity.
- At the end of his mission, the Prophet was blessed with several hundred thousand followers (men and women) of Islam. Thousands prayed with him at the mosque and listened to his sermons. Hundreds of true Muslims would find every opportunity to be with him following five times daily prayers. People used to seek his advice for their day to day problems, and listened attentively to the interpretations and applications of revealed verses of the Quran. They followed the message of the Quran and the Messenger of Allah with utmost sincerity, and supported him with everything they had. A dedicated band of followers indeed.

(II) The Quran and Muhammad – the Inter-relationship

[Quran 7:158] Say: "**O mankind! I am sent unto you all, as the Messenger of Allah**, to whom belongs the dominion of the heavens and the earth: there is no god but He: it is He Who gives both life and death. So believe in Allah and His Messenger, **the Unlettered Prophet**, who believes in Allah and His words: **follow him that (so) you may be guided**."

The Quran and Muhammad (pbh) are Intertwined

The Quran and the prophet (pbh) are interrelated, intertwined, interwoven; <u>one cannot be understood without understanding the other and one cannot be believed in without believing in the other.</u> As we described earlier, as the message of the prophet propagated and permeated through the society, acceptance by a few and rejection by a majority passed through varied phases. Revelations came as per the pressure of the time : sometime to console the Muslims undergoing the turmoil, and as injunctions to them to adhere to the new ideologies of Islam; have faith in Allah and adhere in belief of the hereafter and follow the Prophet staunchly; sometimes to admonish the rejecters and persecutors. The verses revealed in Makkah during the 13 years are mostly related to such topics.

Later on in Madinah, guidance was needed to tackle the fighting enemies and certain rules and regulations were needed to organize a society, quite a new social codes in every walk of life. This explains the different types of the chapters (surahs) called MAKKI surahs (86 in number) and MADINI surahs (28 in number). The verses are called AYATS. There are 6236 verses in the whole Quran, each of varying length.

- There were occasions when the Prophet was at a loss as to what steps are to be taken and just in the nick of time guidance came through the Quran.
- At times people asked certain questions and the prophet did not know the answers then the Quranic verses were revealed as answers.

- ❖ There are occasions when the Prophet took certain steps or acted accordingly but Allah corrected him at the right moments.
- ❖ There are certain guidance of the Quran which are very important to the people but whose practical shape was only to be shown by the Prophet. Here comes the importance of the HADEES (the sayings and the practical directions of the prophet)
- ❖ There are such several verses which demonstrate the interlinking and interdependence when it comes to the interpretations of the verses of the Quran.

[Quran 7:157] "Those who follow the apostle, the unlettered Prophet, whom they find mentioned in their own (scriptures), - in the law and the Gospel; - for he commands them what is just and forbids them what is evil; he allows them as lawful what is good (and pure) and prohibits them from what is bad (and impure); He releases them from their heavy burdens and from the yokes that are upon them. **So it is those who believe in him, honour him, help him, and follow the light which is sent down with him, - it is they who will prosper."**

The pagans of Makkah told Muhammad(pbh) that if he were a Prophet, then like the prophets of old, he should cause winds to blow or rain to fall, or he should revive the dead. To all this Muhammad(pbh) replied, in all humility, 'the only miracles I have are revelations of Allah'. So they damned him and dismissed him as an imposter. Unmindful, he continued to pursue his mission. The Quran asked him to tell the disbelievers:

[Quran 7:188] Say [O Prophet]: "**It is not within my power to bring benefit to, or avert harm from, myself, except as God may please.** And if I knew that which is beyond the reach of human perception, abundant good fortune-would surely have fallen to my lot, and no evil would ever have touched me. I am nothing but a warner, and a herald of glad tidings unto people who will believe."

There could not have been a more straightforward, honest and intelligible explanation of his position. And yet, while other prophets, whose miracles can at best be matters of belief and at worst flights of fancy on the part of followers, are glorified and revered, Muhammad(pbh) is denounced; *this despite the fact that neither science nor philosophy gives much credence to miracles.*

Significance of Muhammad (pbh) in the Whole System of Islam

As we described both Quran and Muhammad(pbh) are inter-related, the importance and significance of the personality of the Prophet is much emphasized in the Quran so much so that it is said "whoever follows obedience of the messenger, he observes obedience to Allah" and at another place it says: S.Nisa 4:65 "But no, by the Lord, they can have no (real) Faith, until they make thee judge in all disputes between them, and find in their souls no resistance against Thy decisions, but accept them with the fullest conviction".

All such verses signify the importance of Muhammad(pbh) in the whole system of Islam, he is like a pivot around which the wheel of Islam is rotating. The Quran presents him as a role Model for all who want to pass their lives in peace and attain success in all walks of life. Such a model is necessary for mankind as then one can easily know how to act on an injunction of the Quran in practical form and also test oneself of his truthfulness to the adherence to Islam.

Despite so much emphasis on the personality of the prophet, the Quran makes it very clear that Muhammad(pbh) is NOT GOD, is not God's son or in any way mortally related to Him or is never to be taken as partner to Him or is in no way God–incarnate. All such beliefs are prevalent in different religions and the Quran emphatically declares what is best described in the Islamic creed **"I affirm that there is none worthy of worship except Allah, that He is One, sharing His authority with no one, and I affirm that Muhammad(pbh) is His Servant and His Prophet."**

Foot Notes:

It should be understood that Muslims believe that the Prophet Muhammad(pbh) was only a man chosen by Allah, and that he is not divine in any way. In order to avoid the misguided wish to deify him, the Prophet Muhammad (pbh) taught Muslims to refer to him as **"Allah's Messenger and His Slave"**. The mission of the last and final prophet of Allah was to simply teach that **"there is nothing divine or worthy of being worshipped except for Almighty Allah**. In simple terms, Allah sent the revelation to Muhammad (pbh), who in turn taught it, preached it, lived it and put it into practice.

In this way, *Muhammad (pbh) was more than just a "prophet" in the sense of many of the Biblical prophets,* since he was also a statesman and ruler. He was a man who lived a humble life in the service of Allah, and established an all-encompassing religion *and a way of life* by showing what it means to be an ideal friend, husband, teacher, ruler, warrior and judge. Muhammad(pbh) faced a great deal of opposition and persecution during his mission. However, he was always patient and just, and he treated his enemies well.

After the death of Muhammad (pbh), some Companions, out of human weakness lost control over their emotions. To console them Abu Bakr, the first caliph, uttered the following remarkable words:

"For him who worshipped Muhammad, Muhammad is dead but as for him who worships Allah, Allah is alive."

Allah tells us: "Muhammad (pbh) is no more than a Messenger. Many were the messenger who passed away before him. If he dies or is slain, will you then turn back on your heels?"

[Quran 3:144] Muslims used to stand up when they wanted to greet him as a mark of respect and he prohibited them saying, *'Do not stand up as the Persians do, some people honoring the others'*.

History tells us that, 'Once he was traveling with some of his companions who began to prepare to cook some food by dividing the work among themselves. Muhammad (pbh) wanted to be in charge of collecting some wood. His companions told him that they could do it for him. Muhammad (pbh) answered back, *"I know you could do it for me,* ***but I hate to have any privilege over you."***

A stranger once came to him almost trembling out of respect. Muhammad (pbh) asked the man to come closer to him and with a compassionate pat on the man's shoulder, told him *"Relax brother, I am only the son of a woman who used to eat dried bread."*

He was consistent in his advice, that *"I am Muhammad (pbh), a slave of Allah and His messenger.* ***I do not like your raising my status above the status which Allah, the Mighty and Glorious, has given me."***

The amazing extent of his humility can be seen in the manner in which he exercised his authority. His followers were always prepared to obey him, but he kept on insisting that obedience should be directed to Allah alone and not to him personally. He categorically warned the Muslims not to over praise him.

"Do not glorify in the same manner as the Christians glorify Jesus, son of Mary, but say, He is a slave of Allah and His Messenger."

- Describing the room of the Prophet (pbh), Umar, his one of the Companions, says,

'I noticed that the contents of his room comprised of only three pieces of tanned skin and a handful of barley lying in a corner. I looked about but failed to find anything else. I began to weep, and he asked, 'Why are you weeping?' I replied 'O Prophet of Allah! Why should I not weep? I can see the mat's pattern imprinted on your body and I also behold all that you have got in this room. O Prophet of Allah! Pray that Allah may grant ample provisions for us. The Persians and Romans who have no true faith and who worship not Allah but their kings – the Kaisers and the Cosroes (the kings of Rome and Persia) could live in gardens with streams running in their midst, **but the chosen Prophet and accepted slave of Allah should live in such dire poverty!'**

The Prophet was resting against his pillow, but when he heard me talk like this, he sat up and said, 'O Omar! Are you still in dark about this matter? **Ease and comfort in the Hereafter are much better than ease and comfort in this world.** The unbelievers are enjoying their share of the good things in this world whereas we have all such things in store for us in the next'. I implored him, 'O Prophet of Allah! Ask forgiveness for me. It was really an error.'

The bedding of the Prophet (pbuh) according to Aisha (ra), 'comprised of leather filled with the bark of date-palm'.

Prof. Ramakrishna Rao in his book '*Muhammad(pbh) – the Prophet of Islam*', vividly describes the frugal life of the Prophet (pbuh) when he writes about the death of the Prophet of Allah as follows.

'The house from which the light spread to the whole world was in darkness that day, because - there was no oil in the lamp.'

An Extra Note:

<u>A clarification regarding use of the word</u> "<u>**Mohammadan**</u>"

This word, "Mohammadan" from "Mohammad", used for a Muslim is equivalent to using "Christian" from "Christ"; *then this word may convey the idea that a Muslim has same faith as regard to Muhammad (pbh) as one Christian has it in regard to Christ. This is totally wrong.* If "Christianity" means a religion originated by Christ then by analogy "Mohammadanism" will mean a religion originated by Muhammad (pbh); which is entirely wrong. Contrary to the concept harbored by many non-Muslims ***The Religion Islam is not founded by Muhammad (pbh)***, it is a religion of all prophets who came to any part of the world; Muhammad(pbh) is only the last one.

(III) How the Quran presents Muhammad?

Does the Quran present Muhammad(pbh):

- As God?
- As God's son?
- As partner of God?
- As God incarnate?
- Or as a messenger of God?

The Quran presents Muhammad (pbh) solely as a messenger of Allah. Several verses in this regard emphasize the messenger -hood of Muhammad (pbh); the Quran also presents him in some other roles so that he could be a practical guide for the believers for all times to come. Following are some of the roles in which he is presented:

(i) <u>As a mortal man like all other people</u>

[Quran 18:110] Say [O Prophet]: "I am but a mortal man like all of you. It has been revealed unto me that your God is the One and Only God. Hence, whoever looks forward [with hope and awe] to meeting his Sustainer [on Judgment Day], let him do righteous deeds, and let him not ascribe unto anyone or anything a share in the worship due to his Sustainer!"

(ii) <u>As a Guide, as a Teacher</u>

[Quran 2:151] A similar (favour have ye already received) in that We have sent among you a Messenger of your own, rehearsing to you Our Signs, and sanctifying you, and instructing you in Scripture and Wisdom, and in new knowledge.

(iii) <u>As a Witness</u>

[Quran 2:143] Thus, have We made of you **an Ummah justly balanced**, that ye might be **witnesses** over the nations and the Messenger **a witness** over yourselves.

The explanation of this verse is best presented in Tafheem-ul-quran by A.A.Maududi:

"The purpose of creating 'the community of the middle way', according to this Quranic verse, is to make it stand as witness 'before all mankind and the Messenger might be a witness before you'. What this means is that when the whole of mankind is called to account, *the Prophet, as God's representative, will stand witness to the fact that he had communicated to the Muslims and had put into practice the teachings postulating sound beliefs, righteous conduct and a balanced system of life which he had received from high.*"

The Muslims, acting on behalf of the Prophet after his return to the mercy of God, will be asked to bear the same witness before the rest of mankind and to say that they had spared no effort in either communicating to mankind what the Prophet had communicated to them, or in exemplifying in their own lives what the Prophet had, by his own conduct, translated into actual practice.

Muslim Ummah as a WITNESS–what does it mean?

This position of standing witness before all mankind on behalf of God, which has been conferred on this community, amounts to its being invested with the leadership of all mankind. This is at once a great honour and a heavy responsibility. For what it actually means is that just as the Prophet served as a living example of godliness and moral rectitude, of equity and fair play before the Muslim community, so is the Muslim community required to stand vis-a-vis the whole world. What is expected of this community is that it should be able to make known, both by word and deed, the meaning of godliness and righteousness, of equity and fair-play.

Furthermore, just as the Prophet had been entrusted with the heavy responsibility of conveying to the Muslims the guidance which he had received; in a similar manner a heavy responsibility has been laid on the Muslims to communicate this guidance to whole of mankind. If the Muslims fail to establish before God that they did their duty in conveying to mankind the guidance they had received through the Prophet they will be taken to task seriously and their honourable position as the leaders of the whole world, far from being of any help to them, will spell their disaster. They will be held responsible along with the protagonists of evil for all the errors of belief and conduct which have spread during their term of leadership.

They will have to face the grim question: What were they doing when the world was surrounded by storms of transgression, injustice and error? http://www.quranenglish.com/tafheem_quran/002-1.htm)

(iv) <u>As a messenger of God</u>

[Quran 4:170] "O Mankind! The Messenger has come to you in truth from Allah, **believe in him**: It is best for you. But if ye reject Faith, to Allah belong all things in the heavens and on earth: And Allah is All-knowing, All-wise."

[Quran 7:158] Say [O Muhammad (pbh)]: **"O mankind! Verily, I am an apostle of God to all of**

you, [sent by Him] unto whom the dominion over the heavens and the earth belongs! There is no deity save Him; He [alone] grants life and deals death!" Believe, then, in God and His Apostle-the unlettered Prophet who believes in God and His words-and follow him, so that you might find guidance!?

(v) <u>As a Role model</u>

[Quran 33:21] "VERILY, in the Apostle of God you have a good example for everyone who looks forward [with hope and awe] to God and the Last Day, and remembers God unceasingly.

(vi) <u>As a Mercy for All</u>

[Quran 21:107] "We sent you not, but as a Mercy for all creatures"

(vii) <u>As a Judge, as an Arbiter but not as a Law giver</u>

[Quran 4:65] " But no, by the Lord, they can have no (real) Faith, until they make you judge in all disputes between them, and find in their souls no resistance against thy decisions, but accept them with the fullest conviction."

At an occasion, the detail of which is given in Hadees Books, the Prophet is told and there by told to all others that he is not entitled to make a permitted ('halal') thing forbidden ('haraam') : Quran (66:1) O Prophet, why do you forbid what Allah has made lawful for you?

(viii) <u>As a Warner</u>

[Quran 33:45] "O Prophet! Truly We have sent you as a Witness, a Bearer of Glad Tidings, and Warner.

(ix) As a Lamp

[Quran 33:46] "And as one who invites to Allah's (grace) by His leave, and as a lamp spreading light."

(x) As one who should be Followed and Obeyed by the believers

[Quran 3:31] Say: "If you do love Allah, Follow me: Allah will love you and forgive you your sins: For Allah is Oft-Forgiving, Most Merciful."

[Quran 4:80] He who obeys the Messenger, obeys Allah.

Extra Note:

The Need of a Model in a Society

There is a need of a model for all adherents of a religion or for that matter for followers of any ideology. One may ask a very general question as to who may be called a good Hindu, a good Muslim, a good Christian or communist or capitalist etc. This is a question which needs a logical answer; there must be a human (not super human or mythological character) IDEAL person whose personality must be taken for two purposes :

- first, taken as a MODEL so that a follower may easily abide by his commands and admonitions in all walks of life;
- second, taken as CRITERION, Standard or Touchstone, who should be taken as a reference for comparison, a reference against whom an adherent or follower can be evaluated of the truthfulness of his claim to be a 'perfect' or 'good' follower. In Islam it is

Muhammad(pbh) who has been authenticated by Allah to be a Perfect Model as described in the Quran 33:21 – "Surely there was a good example for you in the Messenger of Allah, for all those who look forward to Allah and the Last Day and remember Allah much."

The Prophet : A Leader in real sense

Muhammad(pbh) was a leader who was ever ready to act all those commands he gave to his followers, he was not a seeker of personal security, give preference to personal interests to everything else, never showed an inclination to flee danger(in that case it would be reasonable to expect manifestation of such weakness from his followers). **The Prophet (peace be upon him) endured along with others every toil and labor that he asked others to endure, and endured more than others; there was no trouble which others might have experienced and he himself did not. He was among those who dug the trench, and endured hunger and other afflictions just as the common Muslims did. He did not leave the battlefront even for a moment during the siege nor retreated an inch.** After the betrayal of the Bani Quraizah his own family had also been exposed to danger even as the families of the other Muslims were; (see the detail in Surah Ahzaab, 33rd chapter of the Quran). He did not make any special arrangement for his own and his family's protection, which did not exist for others. He was always in the forefront to offer maximum sacrifices for the great objectives for which he was constantly asking others to make sacrifices. Therefore, whoever made a claim of being his follower should have followed the practical example set by the leader.

13

Main theme, Structure and Style of the Quran

(I) Main Theme, Structure and Style of the Quran

Some remarkable points in regard to the introduction to the Quran are as follows:

1. **This book is quite different from other books of the world in regard to the following aspects:**

(*i*) ***Structurally***

It consists of 114 Surahs; with a minor difference of opinions of the scholars, 86 were revealed in Makkah during 13 years and 28 Surahs in Madinah during 10 years of the prophet's stay there till his death in 632.

'Surah' does not conform to the word 'chapter' however in a broader sense it may be taken as that. A chapter has a tag, caption or heading or a name and it is assumed that that chapter conveys the detail of that 'heading'. In the Quran, the name of a 'surah' is just a symbolic one, it does not discuss on that topic; the name is given just to recognize that surah thus the second 'surah' of the Quran 'Baqrah' (cow) does not discuss about the animal cow, this name is used only because this word occurs once in that Surah. However there are a small number of 'Surahs' which confirm the name as for example the very first Surah is named 'Fatiha' (the opening).

Similarly the word "**aayat**" which is translated as 'verse' is not actually a 'sentence' in usual sense, as in various places in the Book there are verses of just single words.

There are no paragraphs in the Quran; the reader himself understands where one topic of description ends and another starts.

However, some modern translators of the Quran have embarked upon presenting the Surahs in paragraphs for ease of understanding.

(*ii*) **In the manner of the presentation of topics**

This is elaborated in a separate sub-article provided as a reference.

(*iii*) **Being directly linked to the changes taking place in the movement undertaken by the Prophet in 23 long years.**

This is also elaborated in the separate sub- article as referred above.

(*iv*) **Being directly linked to the life of the Prophet**

In many cases only guiding principles are given in the Quran, the explanations and the practical applications are available only in the Ahadees (plural of 'hadees', the sayings and actions of the Prophet as recorded by his followers).

e.g salaat and zakaat are mentioned only as commandments to be followed but their practical applications such as how the salaat is to be performed and what percentage of the wealth is to be taken out for charity(zakat) are found only in Hadees this is why it is said that the *Quran & Muhammad (pbh) are inseparable* - one cannot be understood & followed without the other.

2. **Broadly the Quran consists of four topics:**

(*i*) The verses calling attention to the Oneness (tauheed) and existence of Allah.

(*ii*) The verses describing the incidents related to different Prophets and highlighting mainly the struggle of Muhammad (pbh) in the way of establishing the Deen (the system of religion comprising all aspects of life).

(*iii*) The verses which call the people to believe in the life hereafter.

(*iv*) Clear instructions what to do, what not to do most of such verses need the help of 'ahadees' for practical applications.

3. **The Quran's style of presentation is not in the form of that of a *WRITTEN* book but the style of the Quran is that of *ORATION*,** it is this reason that one finds here quick changes in subject matter and addressees.

4. **The Authencity of the Quran;**
   Historically it is a well recorded book, even if one does not believe in this book spiritually; he finds no loophole in its recording and preservation. (We have devoted a separate chapter for this topic in this book.)

5. **Is the Quran a 'complete' & 'sufficient' book?**
   This question itself at first may be rebuffing and repugnant to orthodox Muslims but the aim here is to draw the attention of general readers and highlight different aspects of the Quran *logically*: the words ("complete and sufficient"), are put here merely from the point of view of Logic.

The answer is both Yes and No: the Quran is complete and sufficient in providing mankind the "hidaya" (the Guidance) but it is not sufficient in providing practical applications in some of its injunctions: for that the Prophet's instructions are needed. It is similar to the case that when a machine (entirely new one, a newly invented one) is sent to a workshop, it is necessary that not only a booklet / manual be sent but also some engineer should go to the workshop who may guide in running the machine by demonstration in practice.

'Quran' is a manual to run the most complex machine called 'man' and the Messenger of God is the man sent along with the Quran for practical guidance.

6. **In the course of describing various topics,** the Quran brings about several descriptions connected to modern day scientific facts which are so revealing that they have been discovered only in recent times. (see the detail in a separate chapter - "Scientific Descriptions of the Quran")

7. The Style of presentation of this book is unique:
Some of the styles of presentation of the Quran are as follows:

(*i*) The Quran uses some pertinent clauses at the end of some instructions eg. [Quran2:235] : "And be warned that God knows what is in your minds, and therefore remain conscious of Him; and know, too, that God is much-forgiving, forbearing."

(*ii*) It uses clauses like [Quran: 2:242]: In this way God makes clear unto you His messages, *so that you might [learn to] use your reason.* [Quran 2:266]: In this way God makes clear His messages unto you, *so that you might take thought.* After describing some injunctions or some 'signs' of natural phenomenon the Quran thus asks its readers to ponder, contemplate on the points described.

(*iii*) The beautiful presentation of several 'SIGNS' in nature is worth reading at many places for example in S.Ruum 30:20-25, each verse starting with ***'min aayatihi'* (among His Signs is this)** and ending with such clauses as:

"verily in that are Signs <u>for those who reflect</u>"; "verily in that are Signs <u>for those who know</u>"," there are messages indeed for people who [are willing to] listen! "Verily in that are Signs for those who are wise." Thus it gives emphasis of pondering and analyzing each phenomenon.

(*iv*) At certain places the style of the Quran, to draw the attention of the readers is like these: '*do the disbelievers not see*', '*do you not see*', 'how can you reject the faith in Allah.'

(*v*) At many places, the ending clauses are: "*but none will grasp the Message but men of understanding.*"

(*vi*) At certain places there are glimpses of **beauty of Arabic grammar**: See this example:

[Quran 42:10] **alaihi twakkaltu wa ilaihi uneeb** "in Him have *I placed my trust*, and unto Him *do I always turn*!" this small clause is full of wisdom - the first part is in past tense and the second is in present tense: In the past verb it was said: "In Him did I place my trust," i.e.. "I decided once and for all that as long as I live I have to rely on His help, on His guidance, on His support and protection, and on His decision." Then in the present verb it was said: "To Him I turn," i.e. "Whatever situation I face in life, I turn only to Allah in it. I do not look towards others in an affliction or trouble or difficulty but invoke only Him for help."

(*vii*) **Judicious Combination of Words**

Most of the verses carry at the end attributes of God in: 'ghafoor-raheem', 'azeez-hakeem', 'azeez-raheem' and many such pairs like these; each of the pair conveying a sea of meanings; thus for the pair (azeez-hakeem': the All- Mighty, the All-Wise) (azeez-raheem: the All-Mighty, the All-Merciful). Here, three attributes of Allah have been mentioned: that He is All-Mighty, i.e. none can fight Him and win and that He is All-Wise, i.e. whatever He does, it is always the very demand of wisdom, and His plans and designs are so well-planned that none in the world can hinder and frustrate them". He is merciful - *Mighty without being wise and merciful will turn one a despot,* so this combination of attributes to Allah makes the Quranic description eloquent par excellence. Mostly such pairs are tagged after passing important injunctions thus conveying the meaning that these injunctions are not erratic, irrelevant but well planned by the Most Wise and these are well-suited to you keeping your weaknesses in sight by the Most Merciful.

(*viii*) The Quran describes its other function as the presentation of the Prophetic mission, which is aimed at guidance of humanity, by delivering it from darkness and leading it towards light:

A Book We have sent down to thee that you may bring forth mankind from the darkness into the light. [Quran 14:1]

Light (*Noor*) mentioned as Singular and Darkness (*Zulumat*) as Plural

That you may bring forth your people from the darkness into the light. [Quran 14:5]. The exegesis of the Quran emphasize the point that whenever the Quran mentions **darkness**, it always uses it in **the plural form** although it always uses **light in its singular form**. This means that the word, (darkness) includes all sorts of darkness, all of the evil ways that lead towards darkness, and that (light) signifies one single right path --the path of righteousness, whereas the ways of deviation and perversion are many.

(ix) Prohibition of Alcohols in stage by stage and that of Usury abruptly—why?

We have seen how the alcohol was banned gradually (in the chapter 'Islamic Laws-outdated, barbaric or useful?) because it was a matter of human weakness of physical addiction whereas the usury is rooted in the greed of man which must be removed harshly. See how wisely the injunction of prohibition of usury is passed in [Quran 2:278-279-281] O you who have attained to faith! Fear Allah. And give up all outstanding gains from usury, if you are [truly] believers; 2:279 for **if you do it not, then know that you are at war with God and His Apostle.** But if you repent, then you shall be entitled to [the return of] your principal: you will do no wrong, and neither will you be wronged. 2:281 *And be conscious of the Day on which you shall be brought back unto God, whereupon every human being shall be repaid in full for what he has earned, and none shall be wronged.*

Before passing the injunction it inspires the believers that is if you agreed to submit to Allah's commands then fear Him and follow Him otherwise you are at war with Him and the Prophet. And at the end they are warned to face the consequences on the Day of Judgment.

❖ Thus mark how an injunction purely related to worldly affairs is given a spiritual color to make the believer not only convinced "*with mind*" but to surrender to the command "*with heart*".

The Quran is full of such styles of presentation; a few examples here are sufficient to have a glimpse otherwise a separate book is needed to dwell on this topic.

(II) What kind of a book is the Quran ?

The Quran is not a book in usual sense, as you are accustomed with. We have discussed it earlier that the Quran was revealed during 23 years of the Prophet's life when he along with his followers were passing through different phases of Islamic Movements; guidance were needed as per the situation. This also explains why the mode of address is changed from time to time and the subject matter also changes accordingly - at first glance a reader finds it incoherent and disorganized; but if he keeps in mind the above main motifs, the Quran does not deviate from these anywhere.

To understand this topic in a more elaborate way, we quote here the famous commentator of the Quran, Abul Ala Maududi from his '*Tafheemul Quran*' which is acclaimed as one of the best interpretations of the Quran in present time.

Introduction to the Study of the Quran

A A Maududi
(http://www.quranenglish.com/tafheem_quran/)

We are accustomed to reading books which present information, ideas and arguments systematically and coherently. So, when we embark on the study of the Quran, we expect that this book too will revolve around a definite subject, that the subject matter of the book will be clearly defined at the beginning and will then be neatly divided into sections and chapters, after which discussion will proceed in a logical sequence. We likewise expect a separate and systematic arrangement of instruction and guidance for each of the various aspects of human life.

However, as soon as we open the Quran we encounter a hitherto completely unfamiliar genre of literature. We notice that it embodies precepts of belief and conduct, moral directives, legal prescriptions, exhortation and admonition, censure and condemnation of evildoers, warnings to deniers of the Truth, good tidings and words of consolation and good cheer to those who have suffered for the sake of God, arguments and corroborative evidence in support of its basic message, allusions to anecdotes from the past and to signs of God visible in the universe. Moreover, these myriad subjects alternate without any apparent system; quite unlike the books to which we are accustomed, the Quran deals with the same subject over and over again, each time couched in a different phraseology.

The reader also encounters abrupt transitions between one subject matter and another. Audience and speaker constantly change as the message is directed now to one and now to another group of people. There is no trace of familiar division into chapters and sections. Likewise, the treatment of different subjects is unique. The reader may find all this so foreign that his notion of what a book should be that he may become so confused as to feel that the Quran is a piece of disorganized, incoherent and unsystematic writing.

A Unique Book

What kind of a book is the Quran? In what manner was it revealed? What underlies its arrangement? What is the subject? What is its true purpose? What is the central theme to which its multifarious topics are intrinsically related?

What kind of reasoning and style does it adopt in elucidating its central theme? If we could obtain clear, lucid answers to these and other related questions we might avoid some dangerous pitfalls, thus making it easier to reflect upon and to grasp that meaning and purpose of the Quranic verses. We need, therefore, to be told in advance that this Book is unique in the manner its composition, in its theme and in its contents and arrangement. *We should be forewarned that the concept of a book which we have formed from our previous readings is likely to be a hindrance, rather than a help, towards a deep understanding of the Quran*. We should realize that as a first step towards understanding it we must disabuse our minds of all preconceived notions.

Central Theme

"The way of life which is in accordance with the reality and conducive to human good is that which we have characterized above as "the right way". The real object for the Book is to call people to this "right way" and to illuminate God's true guidance, which has often been lost either through man's negligence and heedlessness or distorted by his wicked perversity."

"The Quran speaks of the structure of the heavens and the earth and of man, refers to the signs of reality in the various phenomena of the universe, relates anecdotes of bygone nations, criticizes the beliefs, morals, and deeds of different peoples, elucidates supernatural truths and discusses many other things besides. All this the Quran does, not to order to provide instruction in physics, history, philosophy or any other particular branch of knowledge, but rather to remove the misconception people have about reality ----"

"This is why the Quran mentions everything only to the extent and in the manner necessary for the purpose it seeks to serve. The Quran confines itself to essentials thereby omitting any irrelevant details. Thus all its contents consistently revolve around this call."

"Likewise, it is not possible fully to appreciate either the style of the Quran, the order underlying the arrangement of its verses or the diversity of the subjects treated in it, without fully understanding the manner in which it was revealed".

"In keeping with the character of the mission at this stage the early revelations generally consisted of short verses, couched in language of uncommon grace and owner, and clothed in a literary style suited to the taste and temperament of the people to whom they were originally addressed, and whose hearts they were meant to penetrate."

Hand in Hand with the Movement of the Prophet

It is now clear to us that the revelation of the Quran began and went hand in hand with the preaching of the message. This message passed through many stages and met with diverse situations from the very beginning and throughout a period of twenty-three years. The different parts of the Quran were revealed step by step according to the multifarious, changing needs and requirements of the Islamic movement during these stages. It therefore could not possibly possess the kind of coherence and systematic sequence expected of a doctoral dissertation. Moreover, the various fragments of the Quran which were revealed in harmony with the growth of the Islamic movement were not published in the form of written treatises, but were spread orally. Their style, therefore, bore an oratorical flavor rather than the characteristics of literary composition.

Oration Presented in the form of Composition

Furthermore, these orations were delivered by one whose task meant he had to appeal simultaneously to the mind, to the heart and to the emotions, and to people of different mental levels and dispositions. He had to revolutionize people's thinking, to arouse in them a storm of noble emotions in support of his cause, to persuade his companions and inspire them with devotion and real, and with the desire to improve and reform their lives. He had to raise their morale and steel their determination, turn enemies into friends and opponents into admirers, disarm those out to oppose his message and show their position to be morally untenable.

Orations revealed in conformity with requirements of a message and movement will inevitably have a style different from that of a professorial lecture.

Why Repetition of the Subjects?

This explains the repetitions we encounter in the Quran. The interests of a message and a movement demand that during a particular stage emphasis should be placed only on those subjects which are appropriate at that stage, to the exclusion of matters pertaining to later stages. As a result, certain subjects may require continual emphasis for months or even years. On the other hand, constant repetition in the same manner becomes exhausting.

Whenever, a subject is repeated, it should therefore be expressed in different phraseology, in new forms and with stylistic variations so as to ensure that the ideas and beliefs being put over find their way into the hearts of the people.

- At the same time, it was essential that *the fundamental beliefs* and principles on which the movement was based should always be kept fresh in people's minds; a necessity which dictated that they should be repeated continually through all stages of the movement... If these ideas had lost their hold on the hearts and minds of people, the Islamic movement could not have moved forward in its true spirit.

Why the Quran was not Arranged Chronologically?

If we reflect on this, it also becomes clear that the prophet (pbh) did not arrange the Quran in the sequence in which it was revealed. As we have noted, the context in which the Quran was revealed in the course of twenty-three years was the mission and movement of the prophet (pbh); the revelations correspond with the various stages of this mission and movement. Now, it is evident that when the prophet's mission was completed, the chronological sequence of the various parts of the Quran - revealed in accordance with the growth of the prophet's mission - could in no way be suitable to the changed situation. What was now required was a different sequence in tune with the changed context resulting from the completion of the mission.

Initially, the prophet's message was addressed to people totally ignorant of Islam. Their instruction had to start with the most elementary things. After the mission had reached its successful completion, the Quran acquired a compelling relevance for those who had decided to believe in the prophet. In the changed context, it had become necessary for the bearers of the mission of the prophet (pbh) to be informed of their duties and of the true principles and laws governing their lives. They also had to be warned against the deviations and corruptions which had appeared among the followers of earlier prophets.

It would be foreign to the very nature of the Quran to group together in one place all verses relating to a specific subject; the nature of the Quran requires that the reader should find teachings revealed during the Madinan period interspersed with those of the Makkan period, and vice versa. It requires the juxtaposition of early discourses with instructions from the later period of the life of the Prophet. This blending of the teachings from different periods helps to provide an overall view and an integrated perspective of Islam, and acts as a safeguard against lopsidedness.

A Misunderstanding to be Removed

The present arrangement of the Quran is not the work of later generations, but was made by the Prophet under God's direction. Whenever a Surah was revealed, the Prophet summoned his scribes, to whom he carefully dictated its contents, and instructed them where to place it in relation to the other Surahs. The Prophet followed the same order of Surahs and verse when reciting during ritual Prayer as on other occasions, and his Companions followed the same practice in memorizing the Quran. It is therefore a historical fact that the collection of the Quran came to an end on the very day that its revelation ceased.

Since Prayers were obligatory for the Muslims from the very outset of the Prophet's mission, and recitation of the Quran was an obligatory part of those prayers, Muslims were committing the Quran to memory while its revelation continued. Thus, as soon as a fragment of the Quran was revealed, it was memorized by some of the Companions. Hence the preservation of the Quran was not solely dependent on its verses being inscribed on palm leaves, pieces of bone, leather and scraps of parchment - the materials used by the Prophet's scribes for writing down Quranic verses. Instead the verses came to be inscribed upon scores, then hundreds, then thousands, then hundreds of thousands of human hearts, soon after they had been revealed, so that no scope was left for any devil to alter so much as one word of them.

How to Approach the Quran

Anyone who really wishes to understand the Quran, irrespective of whether or not he believes must divest his mind, as far as possible, of every preconceived notion, bias and prejudice, in order to embark upon his study with an open mind. Anyone who begins to study the Quran with a set of preconceived ideas is likely to read those very ideas into the Book. No book can be profitably studied with this kind of attitude, let alone the Quran which refuses to open its treasure-house to such readers.

- It should be remembered, nevertheless, that full appreciation of the spirit of the Quran demands practical involvement with the struggle to fulfill its mission. **The Quran is neither a book of abstract theories and cold doctrines which the reader can**

grasp while seated in a cozy armchair, nor it is merely a religious book like other religious books, the secrets of which can be grasped in seminaries and oratories. On the contrary, it is the blueprint and guidebook of a message, of a mission, of a movement. As soon as this Book was revealed, it drove a quiet, kind-hearted man from his isolation and seclusion, and place him upon the battlefield of life to challenge a world that had gone astray. It inspired him to raise his voice against falsehood, and pitted him in grim struggle against the standard-bearers of unbelief, of disobedience of God, of waywardness and error...

➢ How then could one expect to get to the heart of the Quranic truths merely by reciting its verses, without so much as stepping upon the field of battle between faith and unbelief, between Islam and Ignorance? To appreciate the Quran fully one must take it up and launch into the task of calling people to God, making it one's guide at every stage.

The Quran : A National or Universal Doctrine?

Indeed, what marks out a time-bound from an eternal, and a particularistic **national** doctrine from a **universal** one, is the fact that the former either seeks to exalt a people or claims special privileges for it or else comprises ideas and principles so vitally related to that people's life and traditions as to render it totally inapplicable to the conditions of other people. A universal doctrine, on the other hand, is willing to accord equal rights and status to all, and its principles have an international character in that they are equally applicable to other nations. Likewise, the validity of those doctrines which seek to come to grips merely with the questions of a transient and superficial nature is time-bound.

The uneasiness some people feel about (as to why detailed regulations regarding social, political and economic and other matters are not given) this arises because they forget that God did not merely reveal a Book, but that He also designated a Prophet.

- The mission of the Prophet was to give practical shape to the Islamic vision of the good life, by offering the world a model of an individual character and of a human state and society, as living embodiments of the principles of the Quran.

14

Preservation & Authenticity of the Quran

History of Compilation of the Quran

Instead of writing this history in comprehensive form we elucidate below some important points which will suffice for elementary introduction of the subject:

1. Is the Quran in our hands today the same as it was in the time of Muhammad(pbh)?

   - In other words: has the Quran changed from Prophet's time to this day?
   - A hypothetical question: - if a companion of the Prophet comes back today, will he be able to read the present day Quran or will he find it 'different'?
   - Is it true that Usman (ra) the third caliph after the demise of the Prophet selected one out of many versions of the Quran and got all others burnt?

- Is it true that no 'Book' was left by the Prophet?
- As in the case of the Bible, are there different *versions* of the Quran too ?

These questions prompt us to probe into the *authenticity of the Quran* and *history of its compilation.*

2. There are two branches for the preservation of the Quran :

Oral transmission** & **Written transmission

Although the Quran was revealed over a period of roughly 23 years, portion by portion, the Prophet (pbh) took great care that believers be encouraged to memorize that portion of the Quran revealed till then. It was not mere memorization that was emphasized but the companions were inspired to follow the particular tone and temper of recitation as taught by the Prophet. Any reciter learning the recitation of the Quran from the successive companion was enjoined to testify that his recitation was in genuine tradition of the one taught by the Prophet personally. The recitation and memorization of the Quran was fully checked by the lingo-phonetic promptings as required for *prefect* recitation. Even today a certified Reciter has to mention that he learnt the Quranic Recitation from such and such tradition that his teacher was such and such person: the chain should run upward to the Prophet. This '**Oral Transmission**' was a very authentic 'tool' not only in that age of scarcity of writing materials but it has proved to be of immense value in keeping the Quran from getting perverted from the Prophet's time till date.

Getting the revelation in **Written Form** as soon as it came was another means adopted by the Prophet for its preservation. Whenever a revelation came he used to call a scribe, got it written down and tell him to put that portion of revelation in such an such chapter after or before which verses thus virtually he 'edited' the Quran at the same time. Let it be noted that the organization of the verses in a chapter and the sequence of the chapters in the present day Quran are assuredly the work of the Prophet himself and in no way it should be considered a 'fabrication' of later days period.

3. **Historical background** (in regard to the preservation of the Quran) of the Makkan period of the Messenger :

❖ The early followers lived in adverse condition and extreme poverty.

❖ There was much scarcity of writing materials, the scribes also were not in much number.

❖ "Oral transmission" was the main tool of preserving the revelations.

❖ A remarkable helping tool was the extraordinary memory of the common Arabs, men, women & children (as indicated by several instances: a large number of people were enthused to memorize the whole Quran and hundreds and thousands of the "sayings" of the Prophet; it is related that an old woman happened to memorize a chapter, Surah 'QAAF' of 45 verses, only by hearing its recitation by the Prophet in Fajr(early morning) prayer).

- ❖ The situation in Madinah was far more congenial where accessibility to writing materials as well as people capable of copying the Quran grew with time.

4. **Preservation During the Prophet's life time**

The people knew the order of the verses, got them revised, reconfirmed and rechecked by the official scribes (official scribes at the Prophet's time : ZAID BIN TABITH, UBAI BIN KA'AB, MO'AAZ BIN JABAL, ABU ZAID, MOAAWIA BIN ABU SUFIAN, some say there were around forty such scribes, name of 23 are mentioned in a Hadees. Thus it is clearly evident that the whole Quran was well recoded in the hearts of the followers in '**oral form**' and well documented on writing materials of that age in the '**written form**' in the Prophet's own lifetime, but it must be added that the verses were written not in book form but on separate pieces; scrapes of leathers, thin flat stones, palm branches, wooden pieces, shoulder blades of animals, etc. We have indicated the reasons later on why he did not get the Quran in book form.

5. **The time of Abu Bakr**, the first caliph just after the Prophet :

After the death of the Prophet in 632CE in the Battel of Yamama (11 H / 633 CE) many sahaba (companions of the Prophet) who were huffaz, (memorizers of the whole Quran), were martyred then those people who were at the helm of the affairs got alerted about the preservation of the Quran. Zaid bin Thabit, being most prominent of all the scribes, was appointed to head a committee to compile the Quran in Sahifa (book) form.

To safeguard the compilation from error, Zaid accepted only those materials which had been written down in the presence of the Prophet (pbh) himself and which could be verified by at least two (reciters) reliable witnesses who testified that he had **heard** them from the Prophet (pbh) himself and **then memorized**. Theologian of early times, Ibn Hajar's statement affirms this view, that "Zaid was unwilling to accept any written material for consideration unless two Companions bore witness that the man received his dictation from the Prophet himself. Zaid adhered to this principle so much so that he refrained from including the final two verses of *Sura Tauba (chapter 9)* until he came upon it in written form, although he and his fellow Companions of the committee could recall it perfectly well from memory.

Once the mus'haf (Arabic term for 'collection of papers') was compiled and completed in loose sheets of leathers, and unanimously approved by the sahaba(companions of the Prophet), these sheets (tied with ribbon) were kept with Abu Bakr (d13H, 634CE), after his death it was passed on to Umar(caliphate 13-23H, d644CE), and then to Hafsa, his daughter, a widow of the Prophet.

6. **The Time of Usman, the third Caliph** (23 H – 35 H/ 644 – 656 CE)

   Returning from the battle of Azerbaijan (25 H / 645CE) Huzaifa urged Usman "Quick (O, Ameerul Mumineen (Leader of the Believers), help the Muslims before they differ about the text of the Quran as the Christians and Jews differed about their Scriptures ". He was perturbed when he saw the soldiers from different parts of lands meeting together and reading the Quran differently, each considering his reading to be correct. ***What was the problem?*** Let us analyze the whole affair.

(i) Arabic language, even prior to the advent of the Prophet, was highly developed, its poetry in its sublime heights but as it happens with all languages, local impacts give birth to dialects with varying lingo-phonetic distinctions, different Arab tribes were using varying dialects. Although literary aspect of the Arabic language was developed it must be admitted that its script was not perfect; there was no diacritical marks and some alphabets had similar orthography.

(*ii*) Although the Quran in full text in written form was kept with Abu Bakr, but that was not published to the masses.

(*iii*) Many people were in possession of their own pieces of parchment / sheets of writing materials (small portions of the Quran in written form) without getting those verified with the master Record or getting approved by the authentic scribes such as Zaid bin Thabit. And we can easily envisage that such private Quranic portions in various hands might be in circulation among the people and in the absence of authenticity of the written materials, all possibilities of laxness and faults were evident.

iv) As we will explain later in this article, in the absence of diacritical marks, the native Arabs at times differed on pronouncing certain words however it was not a problem for them but for non-Arabs coming to the fold of Islam it turned out be a grave problem in reciting certain verses.

Usmanic Codex(Saheefa-e-Usmani)

Usman appointed a committee of twelve scribes, again under the headship of Zaid bin Thabit and announced to all that whoever possessed even a fragment of a single verse of the Quran it be deposited to the committee. Zaid took utmost care in collecting each surah and each verse contained in it. Each verse was corroborated with a witness who had to declare that he heard it from the Prophet himself. Thus the committee took great pains to collect and compile the scripture in book form. Whenever there was difference of opinion in variant reading, the dialect of the tribe Quraish (in which the Prophet was born) was given preference. At that age of time there was a large number of the companions who had heard the Quran in full or in part from the Prophet himself and had memorized it, so there was little chance of any shortcoming creeping into the manuscript. It must be pointed out that Usman got this Mushaf collected quite independent of the earlier work of Abu Bakr; of course once completed he got it compared with the Mushaf kept with Hafsa, as stated earlier.

One may wonder why Caliph 'Usman took the trouble to compile an autonomous copy when the end product was to be compared with the earlier compiled mus'haf anyway. In the above account no inconsistencies were found between that mus'haf and the independent mus'haf he got compiled. Three broad conclusions emerged:

first, it was checked and rechecked that the Quranic text was thoroughly stable from the earliest days and not erratic. Second, the methods involved in compilation during both reigns were meticulous and accurate. Third, finding no discrepancy between the two Books, Usman and every one of the committee must had had a sigh of relief, a sense of jubilation and most importantly an increase in the credibility of the Divine Book.

Eight (seven, according to some historians) copies were prepared, Usman kept one for him & others were sent to different major cities under the then Muslim rule and very wisely decided to send a Master Reciter along with each Book, who stayed in those cities to teach the recitations and guide the peoples in copying the master codex; in many history books their names are described. It seems certain from various Muslim historical sources that several earliest manuscripts were lost, by natural decay or some other reasons such as through fire amongst other things. There are some copies extant to this day that are attributed to Usmān and they are available in full or in part in different museums of the world, the famous among them are The Topkapi Museum, Istanbul, Turkey, Tashkent (Samarqand), Uzbekistan, St. Petersburg (Russia), Katta Langar, The Egyptian National Library (Dār Al-Kutub Al-Misrīyya), Cairo, (Refer: www.islamic-awareness.org/quran/text/mss)

7. 'Usman Burns All Other Manuscripts: why?

The famous scholar Mustafa Al-Azmi records in his book, "The History of the Quranic Text": With the task complete, the ink on the final copy dry, and duplicate copies dispatched, there was no need for the numerous fragments of the Quran circulating in people's hands. So all such fragments were burned. Mus'ab bin Sa'd asserts that the people were pleased with 'Uthman's decision; at the very least no one voiced any objections. (Abu 'Ubaid, *Fa¢ii'il,* p. 284; ad-

Dani, *al-Muqni'*, p. 18.) Other reports confirm this unanimous approval, including 'Ali bin Abi:Talib who says,

"By Allah, he did what he did with these fragments in the presence of us all [*i.e.* and none of us objected]. [Ibn Abl Dawud, AL_MASAHIF, p. 22; see also pp. 12, 23]

As we described above, right from the time of the Prophet, people were having their own pieces of writings of the Quranic passages, getting these passed to others, hand to hand, being copied, sometimes with errors caused unintentionally. One very important work was done by Usman that he got such copies / parchments in whatever shapes, collected from general people who were keeping the Quranic portions, correct or incorrect, whole or partial; all collected and got them burnt in the presence of and with full approval of all the companions of the Prophet. No one differed or objected rather they were satisfied and they approved such a step. As recorded by Zaid, Mus'ab and Ali: A large number of the Prophet's companions gathered to witness the burning with no one speaking against it.

An instant question sparks in mind as to why he took such a drastic step? He did it for two reasons; first, the people may not fall in disputes in finding differences between the Master Record and the unauthentic parchments in their own hands. Second, for all future generations it was an act of prudence: we can imagine now, how hazardous it would have been, if an incorrect manuscript had appeared today.

The Reaction of the Companions of the Prophet

Some of the missionaries, without proof proclaim that many people didn't like the act of burning. This is wrong as proven by the following: Zaid is reported to have said, "I saw the companions of Muhammad(pbh) (going about) saying, "By Allah, Usman has done well! By Allah, Usman has done well!" [Nisaburi]

Ibn Abi Dawud records Musab ibn Sad ibn Abi Waqqas to have testified: "I saw the people assemble in large number at Usman's burning of the proscribed copies; not a one spoke out against him." Ali commented, "If I were in command in place of Usman, I would have done the same." [Zarkashi]

Almost every companion of the Prophet (pbuh) clealy approved of the act of Usman.

- **A critical note**: A doubt is raised by some orientalists about the credibility of Usman : Is it not possible that he might have used the new 'compilation' to gain some benefits, personal or political to his own ends? The answer is simple and understandable:

How could 'Usman have changed the text that had been in use for twelve years before him, after the death of the Prophet, in the presence of hundreds of memorizer-companions of the Prophet who could easily detect any change, however minor, to the original text and who were prompted by religious compulsions to prevent alterations of any kind in the Word of God?

- And why at all would he want to change it, considering that the extant text says nothing in his favour? It is also important to keep in mind that the vast Muslim world was not homogeneous. There was as much diversity of opinion as one expects from any group of people. There were even conflicts, some of them armed. 'Usman himself had opposition from some groups, one of which actually martyred him. Had the text he promulgated been even slightly less than 100% reliable, his opponents would have made it an issue and accused him of changing the Word of God. But the fact is that these opponents accused him of many things but we do not have any tradition, certainly not an early reliable one, in which they accuse him of changing the Word of God.

Authenticity of the Usmanic Codex

It is indeed true that 'Usman did authenticate and promulgate one particular text and ordered others to be burnt. For differences in script and copying errors during a period of fast conversion (to Islam) might have resulted in many manuscripts with errors. If these manuscripts had been used to make further copies, the errors would have multiplied. The best solution was that certain authenticated copies be sent to various centres of the Muslim world and all others be destroyed. The very fact that the text whose copies were sent by 'Usman was accepted throughout the Muslim world, by both his friends and foes, and the fact that no other text has ever been put forward as an alternative to the existing text proves that the text sent by 'Usman was indeed the authentic one. (Dr. Ahmad Shafaat, 2000, *"Journal of the Muslim Research Institute"*, Canada).

Ahmad Von Denffer aptly concludes in his book about the

Usmanic mushaf that:

The wide distribution of this text and its undisputed authority can also be deduced from the reports on the battle of Siffin (A.H. 37) 27 years after the death of the Prophet, and five years after 'Uthman's copies were distributed, Mu'awiya's troops fixed sheets from the Quran on their spears to interrupt the battle. However nobody accused anyone else of using a partisan version of the text, which would have made a splendid accusation against the enemy. (Uloomul Quran p 56)

8. The Importance of Recitation vis-à-vis the script of the Mus'haf

<u>Al-Rasm- al-Usman (Script of Usmanic codex)</u>

The script in which this Mus'haf (or codex, as some prefer to call) was written, gained significance because of its "official – status". As stated earlier, the script of Arabic had not developed till that age, particularly in two important areas.

(*a*) There was no distinction between letters of the alphabet of similar shape e.g. between *ta* & *tha* ت,ث, and between *fa* & *qaf* ف,ق

(*b*) There were no vowel marks i.e. no indication of differentiation between *zabar,zer and pesh* ; this is elaborated here later on. (,تشدید ,⊠ضم ,پیش ,⊠کسر ,زیر ,⊠فتح,زبر)

The urgency of pronouncing the Quranic Words correctly

❖ At this stage we remind that the urgency of pronouncing the Quranic words in the most perfect way made the Arabic language grow quickly, in a short span of time, to a level, no other language of the world can come even closer to it. After all development of English, there are a thousand words, even simple ones like *but & put*, the utterance of which in correct way, is difficult unless someone guides to pronounce it correctly as there is no diacritical mark on the alphabet 'u' to differentiate the pronouncements.

Indicated above in a) & b), there was no great confusion among the Arabs because they understood without any vowel markings (as people accustomed with Urdu or Farsi read well without vowel marks), however this did create confusion to Non–Arabs. Indeed there was an *urgent need* to update the script of the Mushaf and at the same time to innovate in it some methods to facilitate in reading and reciting in the very manner the authentic reciters were taught by the Prophet. It should be noted that the people attached with the propagation of the Quran in past and in all ages, even today have been in search of techniques to make the written Quran in consonance and concordance with the Recitation. The "Written Transmission" and the "Oral Transmission" have travelled down the ages hand in hand; this has acted well in keeping the Book preserved and authentic.

- In all texts of the history of the Quran it is stated that for ease to all they started to put "dots" of different colors for vowel and diacritical marks, many such changes took place at different stages in history. In early times work was carried out chiefly by **Abu al–Aswad Al –Du'ali (d. 69H/688CE), Yahya bin Ya'mar *(d.* 90 A.H.l708 C.E.), Nasr bin 'Asim al-Laithi *(d.* 100 A.H.l718 C.E.), and Maimun al-Aqran, arriving at Khalil bin Ahmad al-Fraheedi *(d.* 170 A.H./786 C.E.**

Later on this work was modified extensively by two persons Abu Umar Addani and Abu Dauwd, Sulaiman bin Najah around the period 430/450 H. The dots of the colored ink were changed in time by the traditional markings of [zabar(fataha), zeer(kasarah), pesh(dhammah)] etc. These notations continue to this day. Understandably there was some opposition at first to adding anything to the way the Qurān was written. Ibn Umar (73/692) disliked the dotting; others welcomed it, clearly because it was, in fact, doing no more than ***ensuring proper reading of the Qurān***.

Keeping the Usmanic codex (sahifa-e-Usmani), in focus, with the passage of time, grew the grammar of Arabic and other sciences related to the Quran: (Q*irat tajwiz)* different ways of reciting; along with grew calligraphy: different styles of writing e.g. Naskh, Nastaliq, shahmukki, Ruq'ah, Thuluth, Kufic, sini (Chinese) and Hijazi etc.

A.A. Maududi writes in "Rasail wa Masail V. 3"

"In the age of Tabeyeen and taba tabeyeen (students of the companions of the Prophet) the Science of the Qiraat (recitation of Quran) became a specialized field. People traveled, even for a single word far distances to know the pronunciation, accent, the special way of uttering and the notations used, they reached to those teachers who had a near chain of relation to the Prophet (pbh) for each word's pronunciation they noted as to where from they learnt it and further more where from his teacher had learnt it."

9. Three important rules for Acceptance/Non-Acceptance of a Qiraat (Recitation)

(*i*) The Qiraat (recitation) must be according to the orthography of Usmanic Codex.

The condition required the recitation to coincide with the script of one of the copies of the Qur'ân distributed during the era of Caliph 'Usman. It must be emphasised that the orthography of the Usmanic codex is the same as used by the scribes of the Prophet. Hence differences which result from dot placement (for example two dots to be placed above or below in the orthographic of an alphabet would make it ta'lamoon or ya'lamoon)are considered acceptable provided the other two conditions (mentioned below) are complied with.

(*ii*) Qiraat must be conforming to the *lughat, mohawra and Qawaid* (dictionary, proverb and grammar of the Arabic language).

This second condition required that the variations in recitations must match the known Arabic grammatical constructions. Unusual constructions could be verified by their existence in passages of pre-Islamic prose or poetry.

(*iii*)And the most important rule to be observed was that the ***chain of the authenticity*** (sanad) had to be reliable and must reach up to the Prophet (pbh) without any break. Proof must be there that a word or clause under consideration had been verified by the Prophet (pbh) or he had instructed to recite others in the manner which it was being claimed.

To show what a 'chain of authenticity' (sanad) stands for, we give below an example:

Thus a famous Qari Nafi, mentioned above, has this chain: Nâfi' (died in the year 169 H) reported from Yazîd Ibn al-Qaqâ and Abd ar-Rahmân Ibn Hurmuz al-'Araj and Muslim Ibn Jundub al-Hudhalî and Yazîd Ibn Român and Shaybah Ibn Nisâ'. All of them reported from Abû Hurayrah and Ibn Abbâs (very famous two companions of the Prophet) and Abdallâh Ibn 'Ayyâsh Ibn Abî Rabî'ah al-Makhzûmî and the last three reported from Ubayy Ibn Ka'b and he from the Prophet himself. Thus the chain from the Prophet down to Nafi is established.

NOTE no. 1 :- In this manner wherever in the Quran there are differences in the mutwatir (continuous) and mash'hoor (mash'hoor is defined as those Qirats (recitations), in which, nowhere there is conflict or contradiction. An example will clarify this point: In the opening chapter of the Quran, entitled Fatiha (the Opening) there is an orthography of a word that can be read as both "maalik" (master/lord) or "malik" (king, soverign), as we see both words convey the same sense: Every Qirat along with the other one gives new dimension to the meaning.

NOTE no. 2 :- It is this difference of opinion in the Qiraats (readings) which have been called by some detractors of the Quran, among the orientalist as " *versions of the Quran*" and they try to lead the people astray that there *are* different versions of the Quran just like there are "versions of the Bible". Those who know how different are the versions of the Bible, can well understand the deception in this claim. For all this discussion see in the internet www.islamic-awareness.org and Google: *– "all about versions of the Bible and translations".* *And* http://www.gradesaver.com/the-bible/wikipedia/versions-and-t

Note no. 3 William Muir, not a friend of Islam, echoed clearly that there is only one Qur'ân:

"The codex of 'Uthmân has been handed down to us unaltered. So carefully, indeed, has it been preserved, that there are no variations of importance, - we might almost say no variations at all, - amongst the innumerable copies of the Koran scattered throughout the vast bounds of empire of Islam. Contending and embittered factions, taking their rise in the murder of 'Uthmân himself within a quarter of a century from the death of Muhammad(pbh) have ever since rent the Muslim world. **Yet ONE KORAN has always been current amongst them.... There is probably in the world no other work which has remained twelve centuries with so pure a text."** (Sir W Muir, The Life Of Mohammad, 1912, Edinburgh, John Grant, pp. xxii-xxiii)

Similar view are expressed by another Orientalist, Arthur Jeffery who acknowledges this fact, "Practically all the early Codices and fragments that have so far been carefully examined, show the same type of text, such variants as occur being almost always explainable as scribal errors" (Arthurjeffery'sreview of "The Riseof the North ArabicScriptand It's Kur'anic Development by NabiaAbbott", *The Moslem World,* vol. 30 (1940), p. 191. - as quoted in History the Quranic Text –M.Al-Azmi p225)

Note no. 4: A REMARKABLE TRIBUTE TO THE HIST0RIOGRAPHY OF THE MUSLIM SCHOLARS

From an early date Muslim scholars recognized the danger of false testimony and hence false doctrine, and therefore developed an elaborate science for critical study of the tradition. "Traditional science", as it was called, differed in many respects from modern historical source criticism, and modern scholarship has always disagreed with evaluations of traditional scientists about the authenticity and accuracy of ancient narratives. But their careful scrutiny of the chains of transmission and their meticulous collection and preservation of variants in the transmitted narratives give to medieval Arabic historiography professionalism and sophistication without precedent in antiquity and without parallel in the contemporary medieval West. By comparison, the historiography of Latin Christendom seems poor and meagre, and even the more advanced and complex historiography of Greek Christendom still falls short of the historical literature of Islam in volume, variety and analytical depth. (John Burton, The Collection Of The Qur'ân, 1979, Cambridge University Press, pp. 239-240)

Note no. 5

Some clarifications regarding:

1. Number of verses in the Quran
2. Scripts of the Quran
3. Notations used to pronounce correctly
4. Why was no 'Book' left by the Prophet?

(*i*) At the time of the Prophet as the revelations came, he got it written by the scribes and at the same time encouraged his companions to memorize them. They were well versed in their language, they knew well where to start a sentence and where to stop and they memorized the Quranic passages accordingly, however, in writing they did not use any notation for ending of a sentence. This did not hamper them to recite correctly. The manner of recitation they were instructed by the Prophet himself.

As we indicated earlier, to demarcate vowel and diacritical marks some notations were used in the writing, for ending of a verse a mark was also used; such notations were different at different periods of time, these days commonly used, is a big round circle, sometime verse number is written inside sometime outside it. Now a difference of opinion arose; someone marked this symbol at one place in a text where as some other thought that the sentence should end at another place, *but without disturbing the main text.* Take an example: see S.3, v. 3-4. In some Quran you will find these as two separate verses, in some these two are taken as one as verse no. 3 only; although not a single word of the text was disturbed. There are such cases in other places of the Quran. This explains why the famous exegetist (commentator of the Quran) Ibn Kathir, in the preface of his commentary, puts different data for the total number of verses in the Quran. In the present day Quran the number of verses is 6236.

(*ii*) Has the script of the Quran changed from the Prophet's time? Yes, it has changed. The script has changed but not the TEXT, the ways of writing has been changing in the past and it will continue to change in the future for a better and more accurate pronunciation of the words.

There are many different styles of Arabic scripts.

Angular scripts

Kufic developed around the end of the seventh century in Kufa, Iraq (from which it takes its name) and other centres. Until about the eleventh century it was the main script used to copy Qurans. The simple and elegant forms were embellished over time.

Eastern *Kufic* was developed by Persian calligraphers during the tenth century and is distinguished by short, angled strokes.

Maghribi script evolved in North Africa (the Maghreb) and Spain in the tenth century. Forms of this script are still used in this region today.

Square *Kufic* appears from the thirteenth century on coins, tilework and elsewhere in the lands of the Mongols and their successors.

Rounded scripts

As the decorative potential of *Kufic* was increasingly exploited, it became ever more difficult to read and was gradually abandoned for general use during the eleventh and twelfth centuries. **Rounded scripts** were used since early Islamic times for everyday correspondence on papyrus for example, whereas *Kufic* was reserved for more formal public texts.

Naskh is the 'copyists' hand mainly used from the twelfth century for writing government documents and also for copying the Quran.

Thuluth, meaning 'one third', is often used for monumental inscriptions and was particularly favoured by the Mamluk sultans of Egypt (AD 1250-1517).

Nasta'liq is the 'hanging script'. According to legend it was perfected by the fifteenth-century calligrapher Mir Ali al-Tabrizi after dreaming of flying geese. It was popular in Iran and Mughal India from the sixteenth century but is rarely used to copy the Quran.

Divani was developed by Ottoman Turkish calligraphers during the fifteenth century and often used on documents.

In the present day Muslim world there are various scripts, the script, the Indo- pak people are used to is different from what now King Fahad Printing complex, Madinah, is printing for the people of Arab land where as those printed in North Africa are saliently different.

(*iii*) **Notations used in Arabic for better pronouncement of a word.**

It is the only language in the world which takes utmost care to utter a word in the most accurate possible way. For this a specialized science has developed. Right from the time when notations were used In early 1st century Hijra, till today there has been a continuous effort to modify this discipline.

In future there will surely be some more innovations as indicated recently by the induction of **colored Quran** (TAJWEED QURAN) and for recent changes in notation and punctuations of the Qurans published by King Fahad Printing Complex in MADINAH. You can have a glimpse of all these in Google and other sites eg. http://www.quranexplorer.com/Quran-/Default.aspx Recently digital Quran with mp4 and mp5 players have come in the market (http://www.alibaba.com/showroom/colored-quran-player.html)

(*iv*) **Why was no "Book" left by the Prophet?**

[Though the Prophet enlisted all possible measures to preserve the Quran, he did not bind all the suras together into one master volume, as evidenced by Zaid bin Thabit's statement that, "The Prophet was taken [from this life] whilst the Quran had not yet been gathered into a book." (Ibn Hajar, *FathulBari,* ix:12; see also al-Bukhari, al-Quran, hadith no. 4986.)

Note the usage of the word 'gathered' rather than 'written'. Commenting on this, al-Khattabi says, "This quote refers to [the lack of] a specific book with specific traits. **The Quran had indeed been written down in its entirety during the Prophet's lifetime**, but had not been collected together nor were the suras arranged. (As-Suyuti, *al-Itqdn,* i:164.) (as quoted from http://www.islamicsearchcenter.com/library/quran/History_of_the_Quranic_Text_from_Revelation_to_Compilation.pdf)

How you characterize or define a 'book'? It is a number of pages of written or printed work bound together between two covers. In the strict usual perception of a book as we have, Prophet Muhammad(pbh) did not present to his companions the revelations collected and arranged in a single written volume, in book form. There are a number of good reasons for this:

The revelations did not come down in one continuous piece, but at intervals and was received continually until the end of the Prophet's life. As we know and we have indicated this earlier, the Quranic passages were revealed as per changing situations going on in the life of the prophet and his companions. At times, there might be occasions when situations demanded directives simultaneously for two or more quite diverse spheres of life such as war going on and at the same time certain family problem arose in the society. In such cases when the Prophet received revelations, he used to direct the scribes to put the latest passage in such and such Surah, in between or after or before certain verse. Thus in a sense he was editing of the Quran at the same time. The Companions adhered to these sequences in their daily prayers and in memorizing the Book.

As the Prophet himself was not sure as to when the revelations would come to an end so he was in no position to compile and arrange the Quran in a final Book form. The Prophet lived only nine days after the last revelation to him. The matter of leaving no book by him should not be "misplayed" as the *whole revelation* was assuredly there in written form penned on different writing materials and most importantly in the hearts of many of his followers.

15

Translation of the Quran is not the Quran, why?

For those Muslims or non-Muslims who are new to the sciences of the Quran it is a word of caution that the *translation of this Book is* NOT THE QURAN. Why so?

When a translation is done into another language, the translator in fact interprets the meaning and renders it in the new language. It is, by nature, an approximation of the meaning, since words and ideas cannot be expressed identically in different languages. This is a case with any book; the problem is manifolds in case of the Quran in Arabic. A translator faces difficulties at two stages: at first he has to grasp the real meaning of the Arabic word and absorb the nuances of the word, pick up one of the various shades of meaning of the word, understand the context of the verse in which that particular shade of meaning fits. Second, he must be well-versed in the language in which the translation is being made and there again he must be cautious in choosing a pertinent word.

Arabic is a very rich language, and words have many shades of meanings. Thus in many languages it often requires more alertness to get the meaning across, sometimes very difficult to pick up one word of another language to encompass an Arabic word conveying different shades of meaning. Sometimes such statements sound hollow and boastful to outsiders therefore I try to clarify this with an example or two: There is a chapter no. 64 in the Quran named **"TAGHABUN"**, what does this word mean? The famous exegetist A.A. Mududi explains (http://www.islamicstudies.info/tafheem.php?sura=64&verse=1&to=10):

"The word yaum-ut-taghabun (the day of taghabun) as used in the original is too vast in meaning to be explained in a word, or even a sentence, of any other language. Of all the names of the Resurrection that occur in the Quran, this name probably is the most meaningful therefore, a little explanation is necessary to understand its meaning.

'Taghabun' is from 'ghabn', which can be pronounced both as ghabn and as ghaban. Ghabn is mostly used concerning commercial and business transactions and ghaban concerning opinion. Lexically, it has other meanings also, e.g. heedlessness, forgetfulness, a person's being deprived of his share, a man's harming another inadvertently in business or mutual dealing, etc.

The derivative 'taghabun' implies the occurrence of 'ghabn' between two or more persons. Thus, taghabun al-qaum means some people's treating others fraudulently or a person's harming another person and the other's being harmed and damaged by him, or one's taking away the share of another and the other's being deprived of his share, or a person's incurring loss in business and another's gaining a profit, or some people's proving heedless or weak-minded in comparison to others.

Now consider that in this verse it has been said about the Resurrection: 'That will be a Day of **taghabun (mutual loss and gain)** among the people." These words automatically give the meaning that in the world taghabun is a common thing, but this taghabun is superficial and deceptive, not the real and factual taghabun the real taghabun will take place on the Day of Resurrection. There it will become manifest as to who actually incurred the loss and who actually earned the profits, who actually was deceived and who proved to be prudent and sensible. who actually had invested aII his life capital in a wrong bargain and become bankrupt and who had invested aII his energies and abilities. wealth and time, in a good bargain and earned aII the benefits and gains. which the former also could have earned had he not been deceived in understanding the truth about the world."

Example of other Words

There is a word **"kafara"** the derivative of which is "kafir", an infamous word among some people. The famous translator Abdullah Yusuf Ali explains: "the root *Kafara* has many shades of meanings: (1) to deny Allah's goodness, to be ungrateful, (2) to reject Faith, deny His revelation,(3) to blaspheme, to ascribe some limitation or attribute to Allah which is derogatory to His nature, In a translation, one shade or another must be put forward according to the context, but all are implied".

The way in which the fundamental meaning of a root can be brought to light by the practical use of the word by desert Arabs is best illustrated by another example:

[Quran 2:153] **God is with those who are patient.** (innallaha ma'assabireen)

Sabr, commonly translated as patience, is usually applied to a situation from which an individual cannot escape, leading to desperation and helplessness. When there is no hope of actively affecting the situation, the advice given is "have patience," to the extent that even someone suffering great injustice at the hands of another, when he can do nothing to improve the situation, he calms his inner struggle through the magic of "patience." In other words, this interpretation of "sabr" carries a connotation of passivity.

The root meaning of Sabr, however, is constantly and continuously to struggle towards a goal or purpose, to stand steadfastly. This root meaning is derived based on its usage by the desert Arabs in their daily lives. In other words, a connotation of activity.

Need of Knowledge of Arabic as well as Target Language

Another concern is the translator's familiarity with the target language. Some translations are done by individuals who are very knowledgeable in Arabic, but they are not able to render the intended meaning because they are not familiar with the nuances of the other language

Effect of Ill Motive or Absence of Alertness

Every word of the Quranic text is meticulously chosen, chiselled and placed by the All-Wise Himself. They carry

God's 'fingerprint', and are signs of God. But in the translation one can easily twist the meaning if he harbours ill motive or keeps himself not alert even he happens to be sincere. Here is an example:

1. And among His signs is this, that He created for you mates from among yourselves that *you may dwell in tranquillity with them*. And He has put love and mercy between your (hearts): verily in that are signs for those who reflect. (*emphasis added*) Translation by A Yusuf Ali [Quran 30:21]

2. And one of His signs it is, that He hath created wives for you of your own species that you may dwell with them, and hath put love and tenderness between you. Herein truly are signs for those who reflect (*emphasis added*) Translation by Rev. J.M. Rodwell (M.A.)

3. By another sign He gave you wives from among yourselves, that you might live in joy with them, and planted love and kindness into your hearts. Surely there are signs in this for thinking men (*emphasis added*) Translation by N.J. Dawood.

The first example is from the translation by Yusuf Ali, a Muslim. The second is by a Christian priest the Rev. Rodwell and the last example is by an Iraqi Jew, N.J. Dawood.

The Arabic word in the Quran for underlined translation is "li-tas-kunu ilaihaa". See the above translations and compare with the following that by George Sale who made no secret of his antagonism to the holy book of Islam. In his preface to his translation in 1734 he made it known that it was his avowed intention to expose the man Mohammad and his forgery. He records: "who can apprehend any danger from so manifest a forgery?

"And of his signs another is, that he had created you, out of yourselves, wives *that you may* ***cohabit*** *with them*, and hath put love and compassion between you"[Quran 30:21] see the meaning of "cohabit" in **'Wordweb'**—" Share living quarters; usually said of people **who are not married** and live together as a couple. Certainly this translation is unacceptable".

Translation of Scientific Statements

Translation of the scientific statements in the Quran needs more attention. It needs that the translator, apart from being well equipped with the above discussed qualities, be well versed in the scientific background of the words or the statement of the verse under consideration.

Lack of knowledge of even elementary biology has caused widespread fault in translating a famous verse, "khalaqal insane min alaq". Check these well known translations: [Quran 96:2] (Asad) created man out of germ cell, [Quran 96:2] (Y. Ali) created man, out of mere clot of congealed blood, [Quran 96:2] (Pickthall) created man from a clot, [Quran 96:2] (Ahmad Ali) created man from a clot, [Quran 96:2] (Raza Khan) created man from a clot of congealed blood, [Quran 96:2] (Maududi) created man from a clinging substance and [Quran 96:2] (Sarwar) created man from a clot of blood.

Most of the translators have translated "alaqa" as 'clot of blood' – indeed it is one of many meanings of this word as given in "A Dictionary of Modern Arabic by Hans Wehr", - see p 634: most of the meanings are: 'to hang, be suspended, to stick, cling and as noun: medicinal leech, coagulated blood clot. No medical doctor will accept that the origination of man is a blood-clot.

Then from medical point of view what should be the correct translation. See what **Dr Maurice Bucaille**, himself a medical doctor says in his famous book "The Bible, the Quran and Science":

"The implantation of the zygote in the uterus (womb) is the result of the development of villiosities, veritable elongations of the zygote, which, like roots in the soil, draw nourishment from the thickness of the uterus necessary to the zygote's growth. *These make the zygote literally cling to the uterus. This is a discovery of modern times.* **'Something which clings' is the (actual) translation of the word 'alaq'**. It is the original meaning of the word." (p 204)

Further he writes and indeed the following statement is to be read with due attention:

"In fact there are still many translations in circulation today that can give a completely misleading idea of the Quranic revelation on this subject to the scientist who reads them. The majority of Translations describe, for example, man's formation from a 'blood clot' or an 'adhesion'. A statement of this kind is totally unacceptable to the scientists specializing in this field. In the paragraph dealing with the implantation of the egg in the maternal uterus, we shall see the reasons why *distinguished Arabists who lack a scientific background have made such blunders.* ***This observation implies how great the importance of an association between linguistic and scientific Knowledge is when it comes to grasping the (true) meaning of Quranic statements on reproduction." (p 200)***

Concluding Remarks

(*i*) The above descriptions in no way should make one afraid of the translations and be contended with only reciting the Quran in Arabic without understanding it; going to this extreme would be a wrong decision. What is required is to be alert in selecting a good translation. It is quite clear that this quest depends on one's inclination and bent of mind as to how deep he wants to dig into the Quran.

(*ii*) On the contrary this begs a question: does knowing Arabic mean one can understand the Quran? Its answer is 'no'.

(*iii*) Here one more doubt arises: The Quran claims to be a Guide-Book for all mankind then should its guidance must not be understandable in all languages? Its answer is yes.

What I wrote above, the hurdles encountered in translating the Quran and the pitfalls one should be aware of while reading a translation are true but at the same time it must be clarified that "Guidance" from this Book is quite a different thing. Does the guidance depend only on knowing the original Arabic language? No.

The disbelievers of Makkah were expert in the language of the Quran, but they did not understand many of the concepts and similitudes of the Quran. They thus rejected it as being words of a madman. What one needs to comprehend is that understanding the Quran means to understand correctly what is being told in the verses, the concepts, the lessons, the signs, admonitions metaphors and imagery. All of these aspects of the Quran hold true regardless of the language used. When one does not understand the Quran, that is, makes erroneous interpretations, he is incapable of understanding these lessons, admonitions and true purposes of the verses. **One may even be in possession of great Arabic skills, yet be incapable of understanding the verses due to his or her lack of comprehension of what is being told in the verses. Comprehension is something else; it depends on one's sincerity, purity in intention and perseverance and above all "opening of the windows of heart" by Allah.** When the verses of the Quran are explained to such a sincere person by another true knowledgeable believer in his own language, he grasps them correctly, even though he does not know Arabic. An overall guidance can easily be gathered by a good translation however to go deep into the inner meanings, to gather an insight of a word, phrase or similitude one must have the knowledge of Arabic.

Another aspect of sticking to the Arabic Text of the Quran along with the translation is to maintain the purity of the Text of the Book ; it is quite another discussion and this should not be confused at this place; I have discussed it in another chapter " Distinguishing Features of the Quran among World Scriptures".

An Extra Note:

Despite all difficulties **THERE IS A NEED OF TRANSLATION OF THE QURAN** and scholars have translated it in various major languages of the world and they are available in bookshops and in the internet as well. However one should be careful in the selection of a translation. The English translations by Abdullah Yusuf Ali, Muhammad Pickthall and Muhammad Asad are popular translations. See these translations in the following site, here you will find a good tool for search of verses: http://www.islamicity.com/QuranSearch/, www.islam101.com/quran.

Saheeh International (also spelled "Sahih") is a well-known English translation of the Holy Quran by three American female converts. Saheeh International checked many previous translations verse by verse against accepted Arabic tafsir and revised the wording accordingly in clear, contemporary English. This is available in many sites: http://www.faithinallah.org/sahih-international-translation-of-the-holy-quran/ and http://www.saheeh-international.com/

Maulana Maududi's translation and commentary on the Quran **"The Meaning of the Quran"** (originally written in Urdu then rendered into many languages) ranks as one of the best such works in existence today. Unlike many early translators, Maududi uses the standard technique of providing an explanation of the Quranic verses from the Sunnah of the Prophet including the historical and logical reasons behind the verses and **the way of presentation is quite adaptable to modern day educated Muslims and non-Muslims alike**. Maududi's introductions to each chapter of the Quran are very informative and have been used in many web sites.

TAFHEEM-ENGLISH

http://www.quranenglish.com/tafheem_quran/

TAFHEEM-URDU

http://www.tafheemonline.com/tafheem.asp?mode=search&show=intro&s=001&r=1, www.islamicity.com, http://aapkaislam.com/quran-translations.html. It is a very good site, many translations are available here.

"The Meaning of the Quran (Lahore, 1967), the English version of Sayyid Abul A'la Maududi's magnum opus, the Urdu Tafhim al-Quran is an interpretative rendering of the Quran which remarkably succeeds in recapturing some of the majesty of the original. Since Maududi, a great thinker, enjoyed rare mastery over both classical and modern scholarship, his work helps one develop an understanding of the Quran as a source of guidance. Apart from setting the verses/Suras in the circumstances of its time, the author constantly relates, through exhaustive notes, the universal message of the Quran to his own time and its specific problems. His logical line of argument, generous sensibility, judicious use of classical Muslim scholarship and practical solutions to the problems of the day combine to show Islam as a complete way of life and as the Right Path for the whole of mankind." (Dr Rafiq Zakaria: The Quran and Muhammad (pbh) - a Penguin Publication).

16

Distinguishing Features of the Quran among the World Scriptures

All divine scriptures of the world have played significant roles, guiding mankind in different lands in different ages; their adherents are still living under their cool and comfortable shades. By describing the distinguishing features of the Quran, we in no sense, mean to denigrate any other scriptures: the comparison is just academic.

No Intermediary Needed Between the Quran and God

The Quran is the only book accessible to everyone without barricades directly linking its reader to God, no intermediary, no priest needed in between. The Quran teaches its readers directly in plain words, what to do and what not to do.

The novelty of the above fact of the Quran may be evaluated in relative terms when one comes to know that Vedas were forbidden to be 'read' even 'heard' by general masses. At times people of lower strata of the society were penalized for reading or even hearing the Vedas. Reading and learning the Vedas was exclusively reserved for the elite class of Brahmins and Acharyas.

The Most Recited Book

Apart from general instruction to read the Quran whenever one desires, the believers are commanded to recite a portion of it however small but a minimum of three verses, in their daily-five-time prayers. So the Book does not remain exclusive to a higher plane of the elite and scholars of the society but it comes down to the general masses. All over the globe, the daily five times obligatory prayers are being held, so at any point of time a portion of this book is being chanted in some where some corner of the world.

No doubt other religious scriptures are also recited but for comparative analysis we may point out that there is no such binding on the adherents to recite daily at least a portion of it and that too five times a day.

System of Memorization: Unique System of "Oral Preservation"

Right from the time the Quran was revealed; the Prophet very sagaciously established a system (not just recommendation) of *"memorization"* of the Book. There are many scholars called Hafiz (memorizer) who memorize the whole Book, start to end. The number of those who memorize 'some' parts of the Quran, some passages here some there, is innumerable, practically the same as equal to the number of Muslims living on the face of earth because each Muslim, man or woman, youth or old, *has to recite some portions of it in their daily five time prayers*.

Look at another aspect: the way the Muslims deal with the Quran the world over: it is recited by them in prayers, held in congregation, led by an 'Imam', reciting loudly and others standing in rows behind him listening silently. This is the daily practice but in the month of Ramadan the entire Quran is recited. Now the remarkable point is this that during *the prayer if the Imam makes a mistake, any of the persons behind him is entitled to point out the mistake then and there and correct him. This practice has been going on for the last fourteen hundred years.* ***This is a unique process of 'Oral Preservation'***. There has not been any such system among the adherents of other scriptures.

Easy to Memorize

We can call it a miracle that the Quran is easily "memorized". There is a verse Allah says we have made it easy to remember.

[Quran 54:17] "And We have indeed made the Quran easy to understand and remember: then is there any that will receive admonition?"

This is repeated four times in the same chapter: 54:22-32-40.

As told above, those who commit to memory the entire Quran, along with all the accent and punctuation marks, are called the 'Hafiz' or the 'Preservers'. They are not monks or priests given to shun the world and devote themselves to the study and practice of religion rather, they are ordinary men and come from all walks of life. Some of them may be doctors, engineers, lawyers, businessmen, artisans and farmers. No one, not even a single person has ever memorized any other book in the world, religious or secular, scientific or spiritual. This is a striking difference between the Quran and the rest of the books of the world. *The Quran is the only book in the history of mankind that has been committed to memory in its entirety. Today there are hundreds of thousands, if not millions, of people who can recite the entire Quran by memory in its original rhyme and order.*

It is a common experience in Muslim community to find small kids of age ten or so who have memorized the Quran in full and *the amazing part is this that their native tongue is different from Arabic: they don't understand yet they do memorize.*

It can never become extinct, even if all of its written copies are destroyed. The 'hafiz' would be able to reproduce the entire text from memory. The Quran is immortalized in this manner, and preserved for posterity. Such an extraordinary phenomenon is nothing short of a miracle!

In case of other Scriptures there may be a few who might have memorized their scriptures in full. I am unfortunate that I have not met with or heard of a single such memorizer-scholar of other sacred books like Bible, Torah or Veda.

Original Language of the Quran Remains Unchanged

The Quran was revealed in Arabic, the same language which has existed till date without any interlude of time being 'non- existent' from the world.

For a comparison see what happened to other scriptures

(*i*) The Vedas are written in Sanskrit, they are claimed to be given to man since the dawn of the world and they were revealed to not a single person but to several sages through different passages of time, so how one can claim with certitude that all through, the language of the people in the vast land of India in different ages remained the same as today's Sanskrit. This doubt is multiplied by the fact that even today with all the facilities available this language is unfortunately not spoken even in a single township.

(*ii*) Somewhat similar is the case with Torah and 'Psalm' and the books of the Old Testament. They were revealed in different time periods, and compiled by some other scholars in different periods. The history tells that there was a period after 'first diaspora' that the 'Book' was lost when Israelis were driven out of Jerusalem and many years afterwards Prophet Ezra got it compiled from different sources. (see the detail in http://en.wikipedia.org/wiki/Torah)

(*iii*) The original book revealed to Christ was not in Hebrew of today but in a dialect of Hebrew, sometime called 'Aramaic'. It was compiled by not Christ but by some other persons much after he was out of scene and that too not in Hebrew but in Greek language; thus the New Testament is also not available in the Original language of Christ. (http://en.wikipedia.org/wiki/Bible)

The Quran is the only book that has a distinction of being preserved in its original language.

(*iv*) This Quranic experience is intertwined through Arabic literature and civilization and, in an extended fashion, through the arts and civilization of other non-Arab Islamic societies. Quranic calligraphy, the visual manifestation of the Quran, is the basis for Arabic calligraphy and one of the most distinctive features of Islamic architecture. Quranic inscriptions can be found on almost any major work of architecture, offering yet another form of remembrance (**dhikr**). Almost all of the major works of art in the Islamic world draw on Quranic allusion.

Language of the Quran as Lingua Franca

The Quran is in Arabic that is lingua franca of people scattered over a large area of the globe. Another important aspect not to be overlooked is this that Muslims of all over the world, whatever may be their lingua franca; they use Arabic for daily prayers. The modern written language Modern Standard Arabic is derived from the language of the Quran (known as Classical Arabic or Quranic Arabic). It is widely taught in schools, universities, and used to varying degrees in workplaces, government and the media. The two formal varieties are grouped together as Literary Arabic, which is the official language of 26 states and the liturgical language of Islam. Modern Standard Arabic largely follows the grammatical standards of Quranic Arabic and uses much of the same vocabulary. (See Wikipedia http://en.wikipedia.org/wiki/Arabic_language)

No original language of other scriptures is now used as lingua franca (After creation of Israel in 1948, now Hebrew is being tried to implement there. "As of now, there are two official languages in Israel - Hebrew and Arabic. *The language Hebrew, which became extinct for centuries, as it was not spoken after the biblical times, has been revived in the late 19th century*. The language now is the most widely spoken language in Israel" —quoted from: AsiaRooms.com)

Challenge of the Quran

Diction, rhythm, style and a vast number of subjects dealt with and many of the scientific descriptions which proved true, all these make the Quran unparalleled, so much so that it throws challenge to all, to bring a book or even a verse equivalent in diction and structure of it and to show any discrepancy in it.

[Quran 2:23] And if you doubt any part of what We have, bestowed from on high, step by step, upon Our servant [Muhammad (pbh)], then produce a surah of similar merit, and call upon any other than God to bear witness for you -if what you say is true!)

[Quran 2:24] And if you cannot do it-and most certainly you cannot do it-then be conscious of the fire whose fuel is human beings and stones which awaits all who deny the truth! –

[Quran 4:82] "Do they not ponder the Quran (with care)? Had this book been from anybody but Allah, you would have found many inconsistencies."

It is usual for any author of a book to implore its readers to find any discrepancy in his book and suggest him modification required at any place. But the author of the Quran not only does not ask such things but contrary to all usual manners throws challenge to its readers to find any discrepancy in the book. This sends a shock wave in the reader's mind.

There is no such challenge from any of the other religious scriptures.

The Scientific Descriptions in the Quran

There are a number of scientific descriptions in the Quran; they are so pertinent and compatible to the latest knowledge in various fields of Science that make one simply amazed. Many examples we have cited in other chapters mainly, in the chapter "The Scientific Descriptions of the Quran", one is required to see these there. Descriptions of 'Gender determination is based on the semen of man and woman's ovum has no role in it' the 'Space is not Vacuum but filled with Interstellar gas and dust' 'the fetus inside the womb is behind three veils (layers)' are knowledge of only the recent times.

This feature places the Quran on a prominent position among the world Scriptures.

Inseparation of Physical and Spiritual Spheres of Human Life

As opposed to other religious scriptures the Quran strongly puts its view that the two needs of man physical and spiritual are amalgamated and are in no way separate. According to the Quranic thesis of life a man is a whole time slave to Allah, every action of his, even fulfilling the sex desires, if done according to the injunctions of the Quran and guidance of the Prophet, is an act of 'ibaadah' (submitting to Allah) for which act he will be rewarded in the hereafter. There are numerous sayings of the Prophet that a man who toils hard to earn livelihood for himself and his wife and children will be highly rewarded. As indicated in the verse (3:190-191) even doing research in the field of Astronomy, a physical science, is rewarding and spiritually pleasing act in the sight of Allah. This feature makes the Quran unique among all scriptures.

An Extra Note: Why Many of the Scriptures Changed?

There are many factors; we indicate some of them below:

(*i*) Since scribes had to make copies by hand, inadvertent errors often slipped by into the scriptures. Subsequent scribes, then copied the errors of oversight as the word of God, and the mistakes multiplied.

(*ii*) Books could not withstand the pressures of time. They were easy targets during periods of persecution. Scribes copied them one at a time, and the process was painstaking and slow. It took weeks, if not months to produce a single copy, but only minutes to burn an entire roomful of books to ashes. Throughout history, libraries have been ransacked and razed and books have been banned, burnt and banished. Countless number of books have become extinct over the years. They have been lost during forced migrations and exodus due to war, famine, and disease.

(*iii*) Sometimes overzealous defenders of faith interpolated verses to make it more defendable and palatable to the people. This they did with good intention but could not imagine the fatal consequences it cast on the Book.

(*iv*) Sectarian and internecine struggle muddied the Book. All sects fiddled with the text to foster their own beliefs. Counterfeit and corrupted copies of the text crept into circulation, and threw doubt on the validity of all versions.

(*v*) Sometimes kings and rulers appointed councils to alter and edit portions of a Book to cater their own whims and suite their actions. With the absolute power of the state at their disposal, they canonized their own concoction of verses and issued edicts banning all other versions.

How the Quran Could Withstand the Above Mentioned Pressures?

Three systems worked simultaneously right from the day of the first revelation to the Prophet:

(*i*) **Oral transmission**

A unique system of 'memorization' was institutionalised, even the way of utterance of each word was categorised. Muslims males or females, kids or youth, all were inspired to memorise at least some portions of the Quran. Many sayings of the Prophet are there in which he foretells of glad tidings to those who memorise the Quranic verses.

(*ii*) **Written transmission**

The Prophet started to get the verses written right from the first day. Despite scarce writing materials and dearth of scribes, he took utmost care to get each revealed verse in writing, in its proper place in a chapter and he further directed to recite these in daily prayers in the sequence prescribed by him; the same sequence as we see in the Quran today.

(*iii*) **Recitation loudly in three out of five daily prayers**

The five daily prayers were institutionalised to be held in congregation. The leader of the congregation, called 'Imam' who happens to be a Hafiz (memorizer of the whole or part of the Quran) stands in leading position and all others behind him in rows, shoulder to shoulder. If the Imam commits any mistake in reciting, any one behind him is entitled to point out it and the Imam has to re-recite that verse; such is an unique system followed all over the Islamic world.

These three systems have worked well as guards to check the inflow of any deliberate or inadvertent material in the Quran. (A detailed discussion on this subject is given in a separate chapter "Preservation and Authenticity of the Quran")

17

The Quran and Muhammad (pbh) under the scanner of the Orientalists

Any person embarking on a study of the Quran, especially if using books and articles written in European languages, should be aware of the seemingly inherent distortions that permeate almost all writings on the Quran and the Prophet. At least since the Middle Ages, Islam has been much maligned and severely misinterpreted in the West. There are reasons for this bias: a very important reason is historical one.

As Islam came out of Arabian Peninsula, it confronted Christianity; Jerusalem and Damascus, the seat of Christianity and home of Paul were easily taken, Byzantine Empire was shaken, within a short span of time Muslims were knocking the doors of Europe. After the entrance of Caliph Umar to Jerusalem in 637 the city's Muslim masters exhibited a high level of religious tolerance. The situation remained stable for over 400 years. Then, in the latter part of the 11th century, the Turks swarmed westward out of Central Asia overrunning all that lay in their path. Jerusalem fell to them in 1076 and the balance of peace was disturbed. In response to Pope Urban II with the call of a conference at the city of Clermont, France in 1095, a series of crusades was started that lasted for centuries; that sowed the seeds of animosity and hatred in the hearts of Europeans that persists till now, even after the waves of secular ideas swept over the West.

I feel that an elegant summary of the West's ignorance of Islam and the motives of Orientalism are the following words by the Swiss journalist and author, Roger Du Pasquier:

❖ The West, whether Christian or dechristianised, has never really known Islam. Ever since they watched it appear on the world stage, Christians never ceased to insult and slander it in order to find justification for waging war on it. It has been subjected to grotesque distortions the traces of which still endure in the European mind. Even today there are many Westerners for whom Islam can be reduced to three ideas: fanaticism, fatalism and polygamy.

One symptom of this ignorance is the fact that in the imagination of most Europeans, Allah refers to the divinity of the Muslims, not the God of the Christians and Jews; they are all surprised to hear, when one takes the trouble to explain things to them, that 'Allah' means 'God', and that even Arab Christians know Him by no other name.

Islam has of course been the object of studies by Western orientalists who, over the last two centuries, have published an extensive learned literature on the subject.

Nevertheless, however worthy their labours may have been, particularly in the historical and philological fields, they have contributed little to a better understanding of the Muslim religion in the Christian or post-Christian milieu, simply because they have failed to arouse much interest outside their specialised academic circles. ***One is forced also to concede that Oriental studies in the West have not always been inspired by the purest spirit of scholarly impartiality, and it is hard to deny that some Islamicists and Arabists have worked with the clear intention of belittling Islam and its adherents***. This tendency was particularly marked for obvious reasons in the heyday of the colonial empires, but it would be an exaggeration to claim that it has vanished without trace.

These are some of the reasons why Islam remains even today so misjudged by the West, where curiously enough, Asiatic faiths such as Buddhism and Hinduism have for more than a century generated far more visible sympathy and interest, even though Islam is so close to Judaism and Christianity, having flowed from the same Abrahamic source. *Despite this, however, for several years it has seemed that external conditions, particularly the growing importance of the Arab-Islamic countries in the world's great political and economic affairs, have served to arouse a growing interest of Islam in the West, resulting for some in the discovery of new and hitherto unsuspected horizons. (From* ***Unveiling Islam****, by Roger Du Pasquier, pages 5-7)*

The feeling that there is a general ignorance of Islam in the West is shared by Maurice Bucaille, a French doctor, who writes:

When one mentions Islam to the materialist atheist, he smiles with a complacency that is only equal to his ignorance of the subject. In common with the majority of Western intellectuals, of whatever religious persuasion, he has an **impressive collection of false notions about Islam**. One must, on this point, allow him one or two excuses. Firstly, apart from the newly-adopted attitudes prevailing among the highest Catholic authorities, Islam has always been subject in the West to a so-called 'secular slander'. Anyone in the West who has acquired a deep knowledge of Islam knows just to what extent its history, dogma and aims have been distorted. One must also take into account the fact that documents published in European languages on this subject (leaving aside highly specialised studies) do not make the work of a person willing to learn any easier. (From **The Bible, the Quran and Science**, by Maurice Bucaille, page 118)

Other than the Orientalists, today, most Muslims in the West would probably agree that the majority of distortions about Islam come from **the media**, whether in newspapers, magazines or on television channels, of whom some are famous for their notoriety. In terms of the number of people who are reached by such information, the mass media certainly has more of a widespread impact on the West's view of Islam than do the academic publications of *"Orientalists"*, *"Arabists"* or *"Islamicists"*. Certainly, not all Western writings on Islam have the same degree of bias, they run the range from wilful distortion to simple ignorance and there are even a few that could be classified as sincere efforts by non-Muslims to portray Islam in a positive light. However, even most of these works are plagued by seemingly unintentional errors, however minor, due to the author's lack of Islamic knowledge. In the spirit of fairness, it should be said that even some contemporary books on Islam by Muslim authors suffer from these same shortcomings, usually due to a lack of knowledge, heretical ideas and or depending on miss-guided sources.

There is another dimension of "Orientalism", in the words of Edward Said, a renowned Arab Christian scholar and author of several books exposing shortcomings of the Orientalist approach, explains: - the academic study of the Oriental East by the Occidental West was often motivated and often co-operated hand-in-hand with the *imperialistic aims of the European colonial powers*. Without a doubt, the foundations of Orientalism are in the maxim *"Know thy enemy"*. When the Christian Nations of Europe began their long campaign to colonize and conquer the rest of the world for their own benefit, they brought their academic and missionary resources to bear in order to help them with their task.

Actually, quite a few Orientalist scholars were Christian missionaries. One example is that of Sir William Muir, who was an active missionary and author of several books on Islam. Today, these books are viewed as very biased studies, even though they continue to be used as references for those wishing to attack Islam to this very day. (see his views in the book *Orientalism*, by Edward W. Said)

Regardless of the flawed, biased and even devious approach of many Orientalists, they too can have their moments of candour, as Roger Du Pasquier points out:

*In general one must unhappily concur with an Orientalist like Montgomery Watt when he writes that '**of all the great men of the world, no-one has had as many detractors as Muhammad (pbh)**.'* Having engaged in a lengthy study of the life and to understand why this has been the case', finding the only plausible explanation in the fact that for centuries Christianity treated Islam as its worst enemy. And although Europeans today look at Islam and its founder in a somewhat more objective light, '**many ancient prejudices still remain**.' (From Unveiling Islam, by Roger Du Pasquier, page 47 - quoting from W M Watt's **Muhammad (pbh) at Medina**, Oxford University Press)

Now see a few examples of the allegations against the Prophet and the mispresentations of the Quran:

William Muir, one of the widely respected orientalists has made the wildest insinuation that the Prophet (pbuh) was, since his boyhood, a life-long patient of epilepsy of "falling disease."

Rev. J.M. Rodwell has been quoted as saying that,

> *"He (Muhammad (pbh)) was probably, more or less, throughout his whole career, the victim of a certain amount of self-deception. A cataleptic subject from his early youth, born- according to the traditions – of a highly nervous and excitable mother, he would be peculiarly liable to morbid and fantastic hallucination, and alternations of excitement and depression, which would win for him, in the eyes of his ignorant countrymen, the credit of being inspired.."*

R.A. Nicholson is another scholar who seems to propound the religious illusion theory. He says,

> *"Whether we regard it as 'pathological case' or a grand example of mystical ecstasy, the thing outset of his mission a dominating motive can be discerned in his conviction that, the Last Judgment was near and that he must at all costs warn his countrymen of the doom impending."*

Do such types of allegations need clarifications? A book which describes so many scientific facts, historical events unknown to the Arabs then, the injunctions which changed the lives of many, could such a book have been spelt out of the mouth of an epileptic and hallucinated person?

I cite you a very interesting example here; chapter 18 of the Quran answers three questions put to Muhammad (pbh) by the non-believers with consultation with the Jews to test the veracity of the Prophet. One of these questions was "who were the seven sleepers of the Cave and for how long they slept?" This story was completely unknown to the Arabs as it occurred in Ephesus, which was the biggest Roman city and sea-port on the west coast of Asia Minor. The ruins of this city can still be seen 20 to 25 miles south of the modern Turkish city of Izmir. Apart from the details of the sleepers and their beliefs far removed from idolatory, the Quran states:

"So they stayed in their Cave three hundred years and add nine." [Quran 18: 25] The wording is significant. The verses do not say 'three hundred and nine years', but used the apparently cumbersome wording of 'three hundred years and add nine'. Why add nine? This is because their stay was 300 years if one used the solar calendar and 309 years by the lunar calendar. The lunar year is 11 days shorter. Now 11 days times 300 years divided by 365 is 9 years. Just for a moment think how such amazingly accurate calculations can spring from the sub-conscious mind or are these mere products of hallucinations of an illiterate person?

Take another example, an interesting one: the use of word "mulook" in the Quran in the verse 5:20

Allah says in the Holy Quran:

وَإِذْ قَالَ مُوسَىٰ لِقَوْمِهِ يَٰقَوْمِ اذْكُرُوا نِعْمَةَ اللَّهِ عَلَيْكُمْ إِذْ جَعَلَ فِيكُمْ أَنبِيَاءَ
وَجَعَلَكُم مُّلُوكًا وَآتَاكُم مَّا لَمْ يُؤْتِ أَحَدًا مِّنَ الْعَالَمِينَ ⑳

Wa ith qala moosa liqawmihi ya qawmi othkuroo nimata Allahi Alaykum ith **jaala feekum anbiyaa wa jaalakum mulookan** wa atakum ma lam yuti ahadam minal Alameena

This is commonly translated as:

> **"Remember Moses said to his people: "O my people! Call in remembrance the favour of God unto you, when He produced prophets among you and made you kings (mulook), and gave you what He had not given to any other among the peoples."** [Quran 5:20]

Some orientalists allege that the author of the Quran (here the clear indication is to Muhammad (pbh)) erred here for there were no kings/monarchs from amongst the people of Israel before the time of Moses; had this book, the Quran, been from God such clear historical ignorance were not there. Let us examine this charge.

The word "mulook" comes from the word "malak" which means "to own" or "to possess."

John Penrice in his famous Arabic- dictionary writes:

مَلَكَ: To possess, have power or dominion over; to be capable of able to obtain ... مَلِك: One who possess, a king; Plur. مُلُوك

(A Dictionary and Glossary of the Koran, Darul Ishat, Karachi, 1998, p.140) This shows original meaning of "malik" is "one who possesses" and as the monarchs are in a way the possessors of the destiny of the whole nation it is usually used for them.

(see http://www.ghazali.org/arabic/ for many Arabic-English Dictionaries)

Now mark the wordings used in the Quran. It uses "ja'ala **feekum** ambiya" (**He made prophets from amongst you**) which carries the sense that not all of them were blessed with prophethood rather only a few were, and others were required to follow them. But for "mulook" it uses "ja'alakum mulooka" (make a note here "feekum" is not used thus it means "**and made you the mulook**". It means all of them were made 'mulook'. Naturally all could not be made kings; here the original meaning of the word is most befitting: to the children of Israel, Allah favoured them and blessed them with wealth and provisions like He did not bless anyone before thus they were made mulook (POSSESSORS) of wealth and provisions.

A similar interpretation is attributed to the Prophet:

قال ابن أبي حاتم..... عن أبي سعيد الخدری، عن رسول الله ﷺ قال : كان
بنو إسرائيل إذا كان لأحدهم خادم ودابة وامرأة، كتب ملكا۔

Ibn Abi Hatim said: Abu Sa'id al-Khudri narrated from the Messenger of Allah –peace and blessings of Allah be upon him:

> **"With the Children of Israel, a person who had a servant, an animal and a wife was counted as a king."** [Ibn Kathir, Tafsir al-Quran al-'Azim, Dar al-Taybah, Beirut 1999 vol.3 p.73]

In Arabic the use of this word 'mulook' was common as possessors of wealth, power and control; see its use by a famous Jew, hostile to Muslims at the time of Muhammad (pbh). Ka'b bin Al-Ashraf, the infamous member of a Jewish tribe around Madinah, who spent his time inciting the Quraish against the Muslims and calling for the murder of the Holy Prophet–peace and blessings of Allah be upon him-, on learning about the killing of the chiefs of the pagans in the Battle of Badr said:

هٰؤُلَاءِ أَشْرَافُ الْعَرَبِ وَمُلُوكُ النَّاسِ

> **"Those were the nobles of Arabia, the kings of the people (mulook-ul-naas)."** [Sirat Ibn Ishaq, Dar al-Fekr, Beirut 1978 vol.1 p.317]

We know that the Quraish were not monarchs however Ka'b understood that they were highly regarded by the rest of the Arabs and they were prosperous due to their guardianship over the Ka'bah.

Also in the Arabic translations of Bible's Book of Revelation the same word is used:

وَجَعَلَنَا مُلُوكًا وَكَهَنَةً

This is given in the Smith & Van Dyke Arabic Bible. (www.bible.is/arzvdv/rev/1/6)

"And has made us kings and priests... " NKJV, Rev. 1:6

Some English Translation of the above verse 5:20

In the light of all these details we can safely conclude that the best English rendering of the meanings of the verse is given in Saheeh International translation. It reads;

"And [mention, O Muhammad (pbh)], when Moses said to his people, "O my people, remember the favour of

Allah upon you when He appointed among you prophets and *made you possessors* and gave you that which He had not given anyone among the worlds."

Likewise Muhammad Asad translates it as;

"And, Lo, Moses said unto his people:" "O my people! Remember the blessings which God bestowed upon you when he raised up prophets among you, and made you your own masters, and granted unto you [favours] such as He had not granted to anyone else in the world."

It is however important to note that even though some well-known translators have used the word "kings" or "princes" in the translation, they did not mean monarchs.

Abdullah Yusuf Ali did use the word "kings" but in his short commentary note he said;

> **"From the slavery of Egypt the Children of Israel were made free and independent, and thus each man became as it were a king."**

- From the above clarifications one can easily conclude that such types of allegations as leveled against Muhammad (pbh) and the Quran are samples of the human weakness that when one is obsessed with someone's animosity then to what abyss one can fall into. After writing such derogatory sentences against a man who changed the course of human history, these so called scholars must be ashamed of their acts. But I have a quite another feeling, very sad and sympathetic one for such people that not only they let themselves fall into darkness but at the same time, by their erroneous actions they lead many of their readers gone astray!

Word of Caution

So a word of caution to the new seekers after the Quran, whether Non-Muslim or ignorant Muslims must be alert while reading various books authored by them, and the materials available now in the Internet. For a review and critique of many of the views of the Orientalists, the interested reader may consult the following works: Mohammad Khalifa, The Sublime Quran and Orientalism (London: Longman, 1983); Muhammad Mohar Ali, The Quran and the Orientalists (Ipswich, England: Jamiyat Ihyaa Minhaaj al-Sunnah, 2004). New Catholic Encyclopedia (Washington: The Catholic University of America, 1981), vol. 1, p. 715. Quoted from Hamza Mustafa Njozi, The Sources of the Quran: A Critical Review of the Authorship Theories (Riyadh, Saudi Arabia: World Assembly of Muslim Youth, 1991), p. 17.

18

Why the Quran is believed to be a divine book?

Some Logical & Rational Answers

Why the Quran is believed to be a divine book?

Why Muhammad (pbh) is believed to be the Messenger of God?

These two questions are interlinked: logically if one is true, the other is necessarily true. As a premise, if it is proved that the Quran is a divine book, revealed by God then it is logically concluded that the man on whom, it is revealed must be the Messenger of God; conversely if it is proved that Muhammad (pbh) is a messenger of Allah and not a liar or imposter then the claim of his that this Book is from God must be accepted: this argument stands the test of logic; we cannot accept the Message and reject the Messenger, or vice versa. Both must be Accepted or Rejected but not realized singly.

We examine the Divine status of the Quran here rationally. Broadly we may divide the discussion in two categories: External factors and Internal factors.

External Factors:

Various differing views and opinions are presented as to the source of the Quran. The following list of "possible" authors reflects the main theories.

- Under "**external factors**" we present an argument which is called in the science of logic "**process of elimination**", where we get to the answer of the question - "Who is the author of the Quran?" - by eliminating all alternative answers to this question which are definitely implausible. In other words, the definite or (at least) most probable author or **the source of the Quran is identified by eliminating unacceptable alternative candidates:**
- Muhammad(pbh)
- Some other Arab poet (s), scholars, etc.
- Some non-Arab scholars, or poets or religious personalities
- Monks or Rabbis (i.e. from the Bible or Judeo-Christian sources)
- God
- If not God then "who"?

1. Did Muhammad (pbh) Author this Book?

Did the man who presented the Book to the world claim that he was the Author? No, never, rather he disclaimed it although it would have been easier for him to announce the authorship. No one in the history of the world has ever claimed to have written the Quran.

But we know that Prophet Muhammad (peace be upon him) was the only Arabian who first presented, preached and practiced this book, so any detractor may argue that **the first possible source of Quran is one who first presented it to the world. Let us examine this**.

"**Muhammad (pbh) was an illiterate person**. This is a historical fact- had he been a literate one; the enemies might have surely raised this doubt?

- ❖ How can an illiterate person come up with such a vastly rich, supremely poetic, overwhelmingly intellectual and an inspiring text that rocked the entire Arabia nay the entire world?
- ❖ Muhammad (pbh) never attended any school, no one ever taught him. He had no teacher on any subject. How could he have the knowledge of all the science, astronomy, oceanography and metaphysics etc. that is contained in the Quran?
- ❖ For the argument's sake, **suppose he was literate and therefore he had a teacher; who was he and what barred that gentleman to come forward to pat his disciple when he achieved the triumph**.
- ❖ Also how is it that the Prophet's detractors in Makkah could not locate that teacher? It was common knowledge in the township of Makkah that the Prophet was illiterate, and *there is no record of the pagan Arabs in Makkah accusing Muhammad (pbh) of* ***not being illiterate***.

- Allah the Almighty also answered this in the Quran, when it says what means: "***And you were not [able] to recite a Book before this [Book came] nor art thou [able] to transcribe it with thy right hand: in that case indeed would the talkers of vanities have doubted.*** Nay here are Signs self-evident in the hearts of those endowed with knowledge: and none but the unjust reject Our Signs." (S.Ankabut 29:48–49).

If Muhammad (pbh) was illiterate as claimed, he might be dictating the Book with the help of his followers?

This doubt raises a very serious question on the truthfulness of his claim to be the Messenger of Allah: what for he claimed that he is a Messenger of God and what for he claimed that he receives revelations of God?

Was he a liar? An imposter ?

Let us examine this doubt purely on logical basis:

What for one lies?

One lies to gain earthly items: land, riches or such things or gain fame, respect and status in the society; Muhammad(pbh), before proclamation of prophet hood at the age of forty, had a loving wife whose established trade he was handling so he had no dearth of riches rather after being prophet he had to pass through famish situations. Similarly his distinguished high character had earned him the name of "AMEEN"(the trustworthy) People of the city often came to him to seek his advice in matters of their problems to get cases of disputes solved.

Need of such a "lie"?

If we were to say that the Muhammad (pbh) claimed

prophet hood for fame, glory and status, we see that what actually occurred was the exact opposite. Muhammad (pbh), before his claim to Prophet Hood, enjoyed a high status in all aspects. He was of the most noble of tribes, of the most noble of families, and was known for his truthfulness. After his claim, he became a social outcast. For 13 years in Makkah, he and his followers faced excruciating torture, which led to the death of some of his followers, ridicule, sanctioning, and excommunication from society.

Is it possible for a liar to be consistent on his lie for a period of 23 years with unwavering certitude. A liar will falter sometimes, somewhere he will make a mistake and will be caught.

Did he lie to unite all Arabs to become a king or political leader? The book he presented shows no such signs; nowhere one can find a single sentence calling Arab nationalism. In fact the Makkans presented him kingship with a condition that he renounce his Call to Islam, this he kicked out unequivocally.

Can a liar withstand turmoil and show conviction for a long period, as the history tell us, that Muhammad(pbh) endured excruciating pains for his Message? It is simple and plain; if one is liar he will try to grab the glory, the wealth and the worldly gains for which he lied. How and why he will endure pain and labour for his lie? (see the detail of this discussion in my book: "INTRODUCING PROPHET MUHAMMAD (pbh)": http://www.docstoc.com/docs/80753781/introducing-Prophet-Muhammad (pbh)--PDF-)

Dearth of Source Materials

It is a matter of common experience that even to prepare a small article one requires a lot of source materials. As we know Makkah then had hardly any **scholarly figure** to make consultations. There was virtually no existence of **library**. In absence of such source materials it is unimaginable for any person, however intelligent, to compose a book like the Quran, covering varied topics.

In case of falsehood on part of Muhammad (pbh) there must be inconsistency in the language of the Quran, the mood of the author must reflect in his writings and there must be discrepancies in the descriptions of the amazing facts of the universe; all such arguments we will examine under the "**Internal Factors**" discussed below.

If some other persons were helping him? Who were they? In a small township of Makkah how they could not be located and exposed by the enemies of Muhammad (pbh)? Moreover, it is just strange that those people never came forward to claim a share in the authorship of the Book after it became prominent.

What the Quran teaches goes DIRECTLY contrary to the pagan Arab culture, religion, and gods, that existed before the Quran was revealed:

(*i*) Quran condemns ***idol worshipping***, but the Arabs, loved their idol Gods, and worshipped them passionately.

(*ii*) Quran raised the ***status of women***; the Arabs treated women next to animals. At the birth of girl child they felt ashamed so much so that **at times they buried**

them alive which the Quran (and Muhammad (pbh)) rebuked in strongest terms.

(*iii*) Quran condemns and prohibits ***taking interest*** on money, whereas, the Arabs freely charged heavy interest rates in loans and businesses.

(*iv*) Quran condemns and prohibits ***Alcohol drinking***, whereas, the Arabs consumed alcohol freely. The Quran condemns and prohibits ***gambling***, whereas, the Arabs were some of the worst gamblers.

Thus we conclude logically: During the time of the Holy Prophet (pbh), the Arabs would indulge in all the social evils that the Quran condemns and prohibits. ***How can Arabs then write something that would negate their entire social norms and beliefs?***

Judeo - Christian Influence?

We subdivide this argument in two sub-sections:

- ❖ Some Jew or Christian person or persons might have helped Muhammad (pbh) in writing the Quran.
- ❖ Muhammad (pbh) might have plagiarised from the Bible.

Let us examine these:

Go through any biography of the Prophet even by his detractors, no one indicates that there was any Jew or Christian family in Makkah; of course in Madinah there were different tribes of Jews, but no one tells that the Prophet had any contact with any Jew before Migration to Madinah.

What they claim is that he met some Christian monks during his trade travel to Syria who taught him all that is written in the Quran. **Does this argument appeal to you?** Check this rationally:

❖ Did those monks give him all materials in book-form or written on such odd materials as scrapes of leathers, thin flat stones, palm branches, wooden pieces, shoulder blades of animals, etc. And all these Muhammad (pbh) carried with him and no other fellow traveller noticed it ! And more importantly he being an illiterate person what he did with these?

❖ If it is argued that the monks gave him ***only oral sermons*** - then the question arises about the lengths of duration of the meetings and about capacity of an illiterate person to acquire and retain it ? And yet again why these meetings were not noticed by any fellow travellers?

❖ *And most important of all, no enemy of Makkah who all the time spied on him to find faults with him, never claimed that Muhammad(pbh) had made some contact with such and such monks and learnt from them what he was uttering after gaining prophet hood.* (To level such trivial charge never occurred to them !)

❖ *After migration to Madinah the Prophet did come in contact with the Jewish people who after a very short initial amicable period became hostile to him, they were all the time in search of some faults to show him down; in that circumstances the allegation that he took help in writing the Quran does not stand.*

Moreover it seems ludicrous that scholars of the Bible or the Torah were helping Muhammad(pbh) in writing the Quran in which there are a number of verses critical of the actions of the scholars of these two scriptures.

> [Quran 2:79] Woe, then, unto those who write down, with their own hands, (something which they claim to be) divine writ, and then say. "This is from God," in order to acquire a trifling gain thereby; woe, then, unto them for what their hands have written, and woe unto them for all that they may have gained.

There are passages that are highly critical of such Jewish and Christian scholars (for example go through [Quran 2:83-116]

Did Muhammad (pbh) plagiarize from the Bible?

This allegation has been raised by many Orientalists and Missionary people. *Moreover in the western countries, among the masses it is a common perception about the Quran that it is just a plagiarized version of the Bible so they see it as a despised and degraded book.*

We examine this allegation here in depth with logical reasoning.

First, to plagiarize from the Bible, Muhammad (pbh) must be:

(*i*) Literate

(*ii*) if not being literate, he must be helped by a band of Biblical scholars.

(*iii*) An Arabic version of the Bible must be available. The first two points we just discussed above and we saw that they don't stand on logical tests. Examine the third option:

a) It is a historical fact that there was no Arabic version of the Bible at the time of Muhammad (pbh) so where from could he could plagiarize it? Check this fact in the Internet:

There was no Arabic translation of the Bible available during the Prophet's time. For a detailed account of this subject, read the article: **'Is The Bible Really The Source of The Quran?** (www.onislam.net/english, www.islamic-awareness.org/sources/bible.html)

Ernst Würthwein informs us in his book, *The Text Of The Old Testament:* "With the victory of Islam the use of Arabic spread widely and for Jews and Christians in the conquered lands it became the language of daily life. This gave rise to the need of Arabic versions of the Bible, which need was met by a number of versions mainly independent and concerned primarily for interpretation." (Ernst Würthwein, The Text Of The Old Testament (Grand Rapids, Michigan: William B. Eerdmans Publishing Company, 1988, pp. 104.)

The New Catholic Encyclopaedia (Vol. 1, pp. 721-72) confirms that during the time of the Muhammad (pbh) :

"The Hijaz [Arabian peninsula] had not been touched by Christian preaching. Hence organisation of the Christian church was neither to be expected nor found."

- The first translations of the Hebrew Bible in Arabic appeared after the advent of Islam. In fact, the oldest dated manuscript of the Old Testament in Arabic dates from the first half of the ninth century that is about *200 years after the death of Muhammad (pbh)*.

➢ The oldest known, dated manuscripts containing Arabic translations of the New Testament are in the collections of St. Catherine's monastery at Mt. Sinai. Sinai Arabic MS 151 contains an Arabic version of the Epistles of Paul, the Acts of the Apostles, and the Catholic Epistles. It is the oldest dated New Testament manuscripts. **The colophon of this MS informs us that one Bisr Ibn as-Sirri made the translation from Syriac in Damascus during Ramadan of the Higrah year 253, i.e., 867 AD**. [Sidney H Griffith, "The Gospel In Arabic: An Enquiry Into Its Appearance In The First Abbasid Century", Oriens Christianus, Volume 69, p. 131-132]

In such a case where from did Muhammad (pbh) get so many details some of which are even absent in the Bible? **If the Quran was 'principally but not exclusively dependent on Jewish and Christian traditions then how one can explain the following important points?**

❖ Some of the Prophets mentioned in the Quran i.e. Hud for the Thamud and Salih for the Aad people are not even mentioned in the Bible.

❖ Information given in the Quran about Prophet Ibrahim, specifically about his teachings on monotheism and the resultant struggle, is not found in the Bible.

❖ There is no mention of: **Jesus speaking from the cradle** confirming the chastity of his mother, his giving life by God's permission to birds made of clay, the table descending from heaven.

- Moses traveling to the "meeting place of two seas".
- The incident of Pharaoh's plan to kill Moses and that a **"believer" in Pharaoh's court** dissuaded him from carrying out his plan.
- **Moses struck the rock and "12 springs gushed forth for each of the Jewish tribes."**
- **The magicians in Pharaoh's court** declare their belief in God after losing the contest with Moses (pbh) and they were killed for it.

All the above accounts are absent in the Bible.

The Quran <u>contradicts</u> the following accounts given in the Bible:

- **Original sin** of Adam and its consequences on mankind which is the very, if not only, basis of the religion of Christianity. It is a common view held in Christendom there is no such concept in the Quran
- That it was originally **Eve who was led astray by Satan** and she in turn made Adam commit the Sin; the Quran contradicts it very clearly at various places and states that *Satan lead* ***both*** *of them astray*.
- The original sin was passed on to the entire human race, due to which man has to toil for his living and the woman has to give birth to the child in pain according to Bible. The Quran specifically states that Adam sought Allah's forgiveness and Allah accepted his supplications and forgave him.
- The angels visiting Ibrahim on their way to Lut;

- ❖ The preaching of Nuh was specifically monotheism according to the Quran;
- ❖ **The Quran categorically denies the concept of Trinity and confirms that Jesus was no more than a Prophet – not god, not the son of god and not the Trinity.**
- ❖ **The Quran categorically states that Jesus was not crucified nor killed.**
- ❖ The Quran states that all the prophets are noble men sent by Allah and clears all of the prophets from evil intention or evil actions, as charged against them in the Bible.
- ❖ The Quran testifies that all the prophets of God such as Musa or Haroun were sincere to their mission for which they were sent by God, and never betrayed their mission as suggested in the Bible, or sinned as in the case of Lut, David, Solomon and others, who according to the Bible are alleged to have committed different sins and some such sins Muslims can never think of about them.

More details are given in the Quran as compared to the Bible:

en.wikipedia.org/wiki/***Biblical***_narratives_and_the_***Quran***

www.worldevangelicals.org/.../pdf/Quran_and_Bible_Compared.

Based on transcripts of various lectures given by Yusuf Estes & Dr. Gary Miller Source: http://islamtomorrow.com/articles/Bible_vs_Quran.asp Undo

It is quite clear from the above discussions that the Qur'ân is not borrowed from the Bible, neither the Old Testament nor from New Testament in Arabic. This point, although not directly, is also mentioned in the Qur'ân. The Qur'ân defends itself from such accusations.

- If, for the sake of discussion we assume that Muhammad (pbh) copied some passages and facts from the Bible, how it is that he did not copy the incorrect information contained in it.
- **Dr Maurice Bucaille** argues this point well in his famous work, "The Bible,TheQuran and Science":
- "Furthermore the scientific errors contained in the Bible - such as those describing man's first appearance on earth, which, as we have seen, may be deduced from the Genealogies that figure in Genesis are not to be found in the Quran.
- Thus, if Muhammad (pbh) were the author of the Quran (a theory upheld by some people), *it is difficult to see how he could have spotted the scientific errors in the Bible dealing with such a wide variety of subjects and have proceeded to eliminate every single one of them* when he came to compose his own text on the same theme".

Internal Evidences

Internal Evidences are based on the statements available in the Quran itself

As to the form of the Quran—i.e., linguistic and literary features - any strict comparative analysis identifies the Quran to be not only superior to any other text - preceding or following, including the sayings of the Prophet himself, who received and delivered the revelation - but also to be a perfect, flawless and the most eloquent composition. This perfection can be witnessed and proved on the levels of the individual words (semantics), sentence (grammar and rhetoric), and whole surahs (chapters). A thorough examination of the Quran shows that each of the words was selected and phrased in the most appropriate manner to fulfil the most precise meaning and most effective impact, whether cognitive, psychological, passionate, or phonetic, on the reader or listener.

1. **The structure and style of the Quran - the absence of inconsistencies.**

The Quran is the book without inconsistencies; one part of its text (or doctrine) does not clash with the other. In fact, it sets the absence of contradiction, irrationality, and incoherence, as one of the criteria for checking the authenticity of any divine revelation. It states "**Do they not ponder the Quran (with care)? Had this book been from anybody but Allah, you would have found many inconsistencies.**" (S-Nisa4:82).

If the allegation against Muhammad (pbh) that he imitated from several books like the Bible, the Torah etc, or that some anonymous persons helped him in supplying the source materials then he must have been adopting a *"pick and choose" technique in writing the Quran. If that had been the case such a technique must have led to a large number of discrepancies. But to the surprise of all there is none.*

2. **The style of the Quran is quite different from that of Muhammad (pbh)'s own speech.**

The people living along with him and observing him all

through long years up to the age of forty when Muhammad (pbh) (pbuh) was bestowed with prophet hood, were accustomed to his own style of talks - *and suddenly they found him uttering a speech quite different. There was a marked difference between the speech of Muhammad (pbh)'s own day to day talk and that of the Quran*. This difference can be seen and checked even today by comparing the narrations of the Quran and the collections of his sayings called "Ahadees".

- It does not make sense that a man may have two UNIQUE, distinguishable and completely different styles of speech in Public. This is yet another reason why Muhammad (pbh) couldn't possibly have written the Quran.
- Quran was revealed over a period of 23 years. A very long period indeed! Is it possible for someone to maintain the same linguistic cadence in his spoken language and the style used in the Quran, which has no match in between them.

3. The mood of the author must reflect on his writings: Test the Quran on this criterion.

As we have described Quranic verses were revealed at different situations and circumstances in the long 23 years of prophet hood. At times, as a human being, Muhammad (pbh) was under much physical and mental stress. it was natural that his anguish would reflect in the Quranic verses if those were written by him.

Take an example. Surah Ahqaf, the 46th chapter of the Quran was revealed at the time of his coming back from Tai'f, a city 65 km from Makkah where he went, after being persecuted and rejected by Makkans in the Year of Sorrow

(***The Year of Sorrow*** The 10th year of the Prophet hood was a year of extreme persecution and distress in the Holy prophet's life. The Quraish and the other tribes had continued their boycott of the Bani Hashim and the Muslims for three years and the Holy Prophet and the people of his family and Companions lay besieged in Shi'b Abi Talib, a valley in Makkah. The Quraish had blocked up this locality from every side so that no supplies of any kind could reach the besieged people; many a times they had to eat even grass and leaves out of hunger. At last, when the siege was lifted this year, Abu Talib, the Holy Prophet's uncle, who had been shielding him for ten long years, died, and hardly a month later his wife, Khadijah, who had been a source of peace and solace for him ever since the beginning of the call, also passed away. Because of these tragic incidents, which closely followed each other, the Holy Prophet used to refer to this year as the year of sorrow and grief.) He went to Taif with a hope to find a refuge there. But therefrom he was compelled to leave. When he was leaving the city, the chiefs of the city set their scoundrels behind him, who went on hurling abuses on him and pelting him with stones for a long way from either side of the road till he was covered with wounds and his shoes were filled with blood. Wearied and exhausted he took shelter in the shade of the wall of a garden outside Ta'if, and prayed:

"O God, to Thee I complain of my weakness, little resource, and lowliness before men. O Most Merciful, Thou art the Lord of the weak, and Thou art my Lord. To whom wilt Thou confide me? To one afar who will misuse me? Or to an enemy to whom Thou hast given power over me? If Thou art not angry with me I care not. Your favour is wider for me. I take refuge in the light of Thy

countenance by which the darkness is illumined, and the things of this world and the next are rightly ordered, lest Thy anger descend upon me or Thy wrath light upon me. It is for Thee to be satisfied until Thou art well pleased. There is no power and no might save in Thee." (Ibn Hisham: A. Guillaume's Translation, p. 193).

Every word of this supplication makes it clear that he as a mortal being, was in much physical and mental stress. *But, amazingly, the Surah al- Ahqaf (46th chapter of the Quran) revealed at the very same time is free from such human feelings. This and other instances in various places of the Quran clearly indicate that Muhammad (pbh) is not the author of this Book.*

Take another example which vividly clarifies the same point : the Revelation of the 48th chapter, "THE VICTORY". The prophet at the seventh year of Hijrah travelled towards Makkah with 1400 of his companions with an intention of performing Umrah in the sacred Kaaba located in Makkah, the home of his blood thirsty enemies. They carried no weapon with them except one traditional sword yet they were barred to enter the city. They were subjected to agree to a treaty which was, outwardly, in total favour of the enemies. The companions of the Prophet felt humiliated and dejected so much so that they did not carry out his orders of offering ritual sacrifices of the camel they had taken with them. This was very shocking to the Prophet; this was the first time in his life that his companions did not even move to carry out his orders.

In such a situation, on the return to Madinah, the **surah Fatah (victory)**, the 48th chapter of the Quran was revealed - the opening line itself declares [Quran 48:1] *"(O Prophet), surely We have granted you a clear victory"*. There was nowhere victory seen. The dejected companions asked what sort of victory is this ? We were debarred from the House of Allah; our sacrificial camels also could not go to their right places; the Holy Messenger of Allah had to halt at Hudaibiyah, and in consequence of this truce two of our oppressed brothers (Abu Jandal and Abu Basir) were handed over to their oppressors."

But this declaration was not from the Prophet but from Allah who knew the Unseen future that victory was surely nigh. Had this been from the authorship of the Prophet, such confident declaration - could not have been pronounced. (Not long after this truce victory began to become manifest, and everyone realized that the triumph of Islam had begun with the treaty of Hudaibiyah. Almost one and the same thing has been related from Abdullah bin Masud, Jabir bin Abdullah and Bara bin Azib. They are reported to have said: The people look upon the conquest of Makkah as the victory, but we regard the truce of Hudaibiyah as the realvictory. (Bukhari, Muslim, Musnad Ahmad, IbnJarir). (http://www.islamicstudies.info/tafheem.php?sura=48)

4. Some Recordings of the Quran hitherto Unknown to the Arabs and some Predictions.

Within the Quran are recorded facts about ancient times that were unknown to Muhammad (pbh)'s contemporaries e.g. the story of Joseph. In certain cases the prediction of the Quran was fulfilled although there was not even an inkling at the time of prediction e.g. victory of Byzantines over Persians after initial defeat (see its detail in the preface of 30th chapter named Rum(v.2-4) "The Romans have been defeated in the neighbouring land; but after their defeat they shall gain victory in a few years. All power belongs to Allah both before and after. On that day will the believers rejoice".

(http://www.quranenglish.com/tafheem_quran/030-1.htm.com by A.A.Maududi)

5. Unique Impartiality in the Quranic Descriptions.

We must consider this factor also, Muhammad (pbh) was an Arab, the Arabs & Jews are noted for their rivalry, and despite this the name of Jesus (a Jew) is mentioned 25 times, Moses far more than this but the name of Muhammad (pbh) in the Quran is mentioned only 4 times. Once again reason dictates that if the Quran was written by Muhammad (pbh) he would favour himself more than others. The mother of Muhammad (pbh) is not mentioned by name even once in the Quran, nor the name of the most loving wife Khadija who supported him at times of distress; far from mentioning their names even no indication is there. Mary the mother of Jesus on the other hand has a whole chapter by her name, the 19th chapter of the Quran. See with what reverence the Quran describes Mary in the following verse: "Behold! The angels said: "O Mary! God has chosen you and purified you - Chosen you above the women of all nations." [Quran-3:42]

The above verse refers to Mary the mother of Jesus (PBUH). Such an honour to Mary is not to be found even in the Christian Bible.

The famous orator ***Ahmad Deedat*** elaborates this point well: The Jews are told in Bible that their father, Abraham, had two wives -Sarah and Hagar. They say that they are the children of Abraham through Sarah, his legitimate wife;

that their Arab brethren have descended through Hagar, a "bondwoman", and as such, the Arabs are of inferior breed.

Will anyone please explain the anomaly as to why Muhammad (pbh) *(if he is the author) chose this Jewess Mary for such honour? The answer is simple – He had no choice - he had no right to speak of his own desire. (He had to submit to The Will of Allah)."* It is no less than an inspiration sent down to him. [Quran, 53:4].

6. Quran's scientific Information.

Let us examine the Quran more closely. Starting with the content, could the knowledge therein have been within the reach of any human source, i.e., the Prophet Muhammad (pbh), his contemporaries, or the whole human civilization and for several centuries ahead? How could a book revealed at that point of history refers —in precise terms—to scientific phenomena and historical events—that were unknown or misunderstood before their subsequent verification?

The Quranic references cover such wide spectrum of topics as the nature of space, relativity of time, the shape and motion of the earth, the role of mountains, water for life, the water cycle, the sources of rivers and groundwater, sea depths, embryology, hygiene and proper health practices, prophecies fulfilled (after revelation), etc.

In scores of verses we find references to scientific wonders, some only recently discovered or confirmed, regarding, the creation of the Universe, certain very fine description related to Biology, cosmology, geography, embryology and meteorology etc.

These we have elaborately explained in a separate chapter (Scientific descriptions in the Quran)

At this place, as an example, we present the following passage from the Quran:

1. Does Man think that he will be left uncontrolled, (without purpose)?
2. Was he not a "Nutfah" of sperm emitted (in lowly form)?
3. Then did he become a clinging "Alaquah"; then did (Allah) make and fashion (him) in due proportion.
4. And of that "Nutfah" He made two sexes, male and female.
5. Has not He, (the same), the power to give life to the dead?

In the above verse, it is "of that "Nutfah" (part of semen) that Allah made the two sexes, male and female. Hence human male is responsible for the birth of a male child or a female child. The human female is not responsible for the sex determination of the child. However, in many nations the woman is blamed for the birth of a female child as in these countries they welcome the arrival of a male child.

The year 1956 is considered to mark the beginning of modern human Cytogenetics. The sex of the foetus is determined by the father's sperm. The female ovum contains only the X chromosomes. If the sperm, or the emitted drop of semen contains the Y chromosome, then the baby will be a male, otherwise the baby will be a female. None of the information as above exists in the Bible or any other religious book. None of this was known until the discovery of genetics in the 20th century. Indeed, in many cultures, it was believed that a baby's sex was determined by the female's body. That was why women were blamed when they gave birth to girls. Thirteen centuries before human genes were discovered, however, the Quran revealed information that denies this superstition, and referred to the origin of sex lying not with women, but with the semen coming from men.

There is no way Prophet Mohammad peace be upon him could have guessed it all 1400 years ago. It had to be a Divine Revelation from Allah Almighty.

7. Theory of Probability applied to the Quran.

Let us discuss the question raised by some sceptics *that Muhammad (pbh) being an intelligent and wise man* ***might have guessed correctly*** *all the facts which are compatible to modern Science.* Is it possible for some person however intelligent to guess correctly so many facts? Let us examine this with mathematical theory of probability.

According to this theory if one guesses one thing out of two, the probability that the guess to be correct is 1/2; that is 50 %.; two separate facts to be correct is 1/2 x 1/2. In terms of percentage it is 25 % chance that he is correct. Continuing on with the example, if the same person now has three situations in which to make blind guesses, then he will only be right one eighth of the time (i.e., one time out of eight or 1/2 X 1/2 X 1/2= $\frac{1}{2}^{3.}$ In terms of percentage it comes 12.5%. Again, the odds of choosing the correct choice in all three situations have decreased his chances of being completely correct to only one time in eight. It must be understood that as the number of situations increases, the chances of being right decrease, for the two phenomena are inversely proportional. ***Thus for 10 situations the guess to be correct is $1/2^{10}$, the percentage to be correct is 0.097 5 %; thus the probability to be correct diminishes.***

Now have a look on the scientific descriptions of the Quran, there are several descriptions in different fields of Science, even if you take 20 such descriptions, the percentage of guess for all to be correct comes next to zero.

It concludes that no human however intelligent can ever describe so many scientific facts all correctly just by guessing.

Conclusion

By 'Logical Process of Elimination' of all the options indicated at the beginning, we come to conclude that the only option left is : 'God'. To some it will be a pleasant conclusion but to many it may be abhorrent. If one agrees with the arguments in eliminating all the options presented above logically but is not ready to accept the one final option left, --- "that the Quran's author must be God" ---

- *Then all principles of logic and rationality demand from him to put forward an 'another option' and present logical arguments in its favour.*

To find an author of the Quran other than God remains a challenge to all sane persons.

As we indicated in the beginning of this article, if either of the two claims: (the Quran is a divine book and Muhammad (pbh) is the Messenger of God) is established, logically it proves the other. If one agrees that the Quran is a

Divine Book then he must submit that the man who presented it to the world must be the Messenger of God. One cannot be understood without understanding the other, one cannot be believed in without believing in the other. The Quran and Muhammad (pbh) are intertwined.

In this article we have shown logical points in favour of this argument. I hope this will satisfy many and at least it will open new windows of knowledge for inquisitive minds.

19

Present day World: Why it needs the Quran?

The modern world of today is living in a NEW DARK AGES. Surprised? How one can dare say such words for this highly progressive, scientific world! Well, I change my words: the modern world is living in a very shining world - so much dazzling that it has made man blind. I know these words also will not be digested but I will explain and show that the modern man is behaving in the same manner as a pagan at the time of Muhammad (pbh). The modern man is harboring a false pride of attaining intelligence and knowledge but in actuality the outcome results of his actions in recent times show just the opposite. Have a look on a few follies of the modern man:

In the Field of Science

- Regardless of all developments of tools, devices and appliances with the help of 'science', the man has not been able to stop the abuse of science in killing 'himself'.

- He could not stop developing nuclear bombs and weapons of mass destructions.
- He is so massively obsessed in procuring 'luxury items' that he could not see what damage he is inflicting upon the eco–systems.

In the Field of Politics

- How many 'wars 'Man has fought after the so called 'Renaissance'? Forget the old ones. What happened in the 'modern world wars' - what for were they fought? If man had become wise ------- why could he not 'avoid' the causes of wars, why he could not suppress his lust for homicide?
- Why the wise men of Germany obeyed Hitler like slaves obey their master?
- Why the wise men of enlightened America did not raise a voice against their 'wisest man' who recklessly decided and ruthlessly dropped Atom Bombs and wiped out a city in minutes?
- For what service of mankind the wise men of America, Russia, Britain and France spent 'unaccountable' amount of huge money in developing thousands of atomic war-heads, the keeping of which in silos 'safely', requires as much fund which can feed people of some hungry countries of Africa for years.
- Pharaoh of Moses, you know but what about modern pharaohs, some mighty countries being able "to gather more power" were clever enough to subjugate the whole world by wielding the 'veto power' in UN;

how many times you have seen, any of these pharaohs stands and kicks out the world opinion ?

- There are more than one cases, from Vietnam, Korea to Palestine, Iraq and Afghanistan when 'enlightened men' of one nation tramples other nation and the "wise men" of the whole world just watch the whole drama dumbfounded like fools ------- offending words?! But sadly true.

In Economics

- Right from the time of Renaissance when man thought himself 'wise enough' he started to subjugate another fellow being economically. You know the history of Europe's industrialization - how "man of today" was compelled to undergo "forced labor" in the wilderness of Siberia and how the very wise man of today is 'robbed' in Wall Street, New York : these are the outcomes of modern economics, man is hanging like a pendulum bulb between the extremes of communism and capitalism.

- How some wise men evolve and experiment new formulae in forms of Globalization 'World Trade, Kyoto Protocol and so on only with the motive of finding ways to subjugate others --------- they are playing games like chess players.

Emancipation of Women

- In the name of liberalization and 'progressive forwardness 'the woman of today is tangled in the web-net of lust engineered very wisely set by the modern man. It is a tragic irony that in the chill of

Northern Europe, the woman is pampered to keep her body half-clad or one fourth clad while her male admirers enjoy dressing to the full.

- ❖ There are chains of stories in almost all western families of home- breaking and sexual harassment of the women. Women alone are victims of onslaughts at homes, at work sites and even on roads and elevators.
- ❖ With all loud claims of reaching zenith of intellect the man could not learn how to behave with women.
- ❖ The man thought he has acquired much knowledge and power and in his vanity he literally shed off the so-called "shackles of religion" and ran in quest of freedom--- unlimited freedom! But what is freedom? Freedom from what? And freedom to do what? Does the eagle pin to swim in a sea? Does the fish long to dance in air? Such freedom is lethal. We must know the bounds of freedom as per our nature we are created.

The lesson is simple: MAN as such has not changed, his instinct, aspirations, lust, and all his qualities and shortcomings have not changed. With all his 'wisdom' and 'knowledge' acquired through advancement of science he requires to be guided by His creator -------- here comes the role to be played by the Quran. The Quran? Yes but unfortunately so much has been said against 'Religion' as such and more against 'the Quran' that at first it seems a call of an insanity but it is the call of real prudence; and Man has to come back to it one day.

Broadly, we divide the problems, man of today are facing, in two categories: <u>Individual problems</u> and <u>Collective problems</u>.

Individual Problems

- Man today is maddening after innumerable material gains; they hurry after several aims, stricken by a desire to attain all of them at the same time. And the result is often stress, depression, and despair, at times leading to severe psychic disorders.
- It is also worth remembering that another characteristic of modern life is the cult of speed. People today have no time to rest, as they are morbidly engaged in a rat race for money, fame, fashion, and power.

We have devised swift means of transport, though often we have little sense of direction. We have most efficient machines for doing cumbersome work; but we have forgotten the simple joys of handicraft. We have giant organizations and systems; but we have no sense of community and no sympathy for our ailing brothers, just in neighbour. There are several injunctions in the Quran and hadees referring to man's malaise of soullessness.

S. Takathur 102nd Chapter of the Quran: and its Explanations

- (102:1) The craving for ever-greater worldly gains and to excel others in that regard keeps you occupied (102:2) until you reach your graves (102:3) Nay, you will soon come to know (102:4) nay, again, you shall soon come to know. (102:5) Nay, would that you knew with certainty of knowledge (what your attitude will lead to, you would never have acted the way you do). (102:6) You will surely end up seeing Hell; (102:7) again, you shall most certainly end up seeing it with absolute certainty. (102:8) **then, on that Day, you will be called to account for all the bounties you enjoyed.**

➤ Explanation A.A.Maududi (http://www.quran-english.com/tafheem_quran/102.htm):

"Takathur is from kathrat, which has three meanings: (1) That man should strive to gain more and more of everything; (2) that the people should vie with one another for gaining more and more; and (3) that they should brag and boast of possessing greater abundance of things than others.

Therefore, alhakum at-takathur would mean: "Takathur (greed for more and more) has so occupied you that its pursuit has made you heedless of every higher thing in Iife."

"They desire to have more and more means of comfort and physical enjoyment and, overwhelmed by this greed, they have become wholly insensitive as to the ultimate end of this way of living. They are engaged in a race with others to acquire more and more of power, more and more of forces, more and more of weapons, and they have no idea that all this is a means of filling Godś earth with tyranny and wickedness and of destroying humanity itself. In short, takathur has many forms, which have engrossed individuals as well as societies so completely that they have become heedless of everything beyond the world, its benefits and pleasures."

These Ahadith (Prophet's sayings) make it explicit that not only the disbelievers but the righteous believers too will be questioned. As for the blessings which Allah has bestowed on man, they are unlimited and countless. There are many blessings of which man is not even conscious. The Quran says: "If you try to count the blessings of Allah, you will not be able to calculate them."

(Surrah Ibrahim : 34). Countless of them are the blessings which Allah has granted directly to man, and a large number of these are the blessings which man is granted through his own skill and endeavour. About the blessings that accrue to man in consequence of his own labour and skill, he will have to render an account as to how he acquired them and in what ways he expended them".

According to Mu'adh ibn Jabal, when the Prophet (SAW) appointed him governor of Yemen, he said, 'Abstain from luxuries, for those who live luxurious lives are no servants of God.' (Hadith of Ahmad ibn Hanbal)

No Peace of Soul

Carl Jung, the famous Swiss psychologist, has written that the root cause of the disease of modern man is that he has forgotten his soul. According to him, man is in such a state today that he cannot find any solace in his life, because he has ignored his soul. (Carl Gustav Jung, Modern Man in Search of a Soul, Harvest Books- New York, 1955)

- ❖ For the above problems, the Quran suggests in several verses how a man believing in the here -after should pass his life with contentment. It instills in the mind of man that this world is a transitory phase and the real abode is after death. One should be contented with what he has; he must strive for a better status but he must surrender to God for the result. This keeps the man, psychologically, tension free. More over the Quran puts a responsibility on man to pay attention to and help the needy.
- ❖ For peace of soul the Quran prescribes a very psychological remedy: five times prayer with ablution

(washing of one's hand, face and feet – this physically and spiritually helps in keeping one calm and peaceful).

Collective Problems

Most conflicts of the contemporary world stem from two roots: ethnic and economic.

Let us consider the question of ethnic violence. Its most notable characteristic is the violence and the rage it evokes. How can such conflicts be resolved? The Prophet Muhammad (pbh) effectively instilled into his followers the idea that all humans are progeny of Adam and there is no distinction based on colour and ethnicity. There are several Hadees in this regard and anecdotes which indicate perfect harmony among his followers coming from different ethnic and linguistic backgrounds. An excerpt from the Last Sermon of The Prophet:

"All mankind is from Adam and Eve. An Arab has no superiority over a non-Arab, nor does a non-Arab have any superiority over an Arab; white has no superiority over black, nor does a black have any superiority over white; [none have superiority over another] except by piety and good action. Learn that every Muslim is a brother to every Muslim and that the Muslims constitute one brotherhood. Nothing shall be legitimate to a Muslim which belongs to a fellow Muslim unless it was given freely and willingly. Do not, therefore, do injustice to yourselves.

Remember, one day you will appear before God and answer for your deeds. So beware, do not stray from the path of righteousness after I am gone."

Quoting Allah Almighty's own words, he told them that no one is superior or inferior; that differences of skin colour, language, nationality, race, or tribe are God-given; and they do not by themselves represent any sort of superiority or inferiority. They are simply meant for mutual identification and interaction, and not for advancing any claim for precedence.

[Quran 49:13] O mankind! We created you from a single (pair) of a male and a female, and made you into nations and tribes, that ye may know each other (not that ye may despise (each other). Verily the most honoured of you in the sight of Allah is (he who is) the most righteous of you. And Allah has full knowledge and is well acquainted (with all things).

Poverty and Hunger, Unequal Distribution of Wealth

In the contemporary world, the gap between the rich and the poor is evident from the following statistics: The richest 2% of the world's population own half of the world's wealth; while half the world — nearly three billion people — live on less than two dollars a day. (*World Poverty Statistics*, last accessed March 17, 2009)

Why is this happening? Affluent people imagine that they have no responsibility towards the destitute. They ignore the Prophetic teaching that ***the poor and the needy have a claim to a specific share of the wealth of the rich***. Hence, the widening disparity between the extravagant rich and the starving millions, especially of the Third World.

[Quran 51:19] And in their wealth and possessions is the right of him (needy,) who asked, and him (who for some reason) was prevented (from asking).

[Quran 59:7] What Allah has bestowed on His Messenger (and taken away) from the people of the townships,- belongs to Allah,- to His Messenger and to kindred and orphans, the needy and the wayfarer; In order that it (wealth and commodity) may not (merely) make a circuit between the wealthy among you. So take what the Messenger assigns to you, and deny yourselves that which he withholds from you. And fear Allah. For Allah is strict in Punishment.

[Quran 57:10] And why should you not spend freely in the cause of God, seeing that God's [alone] is the heritage of the heavens and the earth?

The Prophet has taught:

"He is not a believer who eats his fill when his neighbour beside him is hungry"

Moreover Zakaat (taking out a certain portion of the wealth and agricultural produce and assets of trade, the detail of which is given in many books), were made obligatory.

The Prophet demonstrated in his own society the validity of these two concepts in realizing rights for orphans, the destitute, and the oppressed. And today we live in a world of terrible inequalities and brutal injustices which have been ironically made acceptable to 'civilized society' by spin and hype.

Today, all thinking humans are painfully aware of the fact that without justice, there is no chance for peace. And the teaching of the Prophet about the overarching importance of justice becomes only too apparent in today's context wide spread use of 'might is right'; be it for individuals, corporates, institutions, countries or even blocs.

But here is Allah's command about justice:

"O you who believe! stand out firmly for Allah, as witnesses to fair dealing, and ***let not the hatred of others to you make you swerve to wrong and depart from justice***. Be just: that is next to piety: and fear Allah. For Allah is well-acquainted with all that you do." (Al-Ma'idah 5:8)

The horrible scenes of atrocities committed by neo-imperialist forces on subject nations for the sake of plundering their resources bring to light the terrible price humans are made to pay, when the world's nations sadly ignore the teachings of Islam as taught by the Quran and Prophet Muhammad (pbh).

Some Doubts Clarified

Is this Book for ALL MANKIND? If so what is the CRITERION?

- ❖ Why this Book deserves the status of leading the mankind?
- ❖ If this book is for all mankind as it claims to be, then
  - Why it was revealed only in Arab land ?
  - Why it describes only the people & prophets of Arabia?
  - Why so much emphasis on Arabic language that daily prayer is said only in Arabic and other language not allowed?

Yes the Quran claims that it is the book meant for all mankind; there are reasons for it:

4:174 - O MANKIND! A manifestation of the truth has now come unto you from your Sustainer and We have sent down unto you a clear light.

4:175 - And as for those who have attained to faith in God and hold fast unto Him - He will enfold them within His grace and bounty, and guide them unto Himself by a straight way.

- At outset let us analyze what should be criterion for a Book to be of Guidance for all mankind ?

  ---- It must be able to bind all the people, all tribes, all nations together; must provide a platform where all classes of people, rich or poor, black or white may stand together.

  ---- It must present principles which may be applicable to people of all lands.

  ---- It must not be time–bound; it must be applicable for all time to come.

  ---- The basic nature of the principles be same to all but there must be flexibility for adoption of the principles according to the variations of lands, geographical conditions and cultures.

  ---- It must present principles which be helpful in establishing a just well-balanced society i.e. it must establish social justice, free of coercion and corruption.

  ---- It must provide the ways and means to meet the basic needs of the people of all lands.

The Quran claims to fulfill all the above criterion. When one reads the Quran with a sincere heart and an open mind, one sees that the models of people and societies described in the Quran existed in every age in history, including that of today. All the disorder, perversion, and mistakes of a society which has strayed from true religious values have been clearly stated in the Quran. The reactions of the people of these societies towards religion have been described with detailed character analyses. These descriptions and analyses are relevant in all respects to the world of today.

Now come to the next questions as to

- **Why it was revealed only in Arab Land; why local color in the book?**
- **Why emphasis on Arabic language?**

These are simple to understand. A Book had to be sent by Allah as it is He Who only can know the needs and shortcomings of man. He had to choose some person through whom Rules and Regulation be promulgated. The land and the people could be any, however as we guess the choice of Arabia may be due to its central location almost same distances to the main inhabited world then: Africa in south, Europe in west and Asia in East and central Asia in North. Even a thousand and half years back Arabic was the most developed language. It is the language which could cope with the conveying the ideas of Allah.

Why adhering rather sticking to Arabic language so much so that daily prayer has to be done only in this?

Al-first thought if seems to be very reasonable to recite daily prayer in local language, so that all men could understand what is being recited. Conversely it looks odd that one utters prayer-words which he does not understand. No doubt it is beneficial to adopt mother tongue or local language in which one is conversant. But there are occasions when a benefit of a thing is to be ignored to save it from a greater calamity. Such is the case with the Quran. Original Language of any Scripture is very important because each word of it connotes a particular shade of meaning ; for example there are about eight words in Arabic for the conveying the meaning of creation ('khalaqa', 'fatara', 'ja'ala', 'ansha', sawwa' falaqa', bad'aa', bara'aa), each having its own nuance. Thus a translation can never convey the very exact meaning and sense. To maintain the purity of the Text of the Quran the scholars of Islam prudently disallowed use of any language other than that of the Quran as revealed to the Prophet. There is not even a single slight difference among the scholars in this regard. However it should be pointed out that this strict order is only for the main salaah (namaaz) and it is surely allowed rather encouraged that translation be used for general understanding and in personal supplications as praising, asking, and seeking forgiveness from Allah in native language facilitates reverence, love, and sincerity with Him.

Here we may remember what calamity befell on the Bible by not adhering to the language in which Prophet Christ spoke; it led to so many versions of the Bible that now Christians are at loss as to which one is the original one.*(It has come to such pass that it is now debatable as to which language Christ spoke*: see Wikipedia (Historical Jesus): Jesus grew up in Galilee and much of his ministry took place there. The languages spoken in Galilee and Judea during the 1st century include the Semitic Aramaic and Hebrew languages as well as Greek, with Aramaic being the predominant language. Most scholars agree that during the early part of 1st century Aramaic was the mother tongue of virtually all women in Galilee and Judea. Most scholars support the theory that Jesus spoke Aramaic and that he may have also spoken Hebrew and Greek.

- Apart from this aspect in daily prayers, if translation were allowed in the daily five-time prayer there would be much infighting among the people as to which language and whose translation be adopted..
- At the same time universal brotherhood would be lost among Muslims: now it happens that a man from Nigeria going to China does not feel alienated at least during prayers, only because of the unique language adopted all throughout the world.

20

The Practicality of the Quran

All religions basically exhort mankind to be righteous and shun evil. But Islam goes beyond that. It guides us towards practical ways of achieving righteousness and eliminating evils from our individual and collective lives. Islam takes into account human nature and the complexities of human society. Islam is guidance from the Creator Himself so He knows well the capabilities as well as shortcomings of man. He has kept due consideration in ordaining the laws. Thus Islam has Practical Solutions for the Problems of Mankind

Which things you call practical?

(*i*) It must be congenial to the human behaviour and psychology.

(*ii*) It must fulfil the needs of man.

(*iii*) It must not go against the nature of man.

(*iv*) It must be adaptable to the man and the society in which he lives so that it makes life more comfortable.

(*v*) It must fit into a larger frame work of the ecosystem.

(*vi*) There must be an element of flexibility to suit all ages.

(*vii*) But in the name of practicality, the flexibility should not lead one to looseness to the extreme.

At the very outset the Quran declares

يُرِيْدُ اللّٰهُ بِكُمُ الْيُسْرَ وَلَا يُرِيْدُ بِكُمُ الْعُسْرَ

"Allah intends every facility for you; He does not want to put you to difficulties" [Quran2:185]

لَا يُكَلِّفُ اللّٰهُ نَفْسًا اِلَّا وُسْعَهَا

On no soul does Allah Place a burden greater than it can bear [Quran 2:286]

لَا يُكَلِّفُ اللّٰهُ نَفْسًا اِلَّا مَآ اٰتٰهَا ۭ سَيَجْعَلُ اللّٰهُ بَعْدَ عُسْرٍ يُّسْرًا ۝

Allah puts no burden on any person beyond what He has given him. After a difficulty, Allah will soon grant relief. [Quran 65:7]

The Path of Moderation

Moderation which leads to balance is a fundamental and distinguishing feature of Islam. Allah tells us:

> ***'We have made you a nation justly balanced'*** [Quran 2:143]

When the Quranic verse ***'As to monasticism which they themselves invented, We did not prescribe any of it for them'*** [Quran 57: 27] was revealed, the Prophet Muhammad (pbh) commented:

'Do not overburden yourselves, lest you perish'. People [before you] overburdened themselves and perished. Their remains are found in hermitages and monasteries' (Musnad of Abu Ya'la). In other words, excesses may eventually develop into large problems and even become a threat to the wellbeing and security of the mankind.

Indeed, the Prophet always resisted any tendency towards religious excessiveness. He once said to his close Companion Abdullah ibn 'Amr: 'Have I heard right that you fast every day and stand in prayer all night?' Abdullah replied, 'Yes, O Messenger of God. The Prophet said, 'Do not do that. Fast, as well as, eat and drink. Stand in prayer, as well as, sleep. *This is because your body has a right upon you, your eyes have a right upon you, your wife has a right upon you, and your guest has a right upon you* (Bukhari, Muslim).

Narrated 'Umar bin Al-Khattab: Narrated Abu Mas'ud Al-Ansari: Once a man said to Allah's Apostle "O Allah's Apostle! I may not attend the (compulsory congregational) prayer because so and so (the Imam) prolongs the prayer when he leads us for it. The narrator added: "I never saw the Prophet more **furious** in giving advice than he was on that day. The Prophet said, "O people! Some of you make others dislike good deeds (the prayers). So whoever leads the people in prayer should shorten it because among them there are the sick the weak and the needy (having some jobs to do)." Shahih Bukhari (1:03:090)

Such easiness is well explained in the hadees reported by Abu Hurairah that the Prophet, said, "Religion is easy..." [Bukhari], he also said; "The best of your religion, is the easiest." [Ahmad]

The easiness of this religion was put into practice by the

best of humanity, the one who came to deliver the message, as Allah, said;

> [Quran 9:128] Now has come unto you a Messenger from amongst yourselves: it grieves him that ye should perish: ardently anxious is he over you: to the Believers is he most kind and merciful.

This understanding is further clarified in a hadith in which the Prophet, said; "… Allah did not send me to be harsh, or cause harm, **but He sent me to teach and make things easy**" [Muslim].

This understanding is further implemented by the Mercy sent to mankind, Muhammad (pbh), reported his wife, 'Aishah, who said: **"Whenever the Prophet, had a choice between two matters, he would choose the easiest, unless it is sinful (act)"** [Bukhari]. Many hadiths have been reported on the matter of easiness: "Allah likes for this nation ease and hates for it hardship and adversity." [Tabaraani].

Abiding by the will of Allah requires that we seek and maintain a delicate balance between the various obligations that demand our attention; between our obligations to Allah, our obligations towards others in our society and our obligations towards ourselves. But contrary to such moderation and balance prescribed by Islam there are extreme approaches observed by different people. Thus on one extreme is the 'liberty and freedom – unlimited' by some sections of the Western society indulging in 'free sex', 'homosexuality, debauchery, materialism and complete nudity. On the other side are sects practising the austerity, asceticism and compulsive celibacy. Islam vouches for the mean–balance.

The Practicality of Islam is Evident in Many Ways

In matters of belief: The tenets of faith in Islam appeal to reason. Islam does not promote superstition, Islam does not promote ideas that fail to satisfy intellect nor does it entertain anything fabulous and flimsy. It is a practical religion, very natural and acceptable if one is ready to evaluate it with little patience and pious intentions.

In matters of worship: The practicality of Islam in matters of worship is evidenced by the fact that Islam takes into account the circumstances of people, their activities, and their human limitations. One important difference with other religion is that here there is no intermediary between Allah and Man - for no ritual, **for no worship is needed any priest**; what you see in congregational prayer, an Imam leading a prayer --- the Imam can be any one from among the congregation.

- ❖ For travellers prayer (salaah) has been curtailed, for sick the ablution (wadhu) is made easy and so on
- ❖ Prayer could be performed practically anywhere.
- ❖ Human psychology and his natural limitations are kept in consideration in Islamic tenets. For this reason, many religious obligations have been spread out over time. Some acts of worship must be performed once a year, while some are required only once in a lifetime, and yet others must be performed many times during the day. Similarly, some forms of worship are purely physical activities, some are exclusively monetary, and some are a combination of the two.
- ❖ Circumstances like sickness and travel are also taken into consideration. For this reason shortening of the

prayers is allowed for the traveller, and a person who is sick or of very old age or a person is on a journey during the month of Ramadân does not have to fast.

In what it permits and prohibits: From the practicality of Islamic Law, we find that only harmful things have been prohibited and they are enlisted in the books of jurisprudence, the rest are in permitted category.

Allah says "permits for them all good things and prohibits for them things that are foul."

Mitigating (partially excusing) circumstances have been taken into consideration. For this reason, **a person can eat prohibited foods in cases of dire necessity**. Allah says: They ask thee (O Muhammad(pbh)) what is made lawful for them. Say: (all) good things are made lawful for you. [Quran 5:4]. They ask you (O Muhammad(pbh)) what is made lawful for them. Say: (all) good things are made lawful for you [Quran 5:3]. Whosoever is forced by hunger, not by will, to sin: (for him) lo! Allah is Forgiving, Merciful."

In family matters: Islamic pragmatism in family matters can be seen in the permissibility of divorce when all attempts to reconcile the husband and wife have failed, in spite of the fact that divorce is disliked in Islamic Law and it is permissible only as a last resort; divorce is the most despised thing but allowed.

In the gradual implementation of its laws. This was applied in establishing many Islamic injunctions, especially prohibitions, such as the *prohibition of alcohol and interest*. This made it easier for people to accept the laws and ensured that they would be more inclined to obey them. Those who know the problems faced by administrations in the US during 1930s in implementing wine prohibitions may just wonder how efficiently Muhammad (pbh) eradicated this evil easily.

Clarity and Rationality

The following are clear examples of the clarity and rationality of Islam:

In Belief: All aspects of the Islamic belief are clear, without any obscurity or ambiguity.

- ❖ Allah is One without any partners. He has the attributes of completeness and perfection. He has no deficiencies or limitations. One has to pray to Allah, bow only to Allah, ask Him only to meet your needs, ask Him directly for forgiveness without any intermediary.
- ❖ Muhammad (pbh) is to be believed in as a servant of Allah, as the last Messenger and is to be taken as the only role model for all practical purposes.
- ❖ One must believe that he is accountable for all his actions here in this world---this makes him a responsible human being
- ❖ These beliefs are simple ones, no philosophical implications - this is one of the beauties of Islam that has attracted people of different lands for ages. Those who know the beliefs in other religions will only appreciate the simplicity of Islam in this regard.

Rationality is something that is found in every detail of Islam. Islam is established upon evidence and prohibits blind following or simply following in the footsteps of one's forefathers without any knowledge. There are strict guidance of the Prophet against superstitions, omens and blind astrology etc. To contemplate and to apply one's reasoning faculty in matters of religion is considered to be one of the most important religious obligations and one of the best forms of worship. Islam contains no tenet, however minute, that contradicts reason or observable reality. The Quran tries to instil in the heart of the believer a love of good conduct towards others and an aversion towards injustice. It calls the individual to abandon fraud and deception. Likewise, it provides specific laws that prohibit certain transactions that are oppressive and take advantage of the poor, like interest, fraud, and hoarding.

- ❖ Following is an example of **comparison with of commandments in other religions**:
- ❖ Unclean Impure Woman?
- ❖ The Jewish code of law, **Halakha**, details strict rules governing every aspect of the daily lives of Jews, including their sexual lives. Jewish law expressly forbids literally any physical contact between males and females during the days of menstruation and for a week thereafter (Keshet-Orr, J. Jewish women and sexuality. **Sexual and Relationship Therapy, 18**(2), 215-224). This includes passing objects between each other, sharing a bed (most couples have two separate beds, which can be pulled apart during **Niddah**), sitting together on the same cushion of a couch, eating directly from the wife's leftovers, smelling her perfume, gazing upon her clothing (whether or not it has been worn), or listening to her sing. According to

stipulated ritual, an Orthodox Jewish wife is responsible for immersing in the **Mikvah**, the ritual bath, following these 2 weeks. This entire period of time, from the beginning of the "bleeding days", until the end of the 7 "clean days", when the woman immerses herself in the ritual bath, is called the "**Niddah** (ritually unclean) period" (Guterman, M. A. (2006). Identity conflict in Modern Orthodox Judaism and the laws of family purity. **Method & Theory in the Study of Religion, 18**(1), 92-100)

Islâm does not consider a menstruating woman to possess any kind of "contagious uncleanness". She is neither "untouchable" nor "cursed". All are allowed to eat the meal cooked by her. She practises her **normal life with only two restrictions**: A married couple are not allowed to have sexual intercourse during the period of menstruation. However any other physical contact such as embracing and kissing between them is permissible. Second; she may not enter any shrine or mosque. In fact, she may not pray or fast during Ramadan while she is menstruating. She may not touch the Qur'anic codex.

Some Doubts Clarified

Well, if the Quran was practicable in Muhammad (pbh)'s time, is it so in modern day world also?

The answer is 'yes' because all the injunctions are within the scope of human bounds: if the 'salah' (namaz) was performed in the mosques, homes, fields, in urgency now it can well be done, in the office–premises; if emergency prayer of 'salatul khouf' (2:239, 4:102) was performed in the battle fields, now it can be done in short in the bunkers and cockpits. It is only a matter of "willingness" ----- where there is a will there is a way. Here again one may ask," In such urgencies why not the salah is waived altogether?" Well, Allah knows well the human weaknesses and capabilities. He waived the 'salah (daily five-time prayer)' for menstruating women but kept the salah, although short, for men in the battle fields. The reason we may envisage is this much that in urgent situations, remembering Allah gives one a psychological boost. (For the strictness in the penal codes such as those for theft and adultery we have discussed these in a separate chapter.)

❖ The obligation of daily prayers that too five times, strict directives what to eat what not to eat, to keep oneself away from enjoyments and entertainments of life such as sun baths at sea beaches and all such bindings -are they not burdensome and extreme of regimentation ?

❖ If the Quran claims to be easy then why is this regimentation in life?

Yes! Islam, being on middle path also has to be strict as well. Let me tell you why!!! What will you call a driver that does not follow the traffic and driving rules? What is a pilot to you that doesn't strictly obey the rules what he is taught? Should not a doctor abide by the rules and teachings that he learnt?

Life is not a game. We don't have it by chance. We have only one chance to spend and lose it. Man is born with a lot of natural, social and psychological complications. It inherits the emotions, feelings, desires. Life must have a proper way and the one who created life, must have the most appropriate knowledge of the creation. He gave us the Life and He told us how to live life. Creator knows what is best for His creation. Now we must have to follow

strictly the rules He defined for us. If we believe in God and believe that he created life, we must follow the rules He defined for us. As driving in a straight line might make one feel constrained but everyone knows it is in a vast interest of everyone's life.

An Extra Note:

In Islam, we avoid extreme conservatism and liberalism. We are not supposed to be so austere on ourselves that we make everything forbidden, nor do we take things so easy as to make everything permissible. We must strike a healthy balance in our lives so that we avoid making mistakes and yet enjoy this life within the limits set for us by Allah.

If we study Islam closely, we find that Allah has only made forbidden those things that are harmful to us. He has done this because He is merciful to His creation and wishes them all that are good in this world.

He set limits for us so that we are not harmed by our own foolishness and ignorance. Also, *if we were to make a list of all that is forbidden by Allah and all that Prophet Muhammad (pbh) told us to stay away from, we would find the list to be very short compared to all the things available to us that are healthy, beneficial, and enjoyable in this life.*

21

How to Study the Quran: a guide to a person quite new to it

In all preceding chapters you have gone through different aspects of the Quran and it is expected that a curiosity to go through the Book directly may have arisen in your heart.

For some, however, the Quran can be difficult to sit down and read from cover to cover. The revelation was given over a period of decades, and each verse has a particular scriptural and historical context. The themes of the Quran are interwoven among the chapters, and the book is not in chronological order. So how does one begin to understand its message? We have identified some points listed below which may be of immense use to any ardent student of the Scripture.

1. Get Acquainted with the One Who Came With the Book

Before embarking on a study of the Quran, it is necessary to have some basic background in the faith of Islam. This will give you a foundation from which to start, and some understanding of the vocabulary and message of the Quran.

It is the first step - to go through **the life sketch of the Prophet**. A short glimpse is given in the chapter (The Quran and Muhammad(pbh)). You may find many articles on this subject in the Net, for ease, I suggest a few sites:

http://www.Muhammad(pbh).net/with-the-prophet-topmenu-63/235-mankinds-debt-to-the-prophet.html (this is a good article by a renowned scholar AAli Nadwi)

http://www.Muhammad(pbh).net/with-the-prophet-topmenu-63/720-the-significance-of-the-hijrah.html (a short essay on how the Prophet changed the course of world history)

http://www.cyberistan.org/islamic/Muhammad(pbh).html

http://wikiz.info/islam/lopm/00cntnts.htm (a detailed study)

2. Get Acquainted with the Companions of the Prophet

To know the social environment and the condition of the society in which the Prophet worked and how he transformed and what impact the Quran had on them one must study the life sketches of the companions; what types of humans were they, how the Quran moulded them into men of steel in face of the enemies and full of compassion among friends; how even one passage of the Book turned them so much loving and submissive to the Prophet and the Ideology he presented that they were ever ready to sacrifice their lives.

http://web.youngmuslims.ca/online_library/companions_of_the_prophet/index.htm and

http://www.alim.org/library/biography/companion/BIO

The above sites will help you in reading the life sketches of the Companions of the Prophet. **Out of the long list at least go through some of them :**

1. Abu Bakr (51 B.H-13 A.H; 573-634 C.E),
2. 'Umar (40 B.H-23 A.H; 584-644 C.E),
3. 'Uthman (47 B.H- 35 A.H; 577-656 C.E),
4. 'Ali (23 B.H- 40 A.H; 600-661 C.E),
5. Talha (28 B.H-36 A.H; 596-656 C.E),
6. Zubayr (28 B.H-36 A.H; 596-656 C.E)
7. *'Abdur Rahman ibn 'Awf (passed away 31 A.H/654 C.E),*
8. *Sa'd ibn Abi Waqqas (23 B.H-55 A.H),*
9. *Sa'id ibn Zayd (passed away 51 A.H),*
10. *Abu 'Ubayda, 'Aamir ibn 'Abdillah ibn al-Jarrah.*

http://en.wikipedia.org/wiki/List_of_non-Arab_Sahaba

(List of non-Arab companions –a good and interesting reading material-especially, Salman the Persian Bilal ibn Ribah, Suhayb ar-Rumi)

3. Understand What Type of Book the Quran is

The revelation was given over a period of decades, and each verse has a particular scriptural and historical context. The themes of the Quran are interwoven among the chapters, and the book is not in chronological order. So how does one begin to understand its message? We have indicated this in chapter (Main theme, Structure and Style of the Quran) elaborately. We request all those who are really interested in seeking guidance or at the least in 'only knowing' the Quran, they must understand the peculiarity of the Book, its theme, structure and style of presentation. We have tried to present all these in a very summarized but lucid manner. Please go through both articles in the chapter "Main Theme, Structure and Style of the Quran" of this book.

4. Where from to Start Reading the Quran

It is my humble advice to a person new to the Quran, not to start reading right from the first paragraph of the first chapter intending to go through to the end of the Book. This is my practical experience that very soon one loses his interest, monotony prevails and he leaves studying the Quran altogether. Then what he should do?

I suggest to pick up **some selected verses and passages** of his/ her choice, interest and temperament; what do I mean by this? If you are an economist, pick up some verses related to economic directives of the Quran; if you are a legal expert, why not to start with the many verses concerned with the social and criminal laws mentioned in this Book ; if you are a scientist, well, there are large number of verses related to your field of choice: astronomy, embryology, meteorology, geology and so on. We have given some such verses and passages in different chapters of the concerned fields. Such type of initiation of going into the Quran, I hope, will pave the way to go ahead and maintain the interest and will create more curiosity to know the details. *(Here we give a short list :* http://www.islamicity.com/mosque/TOPICI.HTM *this site will help you select any topic of your choice)* Here one may ask 'if such selective reading is beneficial, was it adopted by the Companions of the Prophet?'. We must understand that the situation we are living today is entirely different from those prevailing that age: down the passage of time from the Prophet's time till now the history has accumulated many questions and misgivings and also misinformation - so a non-Muslim (or an ignorant Muslim) who approaches the Quran, carries in the backyard of his mind all these questions---his curiosity drives him to know quickly as to what this Book says about all such things. A selective reading will produce a psychological attachment with the Book. Also finding verses of the Quran related to his fields of expertise makes him amazed and he wonders that this Book keeps in it such a treasure hidden in it. Thus 'curiosity' and 'amazement' drive him to come nearer to the Quran.

At hand if you don't have any subject in your mind to hunt you may start with the following:

Go through the following IMPORTANT PASSAGES of the Quran e.g.

- S- Baqrah 1st and last ruku, S- Baqrah V. 164, S- Baqrah V. 153-157, S- Baqrah V. 207-210, S- Baqrah V. 214-216
- S- Baqrah V. 255(ayatul kurshi), S-Al-e-Imraan last ruku, S- Nisa V. 59-70, S- maaida V. 52-56, S- Anaam V. 60 to the End
- S- Ambiya V. 30-33, S- Ruum V. 17-27, S- Fatah V. 28 till End, S- Hadeed V.seven Ayaats of the beginning
- S- Ahzab V. 40, S- shura V. 10-13, S- Hashar last ruku

While reading the Holy Quran be particular to do the following:

- **Have your own copy of the Quran,** try to read only this one, this practice results in much psychological and practical benefits.
- Mark the verses in **your own Quran** which impress you, you may highlight some words etc.
- Write down in the side margins the references of similar descriptions elsewhere in the Quran. If the margin is the less than what you want to write, paste a separate piece of paper (if your noting is more than what the pasted piece of paper can accommodate then use your Note Book. This Note Book may be used for recording other Islamic information as well.)

5. Go to the Selected Short Surahs (Chapters) First

Only then you go to surahs, to those which are medium in length and important eg.

S.49. Hujraat,	S.31. Luqman,	S.36. Yaasin,
S.05. Maida,	S.06. An'aam	S.29. Ankboot,
S.30.Ru'm,	S.75. Qiyamah,	S.61. Saff,
S.03Aale Imran,	S.57. Hdeed,	S.64. Taghabun
S.62. Juma,	S.66. Mulk	

6. Some cautions in the Way of Reading

Look At the Full Verse

Quoting the Quran out of context is by far the single biggest mistake that even sincere students of the Scripture may fall into. This method of quoting is generally used by some biased detractors to present any view no matter how unjustified it may be.

For example, a favourite quote which is repeated by many groups is that the Quran promotes killing and violence as evidenced by the verse:

> "And kill them wherever you find them"
> [Quran 2:191]

However, once we use the method of full context, then a totally different picture appears regarding the same issue:

> "And kill them wherever you find them, and expel them from where they expelled you, and know that persecution is worse than being killed. And do not fight them at the Restricted Temple unless they fight you in it; if they fight you then kill them, thus is the reward of the disbelievers."
> [Quran 2:191]

Look To The Surrounding Verses

Another crucial point to studying the Quran properly is to always look at the verses preceding and following a specific verse/subject. The context of a verse is very important to consider as it indicates the proper meaning of the words used.

Be Aware Of Multiple- Meanings of Words

Some Arabic words, like in English, may have more than one related meaning. Thus ascribing the 'wrong' meaning may sometimes create contradictions between verses in the Scripture or give a strange understanding to the topic the verse is addressing. How a person new to the Quran can save himself form such pitfalls, here comes the need of a reliable 'mufassir' (exegete = an expert in the religious book who explains the meanings of the verses). For this I may suggest:

http://www.islamicity.com/QuranSearch/ (here you find translations by three very renowned scholars :

Muhammad (pbh) Asad (earlier Leopld Weiss, a German Jew, converted to Islam who rose to eminence of Islamic scholarship),

Abdullah Yusuf Ali (his translation and short explanatory notes are in lucid English) and

Marmaduke Muhammad (pbh) Pickthal (a famous Western Islamic scholar), also see the site:

http://www.quranenglish.com/tafheem_quran/ (This is a very famous exegesis (explanatory note), in modern day phraseology by the eminent Islamic thinker A A Maududi.)

"Ulum al-Quran," by Ahmad von Denffer

Authored by a German Muslim, this book gives a good introduction to the disciplines of knowledge needed to understand the Quran. Includes the compilation of the text, abrogation of verses, and the use of allegory and parable.

"The Meaning of the Quran," by A.A. Maududi
(www.dar-us-alam.com/store/main.mvc.)

This six-volume collection of Qur'anic commentary is one of the more popular that has been translated into English, covering in-depth explanation of the entire Quran.

"Way to the Quran," by Khurram Murad
(www.soundvision.com/shop/pview.)

This book is aimed at guiding a person through a personal study of the Quran. It includes practical tips, such as how often to read and for how long, as well as personal advice about how to open your heart to the Qur'anic message.

Arrange Similar Topic Verses Together

Suppose you are interested in finding out what the Quran says about human reproduction (embryology) search such verses and arrange together. To derive conclusions have a glance over all the verses in a sequential manner. There are several websites which will help you in this regard, prominent among them are:

http://www.islamicity.com/QuranSearch/

http://www.searchtruth.com/chapter_display.php?chapter=21&translator=2&mac=&show_arabic=1_;

http://www.isearchquran.com/ ;

http://www.opentruths.com/

Be Patient and Seek God's Help

The Quran is not a general book of knowledge, it is basically a spiritual one so whenever you sit to read it, try to concentrate your mind as well as heart to seek God's help; beseech in the best of words to guide to the right path. At first sight my (this) suggestion may seem to you just a usual passing appeal but when you will ponder deeply, its significance will be revealed. Any good knowledgeable, however well-understood sentence is useless if it touches not one's heart and if it inspires not to act in the right direction. A slight twist in the meaning and connotation may just deviate one that is why it is the instruction of God Himself whenever you sit to read the Quran, seek refuge of Allah from the Satan, the downtrodden.

Do not be afraid to challenge what you read.

The Quran actually invites the reader to do just that, as long as you diligently and earnestly try to find the answers, because in the process, you end up re-discovering your true self.

This rewarding journey of mental and spiritual growth is described in the works of many prominent western Muslims such as American Professor of mathematics Jeffrey Lang, who was challenging the Quran as a fierce atheist, yet couldn't help but surrender to it eventually (*Struggling to Surrende*r, Amana Publications), he writes of his first reading:

"You cannot simply read the Quran, not if you take it seriously. You either have surrendered to it already or you fight it. It attacks tenaciously, directly, personally; it debates, criticizes, shames, and challenges. From the outset it draws the line of battle, and I was on the other side. I was at a severe disadvantage, for it became clear that the Author knew me better than I knew myself. The Quran was always way ahead of my thinking; it was erasing barriers I had built years ago and was addressing my queries".

Allow yourself time to contemplate.

Don't read the Quran like you read the newspaper, rather, read it as a direct message from God Himself to you in particular! When you read verses where God talks to the reader, stop and let the message sink in, then allow yourself time to think of yourself and your life in relation to this divine communication, think of how you could put it to good use to adjust your convictions and behaviour.

When you read stories about previous nations, find contemporary parallels and try to learn the lessons. When you read about God's magnificent creations, think of educating yourself about nature and showing gratitude to Him through respecting life and natural resources. Think of the Quran as a dialogue or a conversation rather than a one-way communication of do's and don'ts. Be brave enough to provide the honest answers to the questions your heart and mind will throw at you while you read.

Final Suggestion

You now should have the necessary tools to educate yourself to the Quran's system and method for deriving meanings and laws. *Try to make it a habit of seeking the answers yourself through the guidance of God. Do not be quick to ask 'others' what God says regarding this or that matter, but try to establish a direct bond with God.. It is only through this self-awareness that people can have a defence mechanism against the misinformation and ignorance that has been spread by many. However if certain verse or word is vexing you and you are not at ease with any explanation available in the Net then find some suitable learned person in your vicinity and discuss with him.*

22

The Quran at the time of despair

Even if one is not a follower of Islam, he can gather solace from the Quran if he follows some principles laid down by it.

1. Trust in Allah

Man is basically weak, he needs support of someone at the time of despair, someone on whom he can trust, someone from whom he may get support and help; who could be better than Allah, the Mighty, All-Knowing, the Most Merciful and Compassionate--so seek support of Allah. Take an example: The Quran relates the story of hiding of the Prophet and his companion Abu Bakr in a cave when the pagan Makkans were running after them blood thirsty ; when Abu Bakr saw them approaching he got perturbed. At that time Muhammad(pbh) consoled him : (la tahzan innallaha ma'ana) **Have no fear, for Allah is with us**":

إِلَّا تَنصُرُوهُ فَقَدْ نَصَرَهُ اللَّهُ إِذْ أَخْرَجَهُ الَّذِينَ كَفَرُوا ثَانِيَ اثْنَيْنِ إِذْ هُمَا فِي الْغَارِ إِذْ يَقُولُ
لِصَاحِبِهِ لَا تَحْزَنْ إِنَّ اللَّهَ مَعَنَا ۖ فَأَنزَلَ اللَّهُ سَكِينَتَهُ عَلَيْهِ وَأَيَّدَهُ بِجُنُودٍ لَّمْ تَرَوْهَا

[Quran 9:40] for Allah did indeed help him, when the Unbelievers drove him out: he had no more than one companion; they two were in the cave, and he said to his companion, **"Have no fear, for Allah is with us"**: then Allah sent down His peace upon him, and strengthened him with forces which ye saw not,

This feeling of Allah being with him gives one a psychological peace.

لَا تَقْنَطُوا مِن رَّحْمَةِ اللَّهِ ۚ إِنَّ اللَّهَ يَغْفِرُ الذُّنُوبَ جَمِيعًا ۚ إِنَّهُ هُوَ الْغَفُورُ الرَّحِيمُ ﴿٥٣﴾

"- do not despair of Allah's Mercy. Surely Allah forgives all sins. He is Most Forgiving, Most Merciful".

2. Consult Others in Cases That Perplex You

Allah suggests that before venturing into a deal to have consultations with others and once a decision is reached he should put his foot forward with firmness putting full trust in Allah.

وَشَاوِرْهُمْ فِي الْأَمْرِ ۖ فَإِذَا عَزَمْتَ فَتَوَكَّلْ عَلَى اللَّهِ ۚ إِنَّ اللَّهَ يُحِبُّ الْمُتَوَكِّلِينَ ﴿١٥٩﴾

[Quran 3:159] "And **take counsel with them in all matters of concern**; then, when you have decided upon a course of action, **place thy trust in God**: for, verily, God loves those who place their trust in Him."

3. Surrender Your Affair Wholly to Allah

This is a mysterious world, with all our expanse of knowledge it is advisable (*I say advisable for the sake of our own mental peace*) to accept the fact that we can never comprehend all the affairs going on in this world... you don't know all the variables of an affair concerned and hence they are out of your control. When you are surrounded with problems from all sides and things seem to be going out of your hands, you are reminded by the Quran and be advised to surrender to Allah (innal amra kull lahu lillah)

قُلْ اِنَّ الْاَمْرَ كُلَّهٗ لِلّٰهِ ؕ

[3:154] "Verily, all power of decision does rest with God"

At another place the Quran suggests to surrender your affair wholly to Allah, this will produce in you a feeling of being relieved of burdens.

وَاُفَوِّضُ اَمْرِيْٓ اِلَى اللّٰهِ ؕ اِنَّ اللّٰهَ بَصِيْرٌۢ بِالْعِبَادِ ﴿۴۴﴾

[Quran 40:44] **my (own) affair I commit to Allah**. For Allah (ever) watches over His Servants"

Submission to Him carries no negative feelings. We must learn to asses in which affair and at what stage we have to submit and where we have to stand firmly to fight back, as amply expressed in the following Hadees:

Abu Hurairah (r) said: "The Prophet, peace be upon him, remarked: 'The example of a believer is like a fresh tender plant; from whichever direction the wind blows, it bends the plant. But when the wind dies down, it straightens up again. (Similarly a believer is tested by afflictions to strengthen his faith and heart, and he remains patient and firm). And an evil person is like a pine tree which remains hard and stiff until Allah breaks it whenever He wills." Source: Fiqh-us-Sunnah, volume 4, #1

At such situations it is also worthwhile to recite the famous prayer couplet:

O Lord!

grant me the **serenity**

to accept the things, I cannot change,

And the **courage**

to change the things, I can,

And the **wisdom**

to know the difference.

Do we know the consequences of anything?

Hardships and trials are part of everyone's life. The important thing is for us to have the right attitude of trusting Allah and His plans when facing such hardships and trials. During such trying times, always remember that nothing happens without the Will of Allah. Second, we may not know that our trials and hardships may be part of a bigger plan of which we may have only limited knowledge. It's only at a later stage when the bigger Plans of Allah reveal themselves to everyone. We can see an example of this from the following verse of Quran-Surah Yousuf that when the step brothers of Prophet Yousuf (pbh) were taking him to throw him into a dark well, Allah revealed to Prophet Yousuf (pbh) that, "Allah will bring about, after hardship, ease." (Quran, 65:7) and this is exactly what happened.

We crave for a thing; we want to achieve a position and status and if we cannot achieve then despair prevails over us. At such time the Quran consoles us:

وَعَسَىٰ أَن تَكْرَهُوا شَيْئًا وَهُوَ خَيْرٌ لَّكُمْ ۖ وَعَسَىٰ أَن تُحِبُّوا شَيْئًا وَهُوَ شَرٌّ لَّكُمْ ۗ وَاللَّهُ يَعْلَمُ وَأَنتُمْ لَا تَعْلَمُونَ ﴿٢١٦﴾

[Quran 2:216] **It may well be that you hate a thing while it is good for you, and it may well be that you love a thing while it is bad for you: and God knows, whereas you do not know.**

This verse is very important in regard to dispelling despair. We have related a true story in the chapter "THE QURAN IS AMAZING", how this verse changed the course of life of a non-Muslim brother. The two words, **"KHAIR"** and **"SHAR"** used here are very comprehensive, they include connotation of all types of good or bad things respectively. One does not know whether a thing however lovely it may look, will prove to be beneficial or harmful in future. Therefore it is taught to us that we must strive for a thing giving due consideration to all pros and cons but if that is not achieved we should not fall in abyss of despair but seek solacement in this thought that perhaps Allah might not had 'khair' in that thing. There is a beautiful prayer "isthikhara" taught by the Prophet the last line of which is "Allahuma aqdir li khaira haso kana summa arzini bih" (**O, Allah grant me *Khair* wherever it may be and make me satisfied with it".**)

"There is a blessing in calamity that the wise man should not ignore, for it erases sins, gives one the opportunity to attain the reward for patience, dispels negligence, reminds one of blessings at the time of health, calls one to repent and encourages one to give charity and endure."

Life is a learning curve and the challenges are there to make us stronger and to condition us and build us emotionally, spiritually and physically for the greater challenges that we will encounter tomorrow. Outwardly circumstances may be perceived as hardships but in reality they may really be ***blessings in disguise***!

4. Strive Hard and Leave the Results to Allah

While we need to carry out our duty to the best of our abilities, always remember that you don't control the outcome of events. Even the Prophets did not control the outcome of their efforts. Some were successful, others were not. ***Once you have done your duty, leave the results to Allah.*** Regardless of the results of your efforts, you will be rewarded for the part you have played. (***assayee minni wal itmam minallah*** which means ***striving from my side, completion from Allah's side.***

However, never underestimate your abilities. Understand the concept of Barakah (blessings from Allah) and remember that Allah can and Insha Allah will expand them if you are sincerely exerting your energies for the right cause and in the right path.

5. The Quranic Concept of Tests and Hardships

> *"Allah does not burden a soul beyond that it can bear…"* [Quran: 2:286]

"Great reward comes with great trials. When Allah loves a people, He tests them, and whoever accepts it attains His pleasure, whereas whoever shows discontent with it incurs His wrath." (Hadith- Tirmidhi)

*"…….If anything befalls you, do not say 'If only I had done (such and such), the such and such would have happened,' rather say: 'Allah has decreed and what He wills He does, for (saying) '**if only'** opens the door to the work of the shaytaan(devil)."* (Hadith-Muslim).

In the perspective of the Quran the problems of life and diseases and afflictions are *TESTS* for us *not the punishment of some previous misdeeds* (as presented by some other religions). They are tests of our faith in Allah as to what degree we trust in Him.

Moreover in the sight of the Quran and as told by the Prophet **problems, illness and such afflictions are <u>redemption for our sins</u> and are the means for going to paradise if we maintain patience keeping faith in Allah.**

In this regard see the following some 'sayings' (hadees) of the Prophet:

"it is reported that the Prophet said: there is no affliction, even pricking of a thorn to a faithful that is not rewarded back by pardoning his sins". (Muatta)

"No doubt that even the fever of one night removes all the sins of a faithful"

It is reported by his companion Au Hurairah that some person abused fever; on that the Prophet said, "Don't abuse fever because it removes sins in a way that fire removes rusting". (Ibn Majah)

It is reported by Anas bin Malik that the Prophet said, "Allah said that if He takes from some person his two things which he loved (his two eyes) but he remains patient, does not lose heart then Allah gives him heaven as a reward." (Bukhari)

Narrated 'Abdullah: I visited the Prophet during his ailments and he was suffering from a high fever. I said, "You have a high fever. Is it because you will have a double reward for it?" He said, "Yes, for no Muslim is afflicted with any harm but that Allah will remove his sins as the leaves of a tree fall down."

- The faith of one that he is being <u>tested</u> by God of his 'submission' to Him and that keeping patience over pains and problems will ensure reward in the life here-after, gives one strength to pass over the tides.

وَلَنَبْلُوَنَّكُمْ بِشَيْءٍ مِّنَ الْخَوْفِ وَالْجُوعِ وَنَقْصٍ مِّنَ الْأَمْوَالِ وَالْأَنفُسِ وَالثَّمَرَاتِ ۗ
وَبَشِّرِ الصَّابِرِينَ ﴿١٥٥﴾

[Quran 2:155] Be sure We shall test you with something of fear and hunger, some loss in goods or lives or the fruits (of your toil), but give glad tidings to those who patiently persevere,

لِّيَبْلُوَكُمْ فِي مَا آتَاكُمْ ۗ

He might try you by means of what He has bestowed upon you [6:165]

فَاسْتَجَابَ لَهُمْ رَبُّهُمْ أَنِّي لَا أُضِيعُ عَمَلَ عَامِلٍ مِّنكُم مِّن ذَكَرٍ أَوْ أُنثَىٰ ۖ بَعْضُكُم
مِّن بَعْضٍ ۖ فَالَّذِينَ هَاجَرُوا وَأُخْرِجُوا مِن دِيَارِهِمْ وَأُوذُوا فِي سَبِيلِي وَقَاتَلُوا
وَقُتِلُوا لَأُكَفِّرَنَّ عَنْهُمْ سَيِّئَاتِهِمْ وَلَأُدْخِلَنَّهُمْ جَنَّاتٍ تَجْرِي مِن تَحْتِهَا الْأَنْهَارُ
ثَوَابًا مِّنْ عِندِ اللَّهِ ۗ وَاللَّهُ عِندَهُ حُسْنُ الثَّوَابِ ﴿١٩٥﴾

[3:195] And thus does their Sustainer answer their prayer: "I shall not lose sight of the labour of any of you who labours [in My way], be it man or woman: each of you is an issue of the other Hence, as for those who forsake the domain of evil and are driven from their homelands, and suffer hurt in My cause, and fight [for it], and are slain - I shall most certainly efface their bad deeds, and shall most certainly bring them into gardens through which running waters flow, as a reward from God: for with God is the most beauteous of rewards."

6. Tie Your Camel Then Trust in Allah

Once you have done your duty, leave the results to Allah.

Tie your Camel: Do your Part

One day Prophet Muhammad, peace and blessings be upon him, noticed a Bedouin leaving his camel without tying it. He asked the Bedouin, "Why don't you tie down your camel?" The Bedouin answered, "I put my trust in Allah." The Prophet then said, **"Tie your camel first, then put your trust in Allah"** (Tirmidhi).

> "Verily Allah does not change men's condition unless they change their inner selves" [Quran 13:11]

7. Seek Help Through Sabr & Salat (<u>Patience and Prayer</u>)

وَاسْتَعِينُوا بِالصَّبْرِ وَالصَّلَوٰةِ ۚ وَإِنَّهَا لَكَبِيرَةٌ إِلَّا عَلَى الْخَٰشِعِينَ ﴿٤٥﴾

[2:45] And seek aid in steadfast patience and prayer: and this, indeed, is a hard thing for all but the humble in spirit,

Seek help through *Sabr and Salat* (patience and prayer) (Quran 2:45).This instruction from Allah provides us with two critical tools that can ease our worries and pain. *Patience and prayer are two oft-neglected stress-relievers*. Sabr is often translated as patience but it is not just that. It includes self-control, perseverance, endurance, and a focussed struggle to achieve one's goal. **Unlike patience, which implies resignation, the concept of 'Sabr' includes a duty to remain steadfast to achieve your goals despite all odds.**

8. Birds Don't Carry Their Food!

Allah is al Razzaq (the Provider). "How many are the creatures that carry not their own sustenance? It is Allah Who feeds them and you, for He hears and knows all things (Quran 29:60)." By reminding yourself that He is the Provider, you will remember that getting a job or providing for your family in these economically and politically challenging times is in God's Hands, not yours.

وَمَا مِن دَآبَّةٍ فِي الْأَرْضِ إِلَّا عَلَى اللَّهِ رِزْقُهَا وَيَعْلَمُ مُسْتَقَرَّهَا وَمُسْتَوْدَعَهَا ۚ
كُلٌّ فِي كِتَابٍ مُّبِينٍ ۝٦

[Quran 11:6] And there is no living creature on earth but depends for its sustenance on God; and He knows its time-limit [on earth] and its resting-place [after death]: all [this] is laid down in [His] clear decree. –

Therefore you are told by the Quran not to lose heart, strive hard and put full trust in God then you will be provided from the quarters you never expected, As Allah says in the Quran: "And He provides for him from (sources) he never could imagine. And if anyone puts his trust in Allah, sufficient is (Allah) for him. For Allah will surely accomplish His purpose. Verily, for all things has Allah appointed a due proportion (Quran 65:3). This type of assurance are not just hollow assurance; mind you it is from Allah, the Creator, the Controller of the universe, the Provider par excellence.

عَلَيْهِ تَوَكَّلْتُ وَهُوَرَبُّ الْعَرْشِ الْعَظِيمِ ۞

[Quran 9:129] In Him have I placed my trust, for He is the Sustainer, in awesome almightiness enthroned."

وَكَاَيِّنْ مِّنْ دَآبَّةٍ لَّا تَحْمِلُ رِزْقَهَا ۖ اَللّٰهُ يَرْزُقُهَا وَاِيَّاكُمْ ۖ وَهُوَ السَّمِيعُ الْعَلِيمُ ۞

[Quran 29:60] And how many a living creature is there that takes no thought of its own sustenance; [the while] God provides for it as [He provides] for you too - since He alone is all-hearing, all-knowing.

9. There is None Who Can Harm or Benefit You Except Allah

There are occasions when we are afraid of losing jobs at the hands of bosses, some mishaps on grounds beyond our control and at many such occasions of peril we are reminded by the Quran that it is only Allah, none else, Who can 'cure' misfortune or alleviate the problems.

وَاِنْ يَّمْسَسْكَ اللّٰهُ بِضُرٍّ فَلَا كَاشِفَ لَهُ اِلَّا هُوَ ۖ وَاِنْ يُّرِدْكَ بِخَيْرٍ فَلَا رَآدَّ لِفَضْلِهِ ۖ يُصِيبُ بِهِ مَنْ يَّشَآءُ مِنْ عِبَادِهِ ۖ وَهُوَ الْغَفُورُ الرَّحِيمُ ۞

[Quran 10:107] And [know that] if God should touch thee with misfortune, there is none who could remove it save Him; and if He intends good for thee, there is none who could turn away His bounty: He causes it to alight upon whomsoever He wills of His servants. And He alone is truly forgiving, truly a dispenser of grace.

10. After Each Hardship Follows A Comfort

It is further stated in the Quran that after each hardship follows a comfort:(65:7)

لَا يُكَلِّفُ اللّٰهُ نَفْسًا اِلَّا مَآ اٰتٰىهَا ۭ سَيَجْعَلُ اللّٰهُ بَعْدَ عُسْرٍ يُّسْرًا ۝

God does not burden any human being with more than He has given him - [and it may well be that] God will grant, after hardship, ease.

فَاِنَّ مَعَ الْعُسْرِ يُسْرًا ۝ اِنَّ مَعَ الْعُسْرِ يُسْرًا ۝

[94:5-6] Verily, with every difficulty there is relief So, verily, with every difficulty, there is relief.

11. Prophet's Life as Solace at the Time of Trial

Many times we may fall into thinking that Allah doesn't love us because of the trials that we are put through but this concept is dispelled by the Quran. The disbelievers and the rejecters of the Prophet charged that if he was a true Prophet, Allah would not had forsaken him to undergo hardships of many kinds, hunger to physical torture. The Quran emphatically clears this doubt: hardships and trials are not the signs of the curse of Allah. As we go through the life of the Prophet and see the many hardships he endured we can see that he was human just as we are: when cut he would bleed, when put in difficult situations he would feel emotional pain. Thus Allah showed in him a lesson for us that regardless of the hardships we must continue to strive in the way of Allah and keep our eye on the ultimate goal, pleasing Allah and entering Jannah. Allah has sent us an example that we can emulate and an opportunity for us to relate to the Prophet on many different levels through our trials.

The Prophet faced almost all types of hardships common men face in their lives : born as orphan, loss of mother at early childhood, loss of patron uncle and comforting wife in the face of hostile enemies, undergoing excruciating pain and hunger while living in a valley under siege, death of children, physical pain in battle fields, treachery of some people, abuse and slander and rumours against own self and wives and many more; in each there is a lesson for us and some material for our solace and comfort. For that we must read his biography earnestly and keep it in our heart as a healing and comforting treasure.

23

Why the Muslims are Lagging Behind?

Muhammad Asad (earlier Leopold Weiss an Austrian Jew), one of the most outstanding scholars of Islam of modern times used the following words at the very beginning of the foreword of his translation of the Quran: The Message of the Quran (available at the site www.islamicity.com):

"Between these first revelation to Prophet Muhammad (pbh) at the age of forty and the last verse just a few days before his death unfolds a book which, more than any other single phenomenon known to us, has fundamentally affected the religious, social and political history of the world. No other sacred scripture has ever had a similar immediate impact upon the lives of the people who first heard its message and, through them and the generations that followed them, on the entire course of civilization. It shook Arabia and within a few decades, it spread its world-view far beyond the confines of Arabia and produced the first ideological society known to man; through its insistence on consciousness and knowledge, it engendered among its followers a spirit of intellectual curiosity and independent inquiry, ultimately resulting in that splendid era of learning and scientific research which distinguished the world of Islam at the height of its cultural vigour; and the culture thus fostered by the Quran penetrated in countless ways and by-ways into the mind of medieval Europe and gave rise to that revival of Western culture which we call the Renaissance, and thus became in the course of time largely responsible for the birth of what is described as the "age of science": the age in which we are now living. All this was, in the final analysis, brought about by the message of the Quran".

Are these words hollow tribute to the Quran? No, how one can deny a clear fact of the history? A common man, Muslim or non-Muslim, asks today: if this book shook Arabia and changed the course of human civilization *then* what happened to it *now* ?

Already having such a fruitful book with them, why the present day Muslims are lagging behind? (Does this not put a question mark on the fruitfulness of the book, the Quran itself?)

Yes it is true and pathetic. There are various reasons and can be explained from different perspectives and it needs much elaborations, beyond the scope of this book. However we can enumerate and consider a few.

- Firstly it is a usual phenomenon in the life cycle of any nation. Nations rise and fall; the famous historian and thinker Ibn Khaldun rightly says that life cycle of a nation is similar to that of a man: it grows from infancy to youth to old age.
- In the teachings of the Quran and the guidance of the Prophet there are those elements that are necessary to build a cohesive, dynamic and prosperous society :

Obedience to a supreme authority, sense of accountability, fraternity, equality of mankind, establishment of a welfare society by taking utmost care of the poor, directives for eradicating superstitions and other social evils and many more directives to uphold the values based on reason and logic.

Those who followed the principles laid out by the Quran under the austere training of the Prophet brought about a revolution not only in the Arabian Peninsula but all adjoining areas. Along with the political sway they opened new vistas in different fields of sciences. Alas, with the passage of time, the Muslims drifted away from the Quran; it became only a thing to be kept in houses at a safe place with decorative coverings, only to be adorned and respected. In most of the countries where Muslims are in the majority, only a small percentage of people know the content of the Quran and ponder on the Quran as required. As a result, people who are ignorant of the real message of the Quran, attribute different meanings to it. Many people believe some traditions to have their origin in the Quran, although they may be contradictory to the very nature of the Qur'anic message. The Quranic directives gave way to local rituals, there are customs which Muslims practice but in fact they are not in the Quran and at times may be contradictory to it. **This shows us that there is a huge difference between the true religion as explained in the Quran and the concept of religion generally prevalent today.** This difference has been caused by abandoning the real source, the Quran. It is this tragic happening of which the Prophet will make a complaint to Allah on the Day of Judgement:

> And the Messenger cried out: O my Lord! surely my people have treated this Quran as a forsaken thing. [Quran 25:30]

The recent decline in the Muslim world has many more causes which can be traced in the history of past two to three centuries. Many historical analyses have been advanced in this regard and many causes have been pointed out such as forsaking the Quran and Sunnah, inadequacy of adaptability of Muslim communities to changing conditions of time, hesitation in adopting new technologies, loss of vision in managing social affairs, giving least or no stress to innovative research in Science and technologies; however one thing is sure that the principles of the Quran and the guidelines of the Prophet are in no way liable to cause such decline as some detractors of Islam refer to. The Quran and the guidance of the Prophet did show and establish their fruitfulness to mankind once and are still calling people to come under its cool shade. Those who understand the power of the Quran and virtues of Prophet's words are drawing closer to Islam, showing a sharp rise in the graph of people to Islamic fold, particularly the coming of Western women in Islamic fold is a positive sign.

- It must be understood that there is a difference between the call of the Quran and the socio-political power of 'so called Muslims' at any period of time. There are many factors which affect the rise of a nation and its downfall. At many places in the Quran it is mentioned that the Muslims must keep taking stock of their conduct otherwise Allah will forsake them and raise another people who will uphold the call of Allah see S.Maida(5:54 O you who have attained to faith! If you ever abandon your faith," God will in time bring forth [in your stead] people whom He loves and who love Him - humble towards the believers, proud towards all who deny the truth: [people] who strive hard in God's cause, and do not fear to be censured by anyone who might censure them: such is God's favour, which He grants unto whom He wills. And God is infinite, all-knowing.)
- For last few decades there have been many movements in different Muslim countries for revival and renaissance of Islam. At many places these movements have been suppressed and at many new places such as in Europe and America it is gaining foothold although in face of resistance.
- Lastly, it is to be remembered that the call of the Quran to mankind is on both individual and collective levels albeit an individual is in primary focus. *One individual has to pay attention to the call of the Quran and decide his steps to be taken on logical and rational basis and not put hold his decision of coming under the shade of the Quran because the social collective life of Muslims at that period of time is not up to the mark of the Quran or is not congenial or*

it is hostile. One has to seek first his own salvation; of course when a band of such individuals are gathered there is a command of the Quran that they should come forward to change the society: S 3:104

- **"Let there arise out of you a band of people inviting to all that is good, enjoining what is right, and forbidding what is wrong: They are the ones to attain felicity".**

APPENDIX 1

Islam Basics

ISLAM—A Unique Name

Adherents of various religions all over the world have named their religions either with the name of a man or a particular race; thus Christianity is named after Christ, Buddhism after its founder Buddha, Zoroastrianism was named after its founder Zoroaster. Judaism had also emerged among the tribe of Judah and so on. Islam is unique in this respect. The word 'ISLAM' comes from two Arabic roots: 'si-la-m' and 'sa-la-m' meaning 'peace' and 'surrender'—both meaning are equally applicable: this gives peace to one who adopts it, calls to all mankind to get peace by coming under its shade. On the other hand it calls man to surrender to his Creator in heart, soul and deed. The one who surrenders to Allah the Creator, is called 'MUSLIM'.

Prophets to All Nations

Let it be clear to all that Prophet Muhammad is NOT the founder of Islam, he is only one and the last in the chain of the Prophets sent by God to different tribes in different parts of the world in different ages. This has been very clearly mentioned in the Quran at various places, their number must be in thousands, only a few are mentioned in the Quran, only those who came in and around the place where the Quran was revealed with the names of whom local people were acquainted. Not all Messengers came with Books. "To every nation a Messenger was sent"(S.Yunus10:47), "There was never a nation without a warner having lived among them" (S.Fatir35:24) They all came with the SAME religion: Worship must be exclusively for Allah to the exclusion of all others –"And verily we have raised in every nation a Messenger proclaiming: SERVE ALLAH AND SHUN FALSE GODS" (S.Nahal 16:36).This answers the frequently asked question, 'did Allah's Messengers come to India?'—yes, sure and certain. But it was not possible nor was it necessary to mention them by name in the Quran, however the abundance of the prophecies present in the Hindu Scriptures of the coming of the last Prophet Muhammad is a clear proof of the coming of Allah's messengers to this land. It is obligatory to all Muslims to pay full respect to all Prophets and all divine books belonged to whichever land; it is this reason that Muslims never thought to show disrespect to them in retaliation to some insane persons' regretful acts against the Quran and Muhammad in recent times.

Basic Creed

In Islam, faith and good works go hand-in-hand. A mere verbal declaration of faith is not enough, for belief in Allah makes obedience to Him a duty. The Muslim concept of worship is very broad. Muslims consider everything they do in life to be an act of worship, if it is done according to Allah's guidance, thus going to office, transacting business, engaging in political forums, contemplating in scientific phenomena even having sexual relations with wives are all acts of 'worship' for which Arabic word used is 'ibadah" coming from the root 'abd' meaning 'slave'— a full time slave to Allah. However there are also five formal acts of worship which help strengthen a Muslim's faith and obedience. They are often called the "Five Pillars of Islam."

Testimony of Faith

- "Ash-hadu an laa ilaaha illallah." (I bear witness that there is no deity but Allah.)

"Wa ash-hadu anna Muhammadan abduhu wa rasuluhu." (And I bear witness that Muhammad is His Slave and His Messenger.)

It needs to make the above declaration with a clear and pure intention in heart. This declaration in plain words means that one has to submit to Allah and in all acts of life he has to obey the commands of the Prophet. Note in the above declaration the word **'slave of Allah' for Muhammad**, this makes it unequivocal that Muhammad is no way to be taken as god or partner of God.

Prayers (Salaat, Namaaz)

Daily there are five time prayers (early morning, noon, afternoon, evening and night time) preferably in congregation in mosques, standing in rows shoulder to shoulder without any discrimination; women have to stand in separate rows(there are separate sections for them in mosques). If not in congregation they are allowed to pray individually anywhere in homes, in offices in business centers.

[29:45] "Recite what is sent of the Book by inspiration to thee, and establish regular Prayer: **for Prayer restrains from shameful and unjust deeds**; and remembrance of Allah is the greatest (thing in life) without doubt. And Allah knows the (deeds) that you do."

In prayer all worshippers have to stand in rows facing one single direction called qiblah (literally this means "orientation,") which is the direction of the Ka'aba in Makkah, in modern-day Saudi Arabia; mosques are constructed in such a way that one side of the building faces the qiblah, to make it easier to organize worshippers into rows for prayer. It should be noted that Muslims do not worship the Ka'aba. The Ka'aba is a capital and focal point of the entire Muslim world, a symbol of Unity.

Congregational prayer is a prelude to unity among the ranks, closeness of hearts, and promotion of the spirit of brotherhood. It is a kind of informal attendance check, and the best way of identifying individuals.

Congregational prayer is the largest, purest and most economical gatherings, it is a sort of free-of-charge meeting, familiarity with each other's problems, and a platform for social cooperation among Muslims. In congregational prayer, individuals stand in a single row, setting aside all distinctions of position, race, language, wealth, etc. Purity and sincerity of affection toward fellow human beings is aroused. Meeting one another in rows of worship, makes believers experience a sense of belonging that engenders courage, power and hope.

Friday Prayer is congregational prayer that Muslims are strictly enjoined to hold every Friday just after noon time (in place of the general noon-prayer on other days). See the wordings of the Quran:

[62:9] Believers, when the call for Prayer is made on Friday, hasten to the remembrance of Allah and give up all trading. That is better for you, if you only knew.

[62:10] But when the Prayer is ended, disperse in the land and seek Allah's Bounty, and remember Allah much so that you may prosper.

Here, a thing worthy of mention is that although in the Quran, Friday has not been declared a public holiday like the Jewish Sabbath and the Christian Sunday, yet no one can deny that Friday is a symbol of the Muslim community precisely in the same way as Saturday is a Jewish and Sunday a Christian symbol. But Muslim Friday is distinctly and essentially different from the Jewish Saturday and Christian Sunday in two ways: first the whole day is not forbidden for mundane affairs but only for that short period when the muezzin calls for Friday prayer and when the prayer ends. Second, Allah did not choose Friday for the day of congregational prayer because He rested on this day after creating the universe. Muslims do not believe in a tired or resting god, as mentioned in the Bible. Indeed it is mentioned in the Quran that Allah created the universe in six days but that does not mean that He rested on the seventh day after completing His work. Allah does not become weary or tired (Quran 2:255). In the Islamic belief, the "six days" is a metaphorical expression for six stages or periods. As for weariness Allah categorically says: "We created the heavens and the earth all between them in Six Days, nor did any sense of weariness touch Us." (50:38)

Zakaat

Giving to charity is one of the five "pillars" of Islam. Muslims who have wealth remaining over the year, after paying for their own basic needs, must pay a certain percentage to help others. This almsgiving is called Zakat, from an Arabic word which means both "to purify" and "to grow." Muslim believe that giving to others purifies their own wealth, increases its value, and causes one to recognize that everything we have is a trust from God. Paying Zakat is required of every adult Muslim man or woman who possesses wealth of a certain minimum amount (called *nisab* in Arabic). The amount of money paid in Zakat depends on the amount and type of wealth one possesses, but is usually considered to be a minimum of 2.5% of a person's "extra" wealth. The specific calculations of Zakat are rather detailed and dependent on individual circumstances, so zakat calculators have been developed to assist with the process.

Sadaqah: In addition to the required alms, Muslims are encouraged to give in charity at all times according to their means. Additional, voluntary charity is called *sadaqah,* from an Arabic word meaning "truth" and "honesty." Sadaqah may be given at any time and in any amount.

[57:10] And why should you not spend freely in the cause of God, seeing that God's [alone] is the heritage of the heavens and the earth?

The Quran specifies eight categories of people to whom Zakat may be donated (in verse 9:60):

- Poor people -- who have few belongings
- Destitute people -- who have absolutely nothing
- Zakat collectors -- for their work in collecting and distributing the zakat
- Muslim converts -- who may be estranged from their families and in need of help
- Slaves -- to free them from slavery in times/places where slavery has existed
- Debtors -- to help free them from insurmountable debts
- Those working in the path of Allah -- soldiers fighting a just war to defend the Muslim community
- Wayfarers -- who are stranded during their travels

Ramdan Fasting

Each year, Muslims spend the ninth month of the Islamic calendar observing a community-wide fast. The annual fast of Ramadan is considered one of the five "pillars" of Islam. Muslims who are physically able are required to fast each day of the entire month, from sunrise to sunset. The evenings are spent enjoying family and community meals, engaging in prayer and spiritual reflection, and reading from the Quran. A special prayer in the night is held in congregation (called *Taraweeh*) in which the Imam recites a long portion of the Quran and all followers listen it in standing; it goes on the whole month till the whole Quran is finished : this is a unique system of preserving the Quran. The fast of Ramadan as observed by all adherents of Islam in all lands of the globe showing a positive communal bonding has both spiritual significance and physical effects: creating in all a feeling what does it mean to be hungry—the Quran at many places urges Muslims to feed others. In addition to the basic requirements of the fast, there are additional and recommended practices in order to gain the most benefit from the experience. For the Muslim, the fast of Ramadan has specific regulations and rules, derived from the Sayings of the Prophet, Islamic scholars have outlined the fasting requirements for the general population, and explain the accommodations that can be made when someone is unable to fast because of sickness, pregnancy or other reasons.

Hajj

Hajj is considered one of the five "pillars" of Islam. Muslims are required to make the pilgrimage once in a lifetime, if they are physically and financially able to make the journey to Makkah. Every year, millions of Muslims from around the world make the journey to Makkah, Saudi Arabia, for the annual pilgrimage (or *Hajj*). All males (females are allowed to wear their own traditional dresses) dressed in the same simple white clothing in two pieces, one tied around the waist another wrapped over upper part of the body, represent human equality and fraternity.

The pilgrims gather to perform rites dating back to the time of Abraham. Hajj is a gathering of humanity in one place, at one time. There are specified days each year to perform the pilgrimage, during the Islamic month of "Dhul-Hijjah" (the Month of Hajj). The diversity and enormity of the crowds of pilgrims in Makkah during the Hajj is something that needs to be seen to be believed.

Renowned activist Malcolm X had a life-changing experience in 1964, when he traveled to Makkah, Saudi Arabia, for the annual pilgrimage. He was especially struck by the true sense of brotherhood and the absolute love between all those assembled, which challenged his previous beliefs that equality among the races was impossible to achieve. He wrote about his experience in a letter, which was later published in **The Autobiography of Malcolm X**.

Day of Judgment

Death is a natural event that none of us can escape. Throughout time, religions have tried to explain what happens to us after death.

Muslims believe that a person's soul leaves the body and awaits a final Day of Judgment before God. At the time of that Judgment, God will show mercy and justice and decide who will be rewarded and who will be punished. He will reward those who have "believed and worked deeds of righteousness" with eternal paradise, called **Jannah** (the Garden). As for those who have rejected faith and done evil, Allah will either forgive them in His mercy, or punish them in eternal Hellfire, called **Jahannam** (a word related to other Arabic words that mean "displeasure," "ignorance," and "frown").

Among Muslims, the Day of Judgment is also known as The Day of Reckoning. It is a day when all beings are raised to life again to face judgment and as to what they had done in their worldly life. Thus it is reminded at several places in the Quran that all are accountable to their deeds.

[31:33] O mankind! do your duty to your Lord, and fear (the coming of) a Day when no father can avail aught for his son, nor a son avail aught for his father. Verily, the promise of Allah is true: let not then this present life deceive you, nor let the chief Deceiver deceive you about Allah.

It is very likely for men to get caught up in the hustle and bustle of life without a thought to what comes next. In Islamic terms, the life we are living now is called the **dunya** — something earthly, temporal, and low. The Hereafter is what Muslims believe is most important; in Islamic terminology, it is called the **akhirah**, "the end" or "the last." The **akhirah** is what is to come at the end of our lives here, and the final aim of all believers is to be in a good place for the rest of eternity. To this end, Muslims try not to get distracted from their true purpose: to worship God and to strive in righteousness. The Quran reminds: "Oh you who believe! Revere God, and **let every soul look to what he has sent forth for tomorrow [the Hereafter]**. Yes, revere God, for God is Well-Acquainted with all that you do. And do not be like those who forgot God, and He made them forget themselves. Such are the rebellious transgressors" [Quran 59:18–19]

Halal and Haram (Permitted and Forbidden)

Halal items are allowed by Allah. Most foods in the world are Halal. Haram means forbidden by Allah. Haram foods are alcohol and other intoxicants, pork, carrion, most carnivorous animals, meat dedicated to idols. For the meat of an animal, other than seafood, to be Halal for a Muslim, it must be slaughtered in a specific manner. The process is called Dhabiha. Basically it is a similar procedure to the Jewish method of kosher preparation. Kosher meat is also allowed for Muslims, as per the Quran. Some Muslims believe that "supermarket" meat and fast food meat is also halal, but Allah said in the Quran that the meat prepared by the Jews and Christians is allowed, whereas almost no one in America practices Christianity anymore, as it was practiced in ancient times. Modern slaughtering techniques, with their attendant cruelty and unsanitary nature, do not pass the halal test for us. It is a bit of a hardship but we believe in the prevention of cruelty to animals and modern slaughterhouses are places of tremendous cruelty. There are detailed books on the subject.

There are also Halal and Haram ways to make money. Any business or activity that involves Interest-money is Haram as is any business involving gambling, alcohol, Haram foods or any business with deceit.

Equality, Tolerance and Unity in Diversity

Islam is known for its teachings about the equality of all people, regardless of race, ethnicity, or linguistic background. Muslims regard the diversity of life as a sign of the beauty of Allah's creation:

> "And among His Signs is the creation of the heavens and the earth, and the variations in your languages and your colors. Verily in that are Signs for those who know" [Quran 30:22]

Many of the first Muslims were from the lowest classes of society — slaves, women, and orphans — who were attracted to Muhammad's message of human worth and equality.

Diversity in Allah's creation is not only in colors and languages, but also in ideas and ways of life. The Quran makes clear that Allah intentionally did not create us all as carbon copies of each other. We have the opportunity to learn from each other and gain a new perspective, particularly when learning about people who are different from ourselves. As the Quran proclaims,

> "Oh mankind! We created you from a single soul, male and female, and made you into nations and tribes, so that you may come to know one another. Truly, the most honored of you in God's sight is the greatest of you in piety. God is All-Knowing, All-Aware" [Quran 49:13]

With this verse, Islam declares equality among people, dose not distinguish between two races, or two groups of people, or between two colors, and the prophet Muhammad (pbh) in his Last Sermon addressed the people signifying that concept during the last pilgrimage, saying: "O mankind, your Lord is One and your father is one. You all descended from Adam, and Adam was created from earth. He is most honored among you in the sight of God who is most upright. No Arab is superior to a non-Arab, no colored person to a white person, or a white person to a colored person except by Taqwa (piety)." [Ahmad and At-Tirmithi]

In another narration, the Prophet was asked: "Who among men is most favored by Allah?" He, replied: "A man who does the most good to people." [At-Tabaraani]

It is one of the most tragic truths of human history that people divided themselves in different segments and assumed someone upper and someone lower on regional, racial linguistic or such other basis. At the time of creation of Adam, Satan showed a similar arrogance that he was superior to Adam: S,Aaraf 7:12

> [7:12] [And God] said: "What has kept thee from prostrating thyself when I commanded thee?" Answered [Satan]: "I am better than he: Thou hast created me out of fire, whereas him Thou hast created out of clay."

In every land they committed this folly in different degrees, somewhere to an extent of tyranny to treat a segment of their own brethren no better than animals. One of reasons why Islam at the earliest time spread so fast was the equality and fraternity shown to all downtrodden people –the equality and fraternity in real Quranic sense; alas which could not be maintained by Muslims of later generations, although it must be said that there are some internal systems in Islam such as Congregational Prayers in Mosques and Hajj that Muslims as a whole are arrested from being fragmented.

Islamic Etiquettes

Civilizations are distinguished by the manners and etiquettes they follow. The Prophet took great care to develop a new society quite distinct from the old one and took great pain in shaping and forming this. He taught all initial manners of living as to how clean oneself after urinating, how to eat, how to live with parents and even how to consummate with spouses. Among all religious or secular leaders of the world it is only Muhammad who taught and cultivated the basics of private life of an individual; it is his great beneficence to mankind that he allowed his own private living manners with his wives to be revealed and described to his followers only to teach them and through them to all mankind—(can you point out a single such leader other than he).

1. Declaring Allah's name before eating and drinking and using the right hand for the purpose

   The first of these is to express thanks to Allah. When anyone among you is about to eat food, he should say *bismillahirrahmanirrahim* (With the name of Allah *the Most Gracious, Most Merciful*) If he forgets to say it at the beginning and [remembers it later on while eating], he should say: "In the name of Allah; [count these words, O Lord!] both at the beginning and at the end of the food [I have eaten]" (Tirmidhi, No: 1858) When anyone among you eats, he should eat with the right hand and when he drinks, he should drink with the right hand. (Muslim, No: 2020)

2. The ceremonial salutation and its response when people meet one another. The ceremonial salutation is

a prayer of peace and well-being for one another in this world and in the Hereafter. The one who initiates the salutation says (*as-salamu 'alaykum*=peace be upon you) and the one who replies says (*wa 'alaykum al-salam*= and on you also be peace).

3. Clipping the moustache, Shaving the pubes, Removing hair from under the armpits, Cutting nails, Circumcising the male offspring.

   All these five things belong to Islamic etiquette. Large moustaches give the impression of arrogance and conceit in a person. Edibles and drinks become contaminated through them when they are put in the mouth. Dirt often accumulates in elongated nails and such nails also have resemblance with savage animals. Consequently, the Almighty has directed us to keep our moustaches trim and to cut our nails whenever they grow. The rest of the three directives are aimed at one's physical cleanliness and hygiene. So strict was the Prophet in observing these norms that for some of them he even stipulated a certain time limit. One of his companions Anas reports : The time before which we must trim our moustache, cut our nails, shave pubic hair, remove hair from under the armpits has been fixed as forty days. (Muslim, No: 258)

4. Cleaning the nostrils, the mouth and the teeth. It is known from the way the Prophet (pbh) did "wadu" (ablution –washing hands, face, feet before salat/namaaz) that he would specially do gargle in order to clean the mouth) and to pour water in the nostrils to clean them). He was also very diligent in cleaning his teeth, and is even reported to have said:

Had I not thought that this would burden my *ummah*, I would have directed them to clean their teeth before every prayer. (Muslim, No: 252)

5. Cleaning the body after urination and defecation. Cleaning carefully the relevant body parts after defecation and urination is another Abrahamic practice. Depending upon the circumstances, these parts can be cleaned by water, mud cubes or other things that can serve the purpose. It is apparent from various Ahadees that the Prophet (pbh) normally used water for this. It is reported: When the Prophet would go out to relieve himself, I would bring some water in a utensil or a water container. He would clean himself from this water and then rub his hands on the mud to clean them. (Abu Daud, No: 45)

6. Taking the ceremonial bath after the menstrual cycle and the puerperal discharge The ceremonial bath has also remained a sunnah of all the Prophets. As soon as bleeding ceases in both these situations, a woman must have this bath to enter the state of purity. The Quran explained the rule regarding this issue in the following words: They ask you concerning women's courses. Tell them: "They are an impurity. So keep away from women in their courses and do not approach them until they are clean. But when they have purified themselves approach them in the manner the Almighty has directed you [in your instincts] – for Allah loves those who constantly repent and keep themselves clean". [2:222]

7. Ceremonial bath after *Janabat* the believers must take the ceremonial bath. (If you are in a state of *janabat*, have a bath., [Quran 5:6]). By janabat is meant the state of impurity that one enters after copulation or after a seminal/ovular discharge whether or not copulation has taken place.

   The way the Prophet set about this directive for such bath as mentioned in various Ahadith, it can be summarized as:

   First the hands should be washed; then the genital area should be thoroughly cleaned by the left hand; then "wadu" should be done except that feet should be washed later at the end; then while inserting the fingers in the hair, water should be soaked into it so that it reaches its roots; then water should be poured all over the body. In the end, the feet should be washed.

8. Sexual Ethics

   Sex is the ultimate expression of love and is a total physical and emotional encounter. In a brief but beautiful expression, the Quran refers to this relation between husbands and wives saying:

   "They are your garments and you are their garments." [2:187]

   The sexual unison between husband and wife is more than seeking a relief from the urge of desire. Indeed, the prophet taught that it is one of the charities in Islam. He said to his companions, enumerating examples of charitable deeds: "And when the one of you makes love (has sex), it is a rewardable charity." His companions were surprised and asked him 'How come that one of us answers the urge of his desire and out of this gets the reward of a charity. To which the prophet answered: "Don't you see that if he does the same but in a forbidden situation it would be counted against him as a sin? And so if he does it in legitimacy it is counted for him as a charity." (Muslim)

In order to maintain the bliss and pleasantness of the relation, both husband and wife should acquire the hygienic and esthetic habits that keep them attractive to one another. It does not behove the woman only to beautify herself for her husband, but this is a reciprocal right. The prophet is reported to have rebuked a man who looked shabby and neglected to tidy his hair and clothing, stating that it was his wife's right that he looks at his best to her, as she to him. Ibn Abbas, a notable scholar of the first Islamic century, stated: Most certainly, I am keen on making myself handsome to my wife, just as I like her to beautify herself for me in keeping with God's saying in the Quran that: "Women have rights even as they have obligations in an equitable way." [2:228]

Monthly Period – the related injunctions

From the biological explanation we know that menstruation is neither "the curse" on woman nor a result of the so-called original sin of Eve. Rather it is a very normal biological process that ensures the perpetuation of the human race.

> Of course, some women feel uncomfortable a few days before and during menstruation. This discomfort is caused by some of the biological changes which take place in the woman's body. Allah says, They ask you about menstruation. (O Muhammad), tell them that menstruation is a discomfort for the women, (it is a period when they pass through physical and emotional tension.) [2:222]

By considering the discomfort of the women during the monthly periods, Islam has forbidden both the husband and the wife from sexual intercourse during the menstruation.

The Quran says,

> They ask you about menstruation. (O Muhammad) tell (them that) menstruation is a discomfort (for the women, it is a period when they pass through physical and emotional tension. Therefore,) do not establish sexual relations with them during the menses, and (again you are reminded that) do not approach them (sexually) until the blood stops. Then when they have cleansed themselves, you (are permitted to) go into them as Allah has commanded you (by placing sexual urge in your nature). [2:222]

Some women asked a Wife of the Prophet Mohammad about what is allowed for them to do with their husbands during their periods. She told them: "Everything but the sexual intercourse".

Narrated Maimuna: (the wife of the Prophet) During my

menses, I never prayed, but used to sit on the mat beside the mosque of Allah's Apostle. He used to offer the prayer on his sheet and in prostration some of his clothes used to touch me." Hadees no. 329

Narrated 'Aisha: We set out with the Prophet for Hajj and when we reached Sarif I got my menses. When the Prophet came to me, I was weeping. He asked, "Why are you weeping?" I said, "I wish if I had not performed Hajj this year." He asked, "May be that you got your menses?" I replied, "Yes." He then said, "This is the thing which Allah has ordained for all the daughters of Adam. So do what all the pilgrims do except that you do not perform the Tawaf round the Ka'ba till you are clean." Hadees no. 302

As we see in Islam the woman during periods will pass a normal life except a few bindings: the regular five time-prayers. Regarding the sexual ethics and menstruation there are many sayings in the Collection of Ahadees, we have given here a cursory glance.

It must be mentioned here that it is a great beneficence and benevolence on the part of the Prophet that he let his private life open only to teach the Muslims and all the mankind as to how to mend their own private lives ; it must be acknowledged that no such Teacher has ever lived, secular or religious in the history.

9. Dead body

Firstly a dead body is not considered 'unclean' (naapaak) nor 'something to be dreaded'; many superstitions are harbored in some cultures. In Islam there are no rituals except 'washing and shrouding the dead', 'special salat (funeral prayer)' and 'burying the dead' by digging a ground: the total cost incurred and time involved is minimal as compared to what is followed in other cultures.

When one hears about someone's death or some tragedy he/she is instructed to utter, "Inna lillahi wa inna ilayhi rajiun." (To Allah we belong and to Him we return.)

In Islam it is taught that upon death, those with the deceased are encouraged to remain calm, pray for the departed, and begin preparations for burial. The eyes of the deceased should be closed, and the body covered temporarily with a clean sheet. It is forbidden for those in mourning to excessively wail, scream, or thrash about. Grief is normal when one has lost a loved one, and it is natural and permitted to cry. When the Prophet Muhammad's own son died, he said: "The eyes shed tears and the heart is grieved, but we will not say anything except which pleases our Lord." One should strive to be patient, and remember that Allah is the One who gives life and takes it away, at a time appointed by Him. It is not for us to question His wisdom.

Washing and Shrouding

In preparation for burial, the family or other members of the community will wash and shroud the body. (If the deceased was killed as a martyr, this step is not performed; martyrs are buried in the clothes they died in.) The deceased will be washed respectfully, with clean and scented water, in a manner similar to how Muslims make ablutions for prayer. The body will then be wrapped in sheets of clean, white cloth (called the *kafan*).

Funeral Prayers

The deceased is then transported to the site of the funeral prayers (*salat-l-janazah*). These prayers are commonly held outdoors, in a courtyard or public square, not inside the mosque. The community gathers, and the *imam* (prayer leader) stands in front of the deceased, facing away from the worshippers. The funeral prayer is similar in structure to the five daily prayers, with a few variations. (For example, there is no bowing or prostration, and the entire prayer is said silently but for a few words.)

Burial

The deceased is then taken to the cemetery for burial (*al-dafin*). While all members of the community attend the funeral prayers, only the men of the community accompany the body to the gravesite. It is preferred for a Muslim to be buried where he or she died, and not be transported to another location or country (which may cause delays or require embalming the body). If available, a cemetery (or section of one) set aside for Muslims is preferred. The deceased is laid in the grave (without a coffin if permitted by local law) on his or her right side, facing Mecca. At the gravesite, it is discouraged for people to erect tombstones, elaborate markers, or put flowers or other momentos. Rather, one should humbly remember Allah and His mercy, and pray for the deceased.

Mourning

Loved ones and relatives are to observe a 3-day mourning period. Mourning is observed in Islam by increased devotion, receiving visitors and condolences, and avoiding decorative clothing and jewelry. Widows observe an extended mourning period *(iddah)*, 4 months and 10 days long, in accordance with the Quran 2:234. During this time, she is not to remarry, move from her home, or wear decorative clothing or jewelry.

Islamic Phrases

One characteristic of Islamic civilization is the use of some phrases used at particular occasions Islam has its own key phrases to use in daily life, some of these are listed below along with the times to use them. Muslims are taught right from the childhood to memorize these.

1. When starting to do something: "Bismillahir Rahmanir Raheem." (In the Name of Allah, the Compassionate, the Merciful.)
2. When mentioning something that will be done in the future. "In shaa-allah." (If Allah wills.)
3. When praising something say, "Subhan Allah." (Glory to Allah.)
4. When in pain or distress. "Ya Allah." (O Allah.)
5. When appreciating something say, "Masha-Allah." (As Allah willed.)
6. When thanking someone. "Jazak Allah." (Allah reward you.)
7. When you see something bad. "Na'oozubillah." (May Allah protect us.)
8. When saying you're sorry to Allah for a sin. "Astaghfirullah." (May Allah forgive us.)

9. When you're happy about something. "Alhamdu-lillah." (Praise to Allah.)

10. When meeting someone. "Assalamu 'alaikum." (Peace be upon you.)

11. Replying to the above greeting. "Wa 'alaykum assalam." (And upon you be peace.)

12. When hearing about a death or tragedy. "Inna lillahi wa innaa ilayhi rajioon." (To Allah we belong and to Him we return.)

13. When you see someone off. "Fee Amanillah." (May (you) be In Allah's protection.)

14. When taking an oath. "Wallah." (I swear to Allah.)

15. When coming out of the toilets. "Alhamdu lillahilazi azhaba annil azaa wa aafaani" (Praise to Allah Who removed from me my ailment and gave me relief.)

16. When going to bed. "Allahumma bismika amootu wa ahyaa" (O, Lord with thy name I die and live.)

17. When one rises in the morning. "Alhamdu lillahilazi ahyaanaa bada ma amaatanaa wa ilayhin nushoor" (Praise to Allah Who brought me back to life after I was dormant)

Note : From above it is noted how the Prophet cultivated a new civilization based on remembering the Almighty on every action and at every step, it is not for any other reason that one of the many names of the Quran is "Zikra" (The Remembrance).

APPENDIX 2

Where to go from here?

A- Know the man who presented the Quran -- the Prophet

A Brief Biography of Prophet Muhammad (part 1 of 2): The Meccan Period
http://www.newmuslims.com/category/177/
by Aisha Stacey

A Brief Biography of Prophet Muhammad (part 2 of 2): The Madinan Period
http://www.newmuslims.com/category/180/
by Aisha Stacey

Muhammad the Greatest by Ahmad Deedat :
www.islam-house.com › English › Books?
http://www.newmuslims.com/index.php?option=com_tree&task=section&id=3

Have you discovered the truth about him? :
by Naji Ibrahim at
www.islamhouse.com › English › Books?

References for Further Search on the Life of Muhammad(pbh)
"islamcity.com, islamreligion.com, prophetMuhammadforall.com, al-islamforyou.org, tafheem.com,Englishtafheem.com, tanzil.info, irf.netlivingislam.org/hadith.html, islamhouse.com

See many Articles here about the Prophet :
http://www.onislam.net/english/readingislam/aboutmuhammad.html

Prophet Muhammad's Leadership: How he brought about the positive changes?:
http://www.onislam.net/english/reading-islam/about-muhammad/464618-how-the-prophet-brought-about-positive-change.html

Muhammad the Benefactor of Humanity
www.al-islamforall.org www.quranforall.org
www.prophetmuhammadforall.org

Many Articles about the Prophet:
www.IslamReligion.com

The Biography of the Prophet and the Orientalists by Muhammad Mohar Ali-King Fahad Printing Complex-Madinah—Download this book here
www.kalamullah.com/.../en_The_Biography_of_the_Prophet_and_the_...?

B- The Quran related articles

1. Guide to the Quran
http://www.newmuslims.com/lessons/32/

2. Amazing Quran by Gary Miller:
   http://www.prophetmuhammadforall.org

3. Preservation of the Quran:
   http://www.newmuslims.com/lessons/54/

4. Scientific description of the Quran :
   http://www.islamreligion.com/category/122/

5. The Quran and modern Science :Dr. Maurice Buccaile (edited by Dr. Bilal Philips) :
   http://www.usislam.org/books/quran_and_modern_science.htm

6. Download the Quran and many other eBooks:
   http://islamicbulletin.org/services/all_ebooks_p1.aspx#link1

7. A word to word translation of the Quran:
   http://islamicbulletin.org/free_downloads/html/complete_quran/complete_quran.htm

8. A short introduction to Islam:
   http://islamicbulletin.org/free_downloads/new_muslim/what_is_islam.pdf

9. Most Common Questions asked by Non-Muslims Zakir Naik :
   http://islamicbulletin.org/free_downloads/new_muslim/most_common_questions.pdf

10. Guide to persons in search of Islam& Quran:
    http://islamicbulletin.org/free_downloads/new_muslim/a_program_of_studies_for_new_muslims.pdf

يَاۤاَيُّهَا النَّاسُ قَدۡ جَآءَكُمُ الرَّسُوۡلُ بِالۡحَقِّ
مِنۡ رَّبِّكُمۡ فَاٰمِنُوۡا خَيۡرًا لَّكُمۡ ‌ؕ

O men! Now that the Messenger has come to you bearing the Truth from your Lord, believe in him; it will be good for you.

[Quran 4:170]

NOTE